AESTHETICS :
MODERN AND POSTMODERN

AESTHETICS :
MODERN AND POSTMODERN

Dr. B. Tirupati Rao

BHARATIYA KALA PRAKASHAN
DELHI (INDIA)

First Published : 2005

Published by **C.P. Gautam**
BHARATIYA KALA PRAKASHAN
3421-A, IInd Floor, Narang Colony, Tri Nagar,
Delhi-110035. Phone : 27393083, 30967505 (O), 27522129 (R)

ISBN : 81-8090-077-0

Cover Painting : Laxman Aley

Laser Type Setting by
A-ONE GRAPHICS
J.D.-18C, IInd Floor, Pitampura, Delhi-88
Ph.: 55640278, (M) 9811167357

Printed by
BDH Printers at Salasar Imaging System,
Delhi-35 Mobile : 9312245804

Contents

In appreciation...

Dr. B.Tirupati Rao's book *Aesthetics: Modern and Postmodern* a major achievement in its own right, is by far the most significant introduction to aesthetics: modern and postmodern. Dr. Rao ventured into a dense but immensely important discipline.

Postmodernism occupies a prominent place in the history contemporary thought. By now, even in India it is a much used and abused word. But Dr.Rao's achievement lies in his explanation of the phenomena of postmodernism in a strikingly creative manner. The thesis studded with interesting debates that went on from Plato to Foucault.

The last three or four decades witnessed some radical changes in the Western social, political and philosophical ideas, with modern and conventional ideas increasingly being called into question. Such questions led to the formation of a significant body of writing called Postmodernism. In Postmodernism one is given the choice to discard old models, practices, values that structured human thinking for centuries. Postmodernism introduced play and experiment in thought. The writings of Foucault, Lyotard, Derrida and Baudrillard exemplify this. The texts by these authors are not light read. Dealing with such complex texts is not an easy task. But, the author of this book made them comprehendable with his analyses. He clarifies the ideas of these notoriously tough authors without diluting them.

Divided into seven chapters, this book covers every aspect of aesthetics and analyses the contribution of Postmodernism to philosophy, sociology and psychology. This traces the unity of Postmodern thought,

thought it is thought to be fragmentary in spirit. It even argues that there is a radical potential in postmodernism, with which the present crisis in the theory can easily be overcome.

Derrida, Lyotard, Foucault and Baurillard developed a radical theory of aesthetics centred on the concept of 'difference'. Derrida explained this in clear terms. The dispute over modernity and modernism refers to conflicting theories of culture and cultural change and related aesthetics developed by a number of Post-Marxists on the basis of polemical interchange with one another, since the 1950s. Dr.Rao has a clear understanding of all these developments. Every page of this is a testimony to that. Combining theoretical discussions with thought provoking analysis of major texts, this book is an ideal introduction to the study of the fascinating subject, aesthetics. We commend Dr. Rao on this well researched work.

A.Venkateswara Reddy
Dr.Siva Nagi Reddy

6th November, 2004.

Acknowledgements

This book would not have been possible without the tremendous academic freedom given me by my research guide Prof.Gangisetti Lakshminarayana. I must thank him, for, he has provided me with information, offered critical insights and stimulated my thought.

Approaching an intricate subject like aesthetics, specifically modern and postmodern aesthetics, is always difficult, but it was made easy by the suggestions of my colleague and an eminent poet Sri. Mohan Prasad (MO), and a well known scholar Sri. Annapareddy Venkateswara Reddy. I owe thanks to both for all their encouragement and gentle reminders and also my level-headed interlocutors on the subject B.Chandrasekar, Dr.V.Chandrasekhar Rao. Prof.Venkat of CIEFL has encouraged me a lot as did my college principal Mr.S.V.Subrahmanya Sastry, Librarian Mr.Prasad Rao and my other colleagues at P.B.Siddhartha College, (Autonomous)Vijayawada.

I can never forget the enormous warmth and affection shown by Mrs.Kanthamma, Mr.Vijaya Kumar Reddy, Mrs.Pavani Vijay Kumar Reddy and their kids Balu and Deepthi. My gratitude to the staff of Indo-American Centre for International Studies (IACIS) is unbounded. My most incalculable debt, however, is to my friends Mr. B.V. Rami Reddy, P.V. Ramana, Jugash, Rathaiah, Sivaiah, Suresh, Uma, M.S. Naidu, V.V.N.V. Prasad and V. Anupama Devi I would also like to thank Mrs. Mrinalini and Mr. Sanjeeva Rao who have been always nice to me. Finally, I would like to thank Dr. E. Sivanagi Reddy for taking interest in getting this book published. I owe a lot to him. My thanks are due to a number of publishers. I have quoted extensively from their publication. They deserve my utmost gratitude.

A note on the book

This book *Modern and Postmodern Aesthetics : A Comparative Analysis* is my thesis for Ph.D. But for a few revisions, the basic structure of the thesis is not changed. All the aesthetic theories discussed in this book are reactions against something which went before; a prior knowledge of these things cannot be assumed, hence, I have given an account of the history of Western aesthetics from Plato to Foucault. Simultaneously, I tried to introduce the modern and postmodern aesthetics and the radical departure from the earlier to the later.

Modernism is a composite term for new aesthetic movements across the arts that date from the late nineteenth and early twentieth centuries. One defining feature of modernism is that it is based on the reaction against the prior aesthetic and philosophical forms of romanticism and classicism. The common feature of modernist art is that it is often referred to as the negative aesthetic or precisely negation of the previous tradition. This negation can be seen in all the art forms.

In painting, it is a rejection of the realist representation and the primacy of subject matter in favour of abstraction and an emphasis on formal and perceptual experiment. In music, it is a rejection of the earlier harmonic, melodic, and sonata forms of tonality in favour of the extension of dissonance and ambiguity. In literature modernism is marked by experimentation, particularly manipulation of form, and by the realization that knowledge is not absolute. In painting, modernism resulted in a profusion of styles and movements in a restless search for new directions and novel principles. Finally in dance, it reflects a rejection of existing traditions and a desire to re-examine the fundamental principles of dance as a medium.

The second characteristic of modernism is linked to the desire for formal experiment, its concern and fascination with new media, technology, and science. The celebration of technology is remarkable in the early twentieth century movements such as Soviet Constructionism and Italian Futurism. Both these movements advocated new media and drew analogies between industrial production and cultural practice. Technologies were new aesthetic stimuli in terms of the subject matter of art.

The third feature of modernism is theoreticism. Modernism invests an unprecedented power in exegetical or interpretative texts. A series of polemical manifestos and writings accompany many of the early twentieth-century movements. In the early period of modernism art theory and practice were linked. This had a profound impact on the creative writing. In fact, theoreticism had been central to the legitimation of the modernist art practice.

The Fourth defining element of modernism concerns its politics and political rhetoric, its vanguard and interventionist aims. There had been a close relation between *avant-garde* and the modernism. The *avant-garde* got radical political connotations. The *avant-garde* artists acted in the name of modernity and by its inspiration. Just like modernity itself, they lived at the front line. They always wanted to transgress the frontiers. As Zygmunt Bauman says, most of them took clues and courage from science and technology : Impressionists from the anti-Newtonian optics, the Cubists from the anti-Cartesian relativity theory, Surrealists from psychoanalysis, the Futurists from combustion engines and assembly lines. In the absence of modernity, modern culture would be unthinkable. The modern artist wanted to serve modernity.

The other important feature of modernism is its deification of reason or rationalism and the division of subjectivism/objectivism and high art/ popular art. In fact this binary nature continues in all the aspects of modernity.

Postmodernism is a term used to denote a multitude of styles and attitudes which exist partly as a response to high Modernism, and partly as a result of post-industrial mass production and late capitalism.

Postmodernism is notoriously difficult to define; indeed, a central tenet is that certain experiences and concepts resist any sort of representation in writing or art. However, one of its most recognizable attributes is certain self-consciousness with regard to the methods of production and to the social contexts of any work, together with a playful incorporation of, or gesture towards, previous styles and modes of thought.

In philosophical terms, Postmodernism is a part of a general attack on Enlightenment truth-claims and values. It displays a preoccupation with language as an inadequate vehicle for expressing any sort of "reality". This mode of thought is sometimes called "the linguistic turn", and it includes the language-games of Ludwig Wittgenstein and the "ordinary language" philosophy of John Langshaw Austin.

Structuralism and Post-Structuralism are closely related to Postmodernism. This relationship is particularly notable in the analyses of society as a system of signs and codes conducted by Roland Barthes, and in the emergence of deconstruction as a method of reading texts and identifying tacit hierarchies within discourses by Jacques Derrida. Michel Foucault also proposed several major theories about the nature of power and repression, and the marginalisation of certain groups throughout history. Jean-François Lyotard's *The Postmodern Condition : A Report on Knowledge* (1979) is an influential explication of Postmodernism's central concerns.

In literary theory, Postmodernism refers in part to the crisis in determining meaning and signification highlighted by Post-Structuralism and deconstruction. The Influential critics in the movement, include Fredric Jameson ,Jacques Derrida, Helene Cixous,Luce Irigaray, and Julia Kristeva.

In the practice of fiction and poetry, Postmodernism has manifested itself in an experimentation and eclecticism which has focused on the nature of fictionality and of writing itself. The term "Postmodernist" can be attached to almost any work that questions the boundaries and possibilities of the fictional enterprise; that attempts to collapse arbitrary borders between genres and to question what constitutes the nature of genre; that refers, directly or by allusion, to other texts; and that makes problematic the idea of "characters" and of a narrative that can lead to a fixed point and convey a fixed meaning. Many novelists and poets writing today incorporate these themes and approaches in their work. Many combined different forms of fictional genre and assimilated many of Postmodernism's theories about the nature of reading.

Lyotard has identified contemporary culture as "junk Postmodernism" or "eclectic Postmodernism" because of its willingness to absorb a variety of styles regardless of their provenance or status. The growing popularity of "camp" and "kitsch" bears witness to this general trend. The explosion of information technology, and in particular cyberculture and virtual reality, has increased a sense of the possible diversification of experience.

The word aesthetic has multiple shades of meanings : in the normal language aesthetic refers to the sensuous. Aesthetics has two sides : it is characterized by a bifurcation of sensation on the one hand and 'perception' on the other. Sensation is related pleasure and is emotional in nature, whereas perception is related to objects and cognitive in nature. Sensation has been understood as related subjective aspect of an individual and the perspective as related objective aspect.

Any genealogical study of the subject 'Aesthetics' reveals the fact that there is neither a single obligating meaning of the expression 'aesthetics' nor there is a semantic element, which would be common to all its multiple meanings. Hence, it is almost impossible to find out a continuous thread through all these multiple meanings and it is equally impossible to locate an essential element of the aesthetics.

In the evolution of Aesthetics various novel ideologies like the Marxian, Freudian and the Feminist are also taken care of giving them their due weight and volume. While dealing with the philosophy of modern aestheticism, the transition from the old to the new is also taken care of by throwing sufficient light on the several modern art forms-like literature, painting, architecture, music and dance.

'Aesthetics' in this book covers several areas of human thought about society, religion, establishments, schools, army, medicine, wealth, thought policing, the writer and writing, speaker and speech, fact, fiction, truth disguised and disclosed, the possibilities and impossibilities of doing so, psychoanalysis and its limitations, the individual and society, economic structures, but not simply truth, beauty, goodness and the permanent values or systems in arts and in all their manifestations.

Wherever and whenever philosophical inquiry went into abstractions, it is not difficult to see that writers brought it down to levels of application to real texts readily available. This has been made possible by philosophers or thinkers who are also creative writers like Sartre. In such cases intuition has become the handmaiden of logical postulations. This aspect is clearer in the feminist studies than in Marxian studies. Culture studies also lent a human angle to philosophical discourses.

Original thinking in a striking manner seems to have come from the French and German language- literature practicioners. A simple and like differance speaks volumes in such hair-splitting arguments.

'Aesthetics' in this thesis is shown as a literature of philosophy and not just 'on' philosophy. As it happens always, it is the latest writer, thinker, aesthetician and philosopher who will have the last laugh in a debate that went on for centuries over the continents!

Though this book is related to aesthetics, it is not simply confined to that discipline only, rather it involves an interdisciplinary method. In fact, the subject 'aesthetics' it self is interdisciplinary in its nature and scope. The term 'interdisciplinary' was first used in the social sciences in the mid 1920s and became common currency across social sciences and humanities in the period immediately after the Second World War. Adopting interdisciplinary approach is not simply bringing different disciplines together. As the comparative nature of the term itself suggests, interdisciplinarity assumes the existence and relative resilience of disciplines as modes of thoughts.

In a sense in which the contemporary cultural studies could be said to synonym with the interdisciplinarity itself, given that it draws variously on philosophy, sociology, history, linguistics, visual culture, politics, economics or even film studies. In this book, I am specifically concerned with the positioning of aesthetic at the intersection between social sciences, particularly philosophy, and the other social sciences. One of the effects of this method has been to question the disciplinary identity of 'aesthetics' by dissolving the category (aesthetics) into the more inclusive notion of culturology.

Even a cursory reading of contemporary literary and cultural studies reveals that it is almost impossible to undertake any serious research work without having considerable exposure to the interdisciplinary studies.

In fact, majority of the literary and philosophical works, that were produced since the Second World War demonstrate the potential of interdisciplinary studies. Roland Barthes' "Mythologies" (1957) is the best example in this regard. "Mythologies" is a seminal work of early structuralism and also a founding text of cultural studies in its pioneering discussion of popular culture.

"Mythologies" deconstructs a whole range of cultural phenomenon from 1950s France, such as wrestling matches, advertisements, soaps, toys and cars. Barthes' structuralism is interdisciplinary, because all kinds of artefacts and phenomenon can be interpreted as 'texts'. For Barthes a text is simply a vehicle for the production and dissemination of cultural meanings and 'a tissue of meanings drawn from the innumerable centres of culture'.

In the typical interdisciplinary method structuralist and poststructuralist approaches tend to emphasize intertextuality. In these analyses, literary and cultural texts tend to be positioned as part of the overall sphere of the language and discourse, and thus as one type of text among many including non-linguistic forms such as cinema, photography, music and fashion.

Derrida's 'deconstruction' is interdisciplinary par excellence. His work fundamentally questions the traditional separation of philosophy from more interpretative and textuality-oriented humanities disciplines. Derrida himself declared in an interview, 'Philosophy in its best tradition has never allowed itself to be put house arrest within the limits of its over discipline, to say nothing of the limits of its profession'.

Freudian and Lacanian psychoanalysis challenged the disciplinary limitation of psychoanalysis and extended it to other disciplines like linguistics. From modern feminism to postmodern feminism we can see feminists bringing together the disparate interests of literary and cultural criticism, the social sciences, philosophy; psychology and psychoanalysis. Feminists not only assimilated these disciplines into their methods, they also challenged even the values and priorities of these disciplines.

The studies related to homosexuality or Queer theory inextricably entangled in much wider issues of sexuality, masculinity, capitalism and national identity. All these examples prove that in the contemporary scenario no intellectual system can escape the interdisciplinarity.

The First chapter deals with origin of the discipline 'aesthetics' and it development. It covers almost all the major schools of aesthetics from Plato to Helene Cixous. However, necessary space is given to Modern and Postmodern aesthetics. Within modern aesthetics, the Phenomenological, Hermeneutical, Marxist, psychoanalytical, Structuralist, Poststructuralist and postmodern aesthetics are discussed at length. The thinkers covered are : Plato, Aristotle, Schiller, Schelling Hegel, Nietzsche, Husserl, Heidegger Sartre, Emmanuel Levinas, Hens-George, Gadamer, Gianni Vattimo, Marx, Lukacs, Goldman, Adorno, Raymond Williams, Herbert Marcuse, Christopher Caudwell, Gramsci, Althusser, Eagleton, Georges Bataille, Barthes, Foucault, Derrida, Paul de Mann, Baudrillard, Gilles Deleuze, Felix Guattari Lacan, Julia Kristeva, Luce Irigaray and Helene Cixous.

The Second chapter traces the historical setting of modernity, its philosophical roots and the emergence of the category of Modernism. Specifically it focuses on the formation of the modernist discourse and its philosophical inspiration, the Enlightenment movement. The chapter concludes by identifying some basic features of modernism.

The Third chapter discusses the formation of modernism as an aesthetics category and how it was inspired by thinkers like Darwin, Marx, Freud, and identifies the manifestation of modern aesthetic philosophy in the five art forms : Literature, Painting, Architecture, Music and Dance.

The Fourth chapter focuses on the reasons- the historical, sociological and philosophical- that are responsible for the transition of the aesthetic category from Modern to Postmodern. This chapter analyses the features of postmodern society in comparison with those of modern society..

The Fifth discusses the genealogy of postmodernism, specifically its relation to the thought of Frankfurt School, Structuralism and Post-Marxism. It even focuses on the importance of 1960s, the period in which there were epistemological shifts in the entire West. After discussing these shifts the major philosophers in the Postmodern and Poststructuralist discourse are introduced. Considerable space is given to focus on the thought of Michel Foucault, Jean Françoise Lyotard, Jacques Derrida, Jean Baudrillard, Gilles Deleuze and Felix Guattari.

The Sixth chapter traces the roots of the word postmodern and analyses various shades of its meaning by borrowing from a variety of arguments that range from Philosophical studies to Film studies. After identifying the postmodern aesthetic in its concrete form, this chapter analyses the postmodern aesthetics as it is manifested in the five art forms.

The last chapter gives a comparative analysis of the two aesthetic categories : the Modern and Postmodern. The focus of the analysis is once again on the five art forms :

This book in its conclusion rejects the transcendental position of any single aesthetic and upholds the typical postmodern spirit 'Celebrate the differences."

Introduction

Man is, in all cultures and languages, known by his capacity to think. Thinking, above all has made man meaningful to him as well as to others. Meaning went with purpose. The purpose itself being embedded in meaning, man has started thinking about thinking. Various thinkers, right from Socrates to Foucault have indulged themselves in the contemplation of thought, and came out from time to time with their own declarations which have mounted up to voluminous discourses over the centuries.

They talked about the mind that thinks. Mind thinks thought. Thus the delicate difference between the thinkers with his own mind thinking about mind has developed fairness in the delineation of the subject and the object, speech and script, talking and writing in an evolutionary process.

Each thinker and philosopher stood on the shoulders of his predecessor and debated the logic of the earlier one. It was not a question of contradicting but complimenting, not a question of negation but a process of contributing by continuation and contradiction. Thus, the classic had the neo-classic, the modern postmodern, and the Structural, Poststructural and so on.

In this book, I have seen myself over the long years of my interest in the subject and the last equally long years of reading, taking notes and writing on the topic, move from path to path, thinker to thinker, writer to writer, text to text with an ever growing interest that never seemed to near any completion though I had to settle down to a certain tentative analysis to the best of my ability and comprehension if only to be able to sum up.

The approach I had followed in my study is- first of all to identify, trace and dilate on the evolution of ideas and then to explicate the contribution of the individual thinkers step by step. The background studies include the Greek, British, French and German thought and the aestheticians in those languages (as translated into English).

Structuralist approaches tend to emphasize intertextuality. In structuralist analysis literary and cultural texts tend to be positioned as part of the overall sphere of the language and discourse, and thus as one type of text among many including non-linguistic forms such as cinema, photography, music and fashion.

What is aesthetics concerned with? What are the characteristic aesthetic problems? Given what has been said about the history of aesthetics, it is, perhaps, not surprising that it would be difficult to list a set of central problems which anyone with any pretensions to being counted as an aesthetician would have had to deal with. The problems vary from age to age. The characteristic preoccupation of the twentieth-century aesthetics has been with the question 'what is Art?" And the reason is the nature of twentieth-century art, which has self-consciously posed the question as a challenge.

The attempts to produce a satisfactory definition of a 'work of art' have often centered upon trying to find some one feature or set of features which all works of art possess, and which constitute the essence of art. The most obvious and most ancient feature is beauty. But it obviously won't do. Many things are beautiful but they are not works of art, so beauty cannot be a sufficient condition of art. And, of course, many things, which are undeniably works of art, are indisputably not beautiful. This isn't because they are poor works of art and simply, as it were, fail to be beautiful, for beauty was not what was aimed at.

But aesthetics is even more of a historically changing subject. The subject-matter of aesthetics has a history, and it doesn't only change, it also grows, for new works of art, and new art forms are constantly being created. And these new works may change our perspective on the past as well. It isn't just that each age has to confront its own contemporary works of art, which previous generations, previous critics, previous aestheticians couldn't have known of, for they weren't yet created : but also that each new age has to re-confront, re-interpret, the artists and works of the past from their own standpoint. Each age re-interprets the art of the past.

Aesthetic concepts have a history. But, the history of aesthetics has a strictly limited relevance to the study of current problems in aesthetics. For those who wrote on aesthetics in the past were not writing about the same things that those who write on aesthetics now are concerned with.

Beauty, not aesthetics is an important aspect of human life. It attracts a large measure of attention and support. But what is beauty? What is art? Why should we value them? These are very old and pestering questions that philosophers have been concerned with over thousands of years. In all these centuries a number of answers have been explored and developed. There have been serious attempts to answer these questions in a coherent and sustained way. Many philosophers devoted much attention to them, often their answers are stimulating.

Philosophers are not the only people to develop theories of art. Sociologists, Musicologists, art critics, and literary critics and theorists have done so as well. All these people of various disciplines are defenders of one or others version of aesthetic cognitivism. They strongly believe and view that aesthetics or art is most valuable when it serves as a source of understanding. Though there are explicit differences between aesthetics on the one hand and science on the other, the former, no less than the latter, is seen to contribute significantly to human understanding. To accept this, it is essential to see that works of art do not expound theories, or consist in summaries of facts. They take the form of imaginative creations, which can be brought to every day experience as a way of ordering and illuminating it. From ancient times there has been an implicit understanding among the people that aesthetic cognitivism can explain more successfully than other theories.

In a way, it would be hard to think of a subject more neurotically self-doubting than aesthetics. No less than a philosopher and mathematician as Wittgenstein said, 'The subject (Aesthetics) is very big and entirely misunderstood as far as I can see'.

Claims that the subject 'Aesthetics' is dreary, irrelevant, muddled and misunderstood have been a persistance themes, not only of recent times, but also from the very beginning of the subject. The word Aesthetic was invented or coined by the German philosopher Alexander Baumgarten, who in his "Aesthetics" used the word to apply to criticism of taste, considered ita science of philosophy. During the nineteenth century, the word was gradually accepted to refer to the philosophy of taste, the theory of fine arts, the science of the Beautiful.

Aesthetics has been approached from two different directions. On the one hand, it has been approached by the philosopher without necessarily having any profound interest in art. Having dealt with truth and goodness, he turns his attention, if he has time, to beauty. In the order of the terms of the philosopher aesthetics has only a marginalized space. What so frequently has resulted have been philosophical works of great generality and abstractness, with very little in the way of examples or references to any actual works of art : perhaps the paradigm case here is Kant's Critique of judgement. One notable exception was Croce, who believed it important to consider the way of thinking involved in the creation and experience of works of art before moving on to consider other ways, such as logical, rational or conceptual thought.

To be clear about the place of art and aesthetic experience in the whole economy of human life, one would have to be clear about many other areas of philosophy. In talking about works of art, and in particular in giving reasons for one's critical judgements, the reasons take their force from the work of art from which the judgements are made.

Notes

1. Wolfgang Welsch. *Undoing Aesthetics*. London : Sage, 1997, p. 10.
2. Roland Barthes. *Image-Music-Text*. London : Fontana, 1997, p. 72.
3. Jacques Derrida. Points...Interviews. Stanford : Stanford University Press, 1995, p. 404.
4. Ludwig Wittgenstein. Lectures and Conversations on Aesthetics, Psychology and Religious Belief (Ed.) C.Barrett, Oxford : Basil Blackwell, 1966, p. 1

I

The evolution of aesthetics

Aesthetics is generally regarded as the philosophical study of beauty and taste. It is immensely difficult to define aesthetics, as it is not confined to any one particular discipline. It includes numerous phenomena like the ugly, the beautiful, the sublime, the elegant, and the taste. It also covers the areas of criticism, the fine art, sensuous joy and charm. Hence, the scope of aesthetics is wider than that of philosophy. It deals generally with nature and value of the arts. In addition to this, aesthetics deals with our responses, which we give to the natural objects. Francis Bacon wrote essays on beauty and deformity, Descartes wrote a treatise on music. But it was only at the end of the seventeenth century that a concrete concern for aesthetics was established.

Aesthetics is a branch of philosophy related to the fundamental nature and perception of beauty and ugliness. It also addresses the question of whether such qualities of beauty and ugliness are objectively there in the things, or whether they subsist only in the mind of the individual. Aesthetics also poses the question whether things are perceived by a particular method, for example the aesthetic method, or, in its place, whether the things have intrinsically special qualities. Aesthetics also inquires whether there is a difference between the beautiful and the sublime.

Though criticism of art and literature are separate disciplines, the two are connected to aesthetics. Colour, sound, line, form, and words are the elements of art. Since Psychology studies human responses to these elements, it is also a part of aesthetics. Criticism studies the structures, meanings, and other problems of literature; hence, it cannot but be a branch of the study of the nature of beauty that had been pursued for centuries. Previously aesthetics was a subject dealt by philosophers only. Since nineteenth century onwards, artists have also added their views.

To be succinct, aesthetics studies arts in general. It compares arts from different cultures and from different periods of history, and in the process it organizes human knowledge of them in an orderly way. In the earlier times, the study of beauty was regarded as the central problem of aesthetics. Whereas, at the present the discipline has widened to include many other dimensions of art. Aesthetics aims to study and understand how art is interrelated to what people experience, what they learn and the cultures in which they live. It also attempts to find whether there are standards of art criticism, which helps people to appreciate or value different kinds of art. Besides trying to study theories concerning works of art, aestheticians want to comprehend artists and audiences. Audiences can understand better if they have learned how artists imagine, produce, and execute, and what makes artist's activities diverse from the work of non-artists. They attempt to examine what happens to people's feelings when they experience art and how art affects the moods, beliefs, and values of the people.

One of the first proponents of aesthetics was Plato. According to Plato, reality consists of prototypes or archetypes, or forms. These forms are beyond the limits of human sensation and are the replicas for all things that survive in human experience. The objects that come into the experience of human beings are imitations of those forms. The philosopher should reason from the object experienced to the reality it imitates, whereas the artist copies the object that comes into his experience. Ultimately, what the artist does is nothing but an imitation of imitation. Plato's aesthetics exhibits some tension because of the contradictory views they contain. At one point he celebrates the great works of art, and at another he sees some artists as rivals to his vision of rational order or society. Plato radically advocates the prohibition of poets and painters from his ideal republic. He provides an extensive theory of imitation (mimesis).

After Plato, Aristotle spoke very consistently on aesthetics in the classical period. Aristotle also considered art as imitation. He thought that the artist divides form from the matter of the objects of experience, like human body, and other objects in the nature like trees, and imposes that form on another matter like canvas and marble. In this way imitation is not just a copy of the original.In fact, it is a particular representation of an aspect of things. Ultimately, each art piece is an imitation of the universal whole.

Both Plato and Aristotle saw aesthetics as an integral part of morality and politics. Aristotle in "Politics" held that art affects human character, hence the social order also. According to Aristotle, the essential function of art is to provide human satisfaction. Even in his "Poetics", Aristotle argued that a tragic drama should stimulate the emotions of pity and fear, which would purge the soul of the audience. In the process of purgation, the spectators become psychologically healthier and are capable of happiness. The concepts of classical thinkers dominated the field of aesthetics until the modern period.

Even in the Middle Ages art was primarily an expression of religion. In the Middle Ages, aesthetic principles were founded basically, on Neo-Platonism. Since fifteenth and sixteenth centuries onwards, Art became somewhat secular. Aesthetics were based on Classical principles rather than religious ones.

Aesthetics was first used in the late 1700s. Philosophers from the ancient Greeks to the present day have talked about the philosophy of art. Almost all the philosophers have written and conversed about whether art is good for people and for society. Despite the fact that there are some detractors who argue that art and artists are so disruptive and that they intimidate the social order, most of them believed that art is good because it allows one to express one's emotions, teaches about the world, or even communicates the traditions of various cultures and times. In fact, aestheticians employ art history to identify or understand the art of earlier times. They make use of the psychology of art to gain knowledge of how our senses interact with our imagination and understanding when we experience art. Critical writings on art help to funnel, to enjoy each independent work of art. Other disciplines of humanities like sociology, anthropology help aestheticians to understand how creating and appreciating art relate to other human activities. The social sciences indicate how art varies in relation to physical, social, and cultural environments.

There are various shades of meanings to the word 'aesthetics'. In one way or the other all of them are related. In ancient Greek philosophy, specifically in the texts of the 'Pre-Socratics', Plato and Aristotle it refers to lived and felt experience. It is the knowledge as it is obtained through the senses. It is not the knowledge acquired from reason. The dichotomy remains even today. Descartes was reasserting the distinction. In fact, he was regarded as the founder of modern philosophy on the grounds that he demonstrated the independence of human rationality from God. Nevertheless, in his declaration that 'I think, therefore I am' in his "Discourse on Method" (1637) he proposes the primacy of thought over sense perception.

The most popular sense of the term 'aesthetics' is the study of beauty and specifically, the beautiful art. This understanding got its roots in the eighteenth century with the emergence of Cartesian individual and the rise of interest in harmonious form. There was a deep relation between this change and the changes of the economic structure of the western society. It was a result of the transition from feudalism to capitalism, which replaced the absolute law of the aristocracy with subjective freedom. Capitalism considered beauty and the other art forms as expressions of its new class identities. Allied to this, we have the romantic theories of beauty, which are in opposition to classical theories. Romantics gave to the artist an important and all most a holistic relationship with nature. They thought that artistic expression and quality go beyond rules or other prescriptive criteria. This gave rise to an excess of individual and subjective autonomy.

In the view of Terry Eagleton, 'aesthetics is born as a discourse of the body. In its original formulation by the German Philosopher Alexander Baumgarten, the term refers not in the primary place to art, but as the Greek *aesthesis* would imply, to the whole region of human perception and sensation, in contrast to the more rarefied domain of conceptual thought'.[1]

Even though questions of beauty and art have played a concrete role in western philosophy since Plato, it is only about the middle of the eighteenth century in Europe that the notion of a distinct area of philosophy called 'aesthetic' develops. Andrew Bowie says, 'Modern philosophy begins when the basis upon which the world is interpreted ceases to be a deity whose pattern has already been imprinted into existence and becomes instead our reflection upon our own thinking about the world'.[2] Descartes prepared the ground in the seventeenth century by declaring 'I think, therefore I am'. He made 'I think' the point of certainty from which philosophy begins.

Descartes had relied upon God to guarantee the order of universe, but at the end of the eighteenth century, Kant made it the task of philosophy to describe the structure of human consciousness. There was no recourse to any divinity with an inherent order. According to Kant, if any cognitive certainty is possible in philosophy, it is grounded in ourselves, but not outside ourselves. To suggest a probable link between the external world of nature and internal world of self-consciousness Kant is concerned with what makes one appreciate and create beauty.

Kant's move from philosophy to subjectivity accompanies the complex and contradictory changes fashioned by modernity : the changes were like the rise of capitalist individualism, the increasing success of scientific method in controlling nature, the decline of long-established and theologically legitimated authorities and simultaneous emergence of aesthetics as a separate division of philosophy and the concept of 'aesthetic autonomy', which means that the works of art have a status which cannot be ascribed to any natural object or human product . Science then onwards, instead of being a part of philosophy related itself to the senses and beauty 'aesthetics' devoted to the significance of natural beauty and art.

Much of the history of western philosophy considered aesthetic experience as a subordinate to reason or rational enquiry. Conventionally, aesthetic or sensory experience is condemned as a source of truth, because it can be befuddled or indistinct or because it is not acquiescent to conceptual analysis. Plato and Descartes are the examples in this regard.

Two German thinkers in the eighteenth century are greatly responsible for making aesthetics vital to philosophy. They are, Alexander Baumgarten (1714- 62) and Immanuel Kant (1724 –1804). Baumgarten deals with the criticism of confusion. 'His book 'Metaphysica' (1739) reconfigures aesthetic confusion as a synthesis ('confusion's field or *campus confusionis*) and, therefore, as a positive epistemological notion'.[3] According to Baumgarten rational judgement divides the world into subjects and objects and predicates, but aesthetic experience allows us to become conscious of these moments as a unified whole.

Kant's writing, however, has overshadowed Baumgarten's contribution because Kant drastically transformed the modern philosophical landscape. His acknowledgement of the finitude of human experience is the most important move in thought. The central problem of Kant's major work, "The Critique of Pure Reason" (1781), is the nature and limits of human knowledge. He declares that human consciousness is not isolated from the world but embedded in it and actively engaged with it. He believed that the mind is actively involved in the objects it experiences. That is, it organizes experience into definite patterns. Therefore, we can be sure that all things capable of being experienced are arranged in these patterns even though we may not yet have experienced them. We can have knowledge of things that have not been experienced as well as those we have already experienced. 'This is 'Copernican Revolution'.[4]

The significance ascribed to art near the end of the eighteenth century has its roots in the decline of theology and the crumbling of theologically legitimated social orders. Marx in his 'Communist Manifesto' described it as "All that is Solid Melts Into Air". The idea of nature with its divinely guaranteed structure and its intrinsic meaning is lost and it ultimately led to a search for other sources of meaning and coherence. The concept that nature is intrinsically beautiful, that it is not just an expression of a divine power, and the idea that humans can create aesthetic products became a vital philosophical problem. It was strongly believed that the coherence of the world and, including ourselves, could no longer be supposed to be guaranteed by God, hence the relation of nature and humans became a major problem. In the view of Andrew Bowie, 'the task set by the philosophy of the time is seen as the creation of a coherent world with whatever natural capacities we possess and whatever innovatory capacities we can develop'.[5]

As soon as philosophy concerned itself with scientific method and the de-mythologizing capacities of science, it began to identify with what is barred by science also. Modern science saw nature as a machine, and the increasing domination of nature by capitalism led to perceive the nature as a profit-making source. However, what makes an object beautiful or ugly has nothing to do with usefulness or uselessness and even its exchange value. Now let us see various schools and individual thinkers in the field of aesthetics in the modern period.

Romantic aesthetics

Romantic aesthetics took different forms in different countries in which it appeared. For example, it was almost an aesthetic movement in England. In France under Rousseau's inspiration, it was mainly a protest against social convention. Finally in Germany it began as an aesthetic movement but quickly broadened out to become an explicit and comprehensive world-view. Many romantics saw art as a manifestation of truth –one that rivalled and ultimately surpassed the analytical reason of the Enlightenment. The Romantics were insistent on the central role poetry played in human culture. Finally, one needs to note how the Romantic idea of genius appeared to suggest that even the artist himself was unequal to his work

Many thinkers proved that many themes that are present in Nietzsche's writings appeared earlier in the writings of Schlegel circle. Schlegel notes a similar cult of myth of the mythical, manifesting itself in the search for a new mythology, a similar divinisation of art, a similar desire for an 'aesthetic revolution' based on a recovery of Greek spirit.

Schiller and Schelling developed and extended Kant's discussions on the aesthetic. Schiller was the first to see that "aesthetic unity" has shown itself to be active not only in art but in thought itself. In his highly influential "Letters on the Aesthetics Education of Man" (1874-95), Schiller puts forward nothing less than a history of the whole of Western Culture.

In fact, Schiller is one of the first theorists of the idea of modern alienation, now a common place cultural commentary. He argues that the cure for alienation lies in art. He holds that there are two drives in man : the sensuous drive (*sinnliche Trieb*), which is always pressing for change; and the formal drive (*form tribe*), which insists on unity and persistence. Both need to have limits placed upon them. The former then does not encroach upon the domain of moral law and the latter does not encroach upon feeling. Stated slightly in different terms, both need to be relaxed, but relaxation must spring from an abundance of feeling and sensation rather than from physical or spiritual importance. Such harmonization can only be accomplished by the operation of a third, "play" drive (*spieltrieb*), which exerts upon the psyche a constraint that is at the same time moral and physical.

According to Schiller, it is in art that the play drive emerges. Whereas the object of sensuous drive is life and that of the formal is form, the play drive has as its object "living form". The concept of living form designates "all aesthetic qualities of phenomenon and, in a word, what in the widest sense of the term we call 'beauty'. Only in the play of art are the sensuous drive and the formal drive are brought together. Only in contemplating the beautiful is man harmonized, for only here does the psyche find a happy medium between the moral law on the one hand and physical exigency on the other. Beauty, Schiller believes, offers us an instant moral freedom being compatible with sense. It leads the sensuous man back to form and thought.

Schiller declares that any blurring of the distinction between art and non-art is dangerous. Schiller does not take up a position where in notions articulated on the basis of a distinction between the aesthetic and non-aesthetic, employed as if those distinctions had not been postulated.

Schiller's "Aesthetic Letters" suggested to a number of younger thinkers that art could in deed be a source of truth, and that philosophy ought in consequence to become aesthetic.

It was Schelling, however, who insisted most on the need to turn philosophy in an aesthetic direction. The crucial work for this theme is his "System of Transcendental Idealism" (1800). Schelling starts out from the problem that Kant's philosophy had made so obvious, that of relating subject and object which is also the problem of relating freedom and necessity, ego and nature, idea and actuality, practical and theoretical.

In Kant, the primacy of the aesthetic is only formal or regulative, whereas in Schelling it is substantive. Schelling intends that nature on the one hand and the work of art on the other are the products of one and the same activity, an activity that is in its essence aesthetic. The only difference between the world and the work of art is that in the former the creative activity is unconscious whereas in the latter it is conscious. In a way, Shelling anticipates Nietzsche's views on the aesthetic character of reality.

Given Schilling's conviction that reality is poetic, we are not surprised to find that he sees philosophy as culminating in art. Philosophy starts out from the principle of absolute identity as in A=A. Absolute identity can be grasped in self-consciousness, the subject of thought and the object of thought are the same : ego=ego. In the view of Schelling the "aesthetic product" starts out from the feeling of a seemingly insoluble contradiction. In other words, the aesthetic product gives us a vision of identity. In deed, it gives us an objectification of identity, since it clearly exists outside the ego. As Schelling puts, the "generally recognized and entirely undesirable objectivity of intellectual institution is art itself". For Schelling, aesthetic institution is nothing other than intellectual institution become objective. In Schelling's view only art can make objective what the philosopher represents in thought. Schelling therefore suggests that philosophy, having completed this task of representation, is about to return, along with all the other sciences, to "the universal ocean of poetry from which it started out". The sciences begin in poetry; in poetry they will conclude.

George Wilhelm Friedrich Hegel, (1770-1831), the German philosopher, is one of the most influential thinkers of the 19th century. He was strongly influenced by Greek ideas. Hegel also read the works of the Dutch philosopher Baruch Spinoza, the French writer Jean-Jacques Rousseau, and the German philosophers Immanuel Kant, Johann Gottlieb Fichte, and Schelling. But he often disagreed with these philosophers. However, the influence of these philosophers is apparent in his writings. Specifically, his philosophy was deeply influenced by Kant's.

Hegel made a systematic study of aesthetics. He produced one of the most important aesthetic documents of the nineteenth century. However, the paradox was that he declared the end of aesthetics. He wanted to make philosophy into a complete articulation of what is inherent in religion and art as expressions of truth. Hegel believed that religion and art do not articulate truth; hence, philosophy is unavoidable to reveal the truth that these two contain. In fact, philosophy for Hegel, is an endeavor to reveal how the process of thinking and the process of reality are ultimately identical.

In his "Aesthetics : Lectures on Fine Art",Hegel asserts that the task of philosophy is 'to show how the idea in logic has, in accordance with its own Concept to transpose itself into natural existence and then, out of this externality, into spirit; and finally to free itself from the finitude of spirit again to become spirit in its eternity and truth'.[6]

Art plays an important role in the system of Hegel. But he never wrote a book on aesthetics. In fact, his work "Aesthetics : Lectures on Fine Art" is a reconstruction made after his death, from the student transcriptions and his own lecture notes. According to Clive Cazeaux, 'Art's ultimate role in Hegel's system is to be the antithesis of thought. A representation which takes shape as an independent object *opposite* consciousness, and which consciousness recognizes as being both of itself and other than itself. This doesn't mean that Hegel has a negative view of art. In the dialectical unfolding of consciousness, there is the necessary antithetical moment when the mind becomes aware that what is immediately before it is not entirely true or adequate, and so it is motivated to utter a further judgment. "Art is the stimulation of enquiry through material estrangement'.[7] "

In the view of Hegel, an art piece is the sensuous display of mind's relationship with the external reality. Art is a material stuff that has permeated with mind. Hegel's division of art is three fold, namely; symbolic, classical and romantic. The subject of symbolic art is the matter itself in its externality. Architecture is an example . The shape is arbitrary and the reality presented opposed to the idea. In the Classical art, material form is peculiarity is suitable to the ideal itself in its essential or crucial nature. The example for this may be shown in the sculpture portraying human form. This is because the artist recreates human forms, which he or she finds in nature. Romantic art, Hegel considers, acknowledges that external representation is inadequate to the demands of thought and seeks to free it from the burden of particularity. This category is represented by those forms, which deny their materiality. For example, painting.

Hegel, in the line of traditional thinking, emphasizes the mental over the physical. That is why he argues that the beauty we perceive in art is higher than that of the real beauty we see in nature. This is because the beauty we perceive is born of the spirit. According to Andrew Bowie, 'Hegel is insistent that the beauty in the works of art has a higher status than the natural beauty, thereby reversing Kant's priorities. Beauty depends upon the development of thought, not upon an immediate pleasurable contemplation of the natural world : ...Hegel's argument about the beauty of nature and the beauty of art suggests that if nature is mainly seen as a threat that must be overcome by *Geist* in the interest of self-preservation it cannot appear beautiful. Beauty is linked to subjective control over nature, which allows thought to move beyond an immediate empirical relationship to nature. When the mountain is no longer just a danger it can become an object of contemplation that makes it more than brute resistant matter'.[8]

However, Hegel does not equate appearance with illusion. In his "Aesthetics Hegel declares, 'Far from being simple appearance the appearance of art should be seen as possessing the higher reality and the truer existence in relation to normal reality'.[9]

After Hegel, it was Frederich Nietzsche who made significant contribution to the study of the category 'aesthetics'. The notion of crisis is crucial for understanding Nietzsche's project, for it is this notion that opens the way to his aestheticism. The paradigm of crisis is the "death of God". Nietzsche's conviction embraces a condemnation of the present world as null. The recognition of this nullity is what we know as nihilism. But as Nietzsche points out there are two kinds of nihilism. On the one hand there is nihilism that fails to respond to what Nietzsche sees as the opportunity offered by the world's nullity. This nihilism views to devaluation of all present values as oppressive and burdensome. We look upon the void, we shudder, and we draw back. We try to dull the reality, pretending that nothing has happened, that the world is still turning on its axis. In short, we adopt a passive attitude. On the other hand, there is an active, aesthetic nihilism. Nietzsche describes this nihilism as appropriate attitude for modern existence. Instead of drawing back from void, we dance upon it. Instead of lamenting the absence of a world suited to our being, we invent one. We become the artists of our own existence, untrammelled by natural constraints and limitations.

Nietzsche exercised considerable influence on twentieth-century philosophy and art. In Nietzsche's view the world is in a constant state of change. In philosophical j–argon it is called becoming. A becoming world can not be known as it is not being. This is the conceptual base of Nietzsche's denial of possibility of knowledge. In his view, 'A world in a state of becoming could not in a strict sense be 'comprehended' or 'known'; only in so far as the 'comprehending' and 'knowing' intellect discovers a crude ready made world put together out of nothing but appearance, but appearance which, to the extent that they are of the kind that have preserved life, have become firm-only to this extent is there anything like 'knowledge' : i.e., a measuring of earlier and later errors by one another'.[10]

According to Nietzsche, the whole apparatus of knowledge is an apparatus for abstraction and simplification. This abstraction or simplification is not aimed at acquiring but at possessing things. As there are no facts, only interpretations, so all knowledge is just interpretation. Words are also the chief agencies in our construction of acts i.e., imposing of 'being' on the flux of 'becoming'. Through words and concepts formed from them humans are continually tempted of things as being simpler than they are.

Nietzsche, in fact, wrote about aesthetics throughout his life . In his view, 'art represents the highest task and the truly metaphysical activity of this life'.[11]

For Nietzsche, beauty is subjective and it exits in the mind of man. But the subjectivity does not imply a limitless arbitrariness in what is found beautiful. Beauty is found in the objects, by people not because it is inherently there in the objects, rather it is in the mind of the beholders. In "The Gay Science", Nietzsche asserts, 'My objections to Wagner's music are physiological objections : why conceal them under aesthetic formulas? My "fact" is that I no longer breathe easily as soon as this music begins to affect me'.[12] Nietzsche reformulated the same sentence later and said that, 'For aesthetics is nothing but applied physiology'.[13]

The most important element in Nietzsche's attraction to aesthetic is the notion of creativity. Time and again, he glorifies the artist. Over-flowing with strength and well-being, the artist transmutes reality. He transforms the brute material of existence into something made after his own image. He sees 'nothing as it is, but fuller, simpler, stronger" This facet of Nietzsche's conception of art is important because he extends it to his own activity, conceiving of himself in his "mature" phase not simply as an observer of art but as an "artist-philosopher'.[14]

As we have discussed already, modernism manifested in various forms and movements in the field of aesthetics . They may be, in philosophical terms classified as the German aesthetics of the nineteenth, the phenomenological and Hermeneutical aesthetics, the Marxists aesthetics,the Postmodern and Poststructuralist aesthetics, Psychoanalytic aesthetics and Feminist aesthetics.

Phenomenological and Hermeneutical Aesthetics

Though Phenomenology and Hermeneutics are independent theories, there is some close relation between them. They concentrate on how words relate to experience.

Fontana Dictionary of Modern Thought defines Phenomenology as, 'In Philosophy, a method of enquiry was elaborated by Edmund Husserl as a development of his teacher Brentano's conception of 'descriptive', as opposed to 'genetic', Psychology. It takes philosophy to begin from an exact, attentive inspection of one's mental, particularly intellectual, processes in which all assumptions about the causation, consequences, and wider significance of the mental process under inspection are eliminated."

In Sociology, Husserl's method was adopted by Alfred Schutz to investigate the assumptions involved in everyday social life. In the sociology of knowledge, phenomenologists have concentrated on the way in which common-sense knowledge about society feeds back through social action, into the moulding of society itself. Other developments range from highly generalized descriptions of how people in different types of society think and feel about the world and their place in it to analyses, in Ethenomethodology, of the unconscious routines by which people manage their inter-personal contacts'.[15]

According to phenomenology, all meaning is to be found in a person's perception of the 'universal essence' of an object or thing. From the perspective, all truth comes out of the ability of human subjects to consider and understand what is going on around them, including their own involvement in the world—their desires, motivations and activities.

Hermeneutics on the other hand is the art of understanding and interpreting historical texts. In the history of hermeneutics three phases are recognized : theological, romantic and phenomenological. Phenomenology, in the twentieth century, is identified with the Germen thinker Edmund Husserl. Husserl has been considered the first to conduct a major phenomenological re-description of the phenomenon. Husserl in his later works, principally in "Ideas Pertaining to a Pure Phenomenology and to a Phenomenological Philosophy" (1913) and "Cartesian Meditations" (1931) performs his phenomenological reduction in order to give verbal expression to mental events as they appear to consciousness, independent of an everyday, uncritical commitment to the existence of other people, places, physical objects causality, etc'.[16] However it is Martin Heidegger, a student of Husserl, who has become a leading phenomenologist of the twentieth century.

Heidegger reasserted the Kantian claim that experience is not the reception of sense impressions but a form of questioning. To have experience is to be in an active state of finding about the world. In his major work "Being and Time" (1927) Heidegger explains how to human being the being itself became an issue. He says, 'Looking at something, understanding and conceiving it, choosing, access to it-all these ways of behaving are constitutive for our inquiry, and therefore are models of being for those particular entities which we, the inquirers, are ourselves. Thus to work out the question of being adequately, we must make an entity-the inquirer-transparent in its own being. The very asking of this question is an entity's mode of being; and as such it gets its essential character from what is inquired about-namely, being. This entity which each of us is himself and which includes inquiring as one of the possibilities of its being, we shall denote by the term *Dasein* '.[17]

Dasein in German, means 'being there'. The concept that being as an issue for humans is very much important for Heidegger. In his view there always has to be an opening up possibilities in advance of existence in order experience to take place. Just as the kind of question asked influences the answer, the way in which one approaches reality affects how it appears. According to Heidegger, phenomenology is the method of enquiries where by some thing is brought out into open. However, his aesthetic ideas are concretely expressed in his essay, "The Origin of the Work of Art". In the view of Heidegger, art is true in that it lets us see the tension between concealment and disclosure. He understands this as the conflict of world and the earth. Ultimately, for Heidegger, the true nature of art is poetry.

He believed that art is truest when it is poetic. Heidegger says, 'All art, as the letting happen of the advent of the truth of what is, is, as such, *essentially poetry*. The nature of art, on which both the artwork and the artist depend, is the setting-itself-into-work of truth. It is due to art's poetic nature that, in the midst of what is, art breaks open an open place, in whose openness every-thing is other than usual'.[18]

Verbal language, Heidegger argues, is the principal form of projection where by a space is opened, allowing an object to appear. When we use words, we are drawing on the associations and significations, which constitute everyday discourse. What the poet does is to work with these in a way which defamiliarizes the familiar, which makes the usual unusual.

An opening appears in the ordinariness of being, allowing new possibilities to come to light. Metaphor is a good example: two familiar but unrelated words are combined to produce a novel description, often leading to a new way of seeing the object in question, e.g., 'time is a river', 'rain is the light of the blind'. Generating 'new' ideas from 'old' concepts reflects the hermeneutic principle of speakers transcending their initial perspectives through conversation.

In Heidegger, the notion of ontologically creative potential of art absolutely is decisive. In the 1930's Heidegger laid a great stress on "the work of art". Extremely important in this regard is his essay " The Origin of the Work of Art" In that he saw art as bringing world into existence. According to him, the work opens up a world and keeps it abidingly in force. After the 1930's Heidegger attributes this world-creating force not just to the work of art but also to "language" in general.

Heidegger expressed the problem of this dichotomy in the thought of Enlightenment. In "Being and Time" (1927) Heidegger is largely concerned with attacking what he sees as the West's deeply ingrained tendency to look at the world in terms of the subject/object division. Heidegger traces this tendency back to Descartes and sees Kant as continuity along the same road. Against the Cartesian and Kantian insistence on looking at the world in terms of the subject/ object division, he proposes the notion of "Being- in – the world". But much of the views of Heidegger on aesthetics can be seen only in his later writings. However, the concern with the subject/ object division so well epitomized in the tension between the practical and the "theoretical" in Kant, is of tremendous importance for Heidegger throughout his career.

In another important work, "Language"[19] (1950) Heidegger propounds his celebrated view, that language speaks man. Language brings man and his world into conscious existence; it is inaugural speaking in that it grants an abode or a dwelling for the being of mortals in the larger context of what Heidegger cryptically calls the "fourfold world" (comprising earth, sky, divinities, and mortals). In this account, language is neither mimetic nor expressive : it does not represent an external reality, nor does it express a pre-existing feeling or thought. Language shapes consciousness and perception, calling things into being; it does not merely designate or label objects. In poetry, Heidegger argues, the essence of language is manifested with particular clarity, since poetry is less concerned with communication and expression than with imaginative creation.

Sartre's Existential Aesthetics

Jean-Paul Sartre and Emmanuel Levinas were deeply influenced by phenomenology. Sartre was known worldwide for his distinct brand of existentialism, which focused on the human experience of freedom and responsibility in a godless universe. The French philosopher and writer Sartre advocated a form of existentialism in which art is seen as an expression of the freedom of the individual to choose, and as such demonstrates the individual's responsibility for his or her choices. Despair, as reflected in art, is not an end but a beginning, because it overcomes the pretexts, alibis, and self-evasions behind which people ordinarily shelter, thus opening the way for genuine freedom.

For Sartre existence is prior to essence : because the world and human nature possess no fixed meaning, they are responsible for their own choices and actions. In the view of Sartre the experience of literature is concretely the experience of freedom. This is an experience that draws together the author and reader into the collaborative feature-oriented project of human existence. This existence is always in a state of becoming.

Sartre presents subjective experience in the form of a question. The question is 'how one should act?' Clive Cazeaux explains Sartre notion of experience in very lucid terms : 'An object does not disclose all its possible appearances in one moment. Experience is successive : a continuum in which aspects appear and disappear, in which appearances are revealed and then withdrawn. Impressions move on : this object is not present to me now in exactly the same way it was a moment ago. The next moment always appears as if it were the answer to a question : it might confirm or confound expectations, or surprise us, or give a negative reply. What is certain is that the next moment won't be the same as before, for even to judge it 'the same' is to give it a different character. It is only in consciousness that the impression of something not being the case can take place, for example, expecting to find thirty pounds in my wallet but finding only twenty, or waiting in a café for a friend who never turns up. It is the possibility of negation, of being surprised by appearances, of having one's expectations confounded, which disengages consciousness from the brute causal order of the world'.[20]

Sartre has specific views on how writing gives shape and form to experience. In his "What is Literature" he argues that, among all the art forms prose is the only form of representation, which returns us to world. Because, for the prose writer words are transparent. The prose writer makes the words transparent so that the readers may assume full responsibility before the object, which has been laid bare. Prose uses words as signs. The ambiguity of sign implies that one can penetrate it at one's will like a pane of glass and pursue the thing signified. In contrast, the other forms like painting, sculpture, music and poetry exist as things and, as such, have a density of their own which withdraws the audience from human situations. Prose, for Sartre, organizes experience in a manner, which does not draw attention to itself as an external or extra-experiential form of organizations.

Levinas' Doubling of Reality

Emmanuel Levinas argues in his "Reality and its Shadow" (1948) that, impedes our openness to others. The most distinctive feature of his writing is the importance he gives to attitude which we can approach others or the 'Other'. Clive Cazeaux says : 'The Other is a technical term from Hegel, denoting that which an individual encounters as distinct from herself, e.g., an object or another person, yet which plays a role in affirming the individual's sense of her own identity. For Levinas, all our dealings with the world, whether they concern art, politics, or science, raise ethical questions of how we ought to behave in the face of someone or something standing before us, and much of his writing is devoted to working out the precise nature of this 'confrontation'.[21]

In the view of Levinas art is a 'doubling of reality'. Like a shadow art has a density of its own. It creates a 'fissure' or an 'interval' (called 'meanwhile') between art and reality. This makes art a dimension of evasion. People are preoccupied with art at the cost of other obligations like, dealing with others. In a way, art obstructs human activity. Levinas says, 'To say that an image is an idol is to affirm that every image is in the last analysis plastic, and that every artwork is in the end a statue – a stoppage of time, or rather its delay behind itself. But we must show in what sense it stops or delays, and in what sense a statue's existing is a semblance of the existing of being'.[22]

Levinas emphasizes that art can be reintegrated into human affairs through conceptual, philosophical criticism.

Gadamer's Hermeneutical Perspective

The German philosopher Hans-George Gadamer has been considered the most important figure to emerge in post-Heideggerian Hermeneutics. In his essay "Aesthetics and Hermeneutics", Gadamer relates the experience of art to the hermeneutic question of how one tradition can understand another. He contests the idea that aesthetic experience is the grasping of an original content, whether this refers to the original experience of the artist or something judged to be specific to the time in which the work was produced. When we study an artwork, he suggests, the artist's intention to speak meets our own projected desire to understand. The encounter does not reconstruct experience but instead surprises us : it generates new experience through the interrelation of perspectives, and draws attention to our own status as beings that interpret the world.

In his essay "Aesthetics and Hermeneutics" Gadamer establishes the close relation between aesthetics and hermeneutics. In his view, when we say that a work of art says some thing to us it belongs to the matrix of things. Here, our assertion is not metaphor but a valid and explainable meaning. Hence, the work of art is an object of hermeneutics. In his view, 'The hermeneutical perspective is so comprehensive; however, that it must even include the experience of beauty in nature and art. If it is the fundamental constitution of the historicity of human Dasein to mediate itself to itself understandingly – which necessarily means to the whole of its own experience of the world – then all tradition belongs to it".[23]

According to Gadamer all human constructions are reflections of a culture's orientation towards the world. This applies to hand tools, to language, and to art. For him, 'the experience of art… becomes the experience of experience, as the distance between ourselves and the artist- necessary for conversation – makes us aware of the temporal, contingent nature of the terms through which we perceive the world'.[24]

Vattimo's Aesthetics of Silence

Another important phenomenological thinker is Gianni Vattimo. Vattimo applied phenomenology and hermeneutics to the question of postmodernity. His essay "The Death or Decline of Art" offers a hermeneutics of the concept of 'end'. The 'end' in a way, indicates Hegel's 'death of art' thesis and even embraces the end of modernity, where 'modernity' is understood as the ultimate dominion of the universal concept over individual phenomenon. According to Vattimo, though art did not turn into thought, it is no longer an independent event. In the process, technological means of production of the art has become kitsch. In that way it refused to engage with mass culture completely. In his view, 'To protest against Kitsch, a manipulative mass culture, and the aestheticisation of existence at a low and weak level, authentic art has often taken refuge in programmatically aporetic positions which deny any possibility of immediate enjoyment of the work (its 'gastronomic' aspect, as it were), refuse to communicate anything at all, and opt for silence instead'.[25]

Marxist Aesthetics

Karl Marx and Friedrich Engels are central figures in the history of literary criticism and theory and in the development of cultural studies, though neither produced a body of literary-critical work. The young Marx wrote lyrics, attempted drama and fiction, and read deeply in eighteenth - and nineteenth-century German philosophy and aesthetics. The writings of Marx and Engels often refer to and quote literature (ranging from classical Greek drama to the novels of Charles Dickens). But as economic historians, social theorists, and revolutionaries seeking to change the world, their main work lay elsewhere, and their direct contributions to literary criticism are scattered and uneven. However, what they contributed allocated for the development of literary criticism on the sociological lines.

Many critics are inspired by the philosophical writings of Marx and Engels. Specifically, Marx's "A Contribution to the Critique of Political Economy" (1858), "Grundrisse" (1857), and "The Germen Ideology" (not published until 1931) gave tremendous impetus to literary and cultural studies. Inspired by the writings of these two philosophers a number of critics and culturologists came on to the scene in the 20th century. The critics, inspired by Marx and Engels produced considerable body of criticism, which exhibits brilliant insights in the analysis of literary and cultural texts.

Lukacs' Aesthetics of Mediated Immediacy

The writings of the Hungarian philosopher George Lukacs (1985-1971) span political theory and literary theory. Lukacs is the first thinker to develop a systematic Marxist aesthetics and thereby to aesthetics as an integral part of Marxist philosophy. Lukacs' original analysis of the commodity form in "History and Class Consciousness" (1923) continues to influence Marxist cultural theory. He was a staunch advocate of realist position. He opposed the experimental aesthetics of modernism by declaring them as obscure and fragmentary. He considered much of the modernist literature a symptom of the alienation, the basic characteristic of life under capitalism. Lukacs believed that the realist literature would counter the decadence of modernist experimentation. In the sense of Lukacs, great literature reflects not the surface reality, but its underline movements. That is why he considered realism a dynamic category.

Lukacs' "The Theory of the Novel" (1960) places the novel in between the epic and tragedy. The former expresses the community where as the latter represents the solitude and death. In "History and Class Consciousness" Lukacs develops the concept of historical "totalities", "actual class consciousness"," maximum possible class consciousness". He distinguishes aesthetic from scientific knowledge. In his view, 'in contradistinction to conceptual abstractions of science, art constitutes an anthropomorphic form of cognition, which truthfully depicts reality with a vivid, human-centered poetic concreteness. Contrary to science, art brings to us the movement of life as motion and makes us grasp it in its living unity. The artist discovers the appearance/essence relationship intellectually and gives it artistic shape, i.e., he conceals the relationship artistically. This tow-fold labour creates a new aesthetically mediated immediacy. However, the fictionality of art differs from that of religion and magic in that art does not lie about its own fictionality.[26]

Lukacs essay "Specific Particularity as the Central Category of Aesthetics (1956) exhibits his interest in aesthetics. He adopts the term 'particularity' to denote the form an artist is able to give reality, a form which avoids both the abstract generality of the universal concept and the uncontextualisable detail of the individual thing. The particular, for Lukacs, exists midway between the individual and the universal. Clive Cazeaux says, 'The 'individual' is what we are immediately confronted with in experience, e.g., 'this stone', 'this chair', 'this colour', where as the 'universal' denotes the abstract, general term, e.g., the concept 'stone', the concept 'colour', which allows us to think of individuals as having certain characteristics'.[27]

The individual-universal relationship has two guises in the essay, "Specific particularity as the Central Category of Aesthetics". The first is the epistemological : in the epistemological, it stands for the distinction between art and science. Both science and art are forms of knowledge, which work in different ways. The scientist passes through particularity; either in abstracting universals from individuals or in using universals to focus on new individuals. In contrast, the artist wants to retain and give expression to a particular tension that exists between sensuous individuality and universal recognition.

According to Lukacs, 'Bourgeois aesthetics values the art work as some thing timeless and ineffable, and takes the emphasis on genre determination to be detraction from the work's ineffability. This treats 'art work' and 'genre' as antithetical poles'.[28]

In the dialectical materialist account of Lukas the two terms are mutually defining concepts. In a way, Lukacs makes 'particularity as the central category of his aesthetics. However he asks, '...does our conception of the central significance of particularity in the system of aesthetic categories not itself run the risk of falling victim to vulgar species of Platonic idealism? We believe that precisely the opposite is, in fact the case'.[29]

However, Lukacs' advocacy of realism came under immediate and persistent criticism. Perhaps the best known is that of Bertolt Brecht, who accuses Lukacs of inadvertently lapsing into formalism by privileging the form of an outdated nineteenth-century genre above all others. More severe are the criticisms directed at Lukacs' central conceptions of totality and typicality.

With the advent of postmodernism, totalising theories in general have come under attack; for instance, the leading philosopher of the postmodern, Jean-Françoise Lyotard, famously urged his readers to "wage a war on totality" and to critique "grand narratives" that purport to explain everything. In spite of all this, Lukacs work has made important contributions to contemporary debates; his influence is clear in the roles reification, realism, and periodisation play in the work of Fredric Jameson, the most important American theorist of postmodernism.

Goldman's Genetic Structuralist Aesthetics

The Rumanian Marxist Lucien Goldman considered himself a disciple of Lukacs'. Goldman substituted 'genetic structuralism' for 'Lukacs' reflection' theory. Goldman's genetic structuralist theory proposed a homology between the form of literary work, and either the 'world view' of a dominant group in pre-capitalist society or economic structure of a capitalist society. He defined 'world views' as, 'ensembles of mental categories which tended towards coherent structures and which were proper to certain privileged social groups, whose thought, feeling and behaviour were orientated, towards on overall organization of interhuman relations and of relations between men and nature.'[30]

According to Goldman the importance of artistic creation is that it is in the great works of art and philosophy that the mental categories of the social groups are fully realized, not through the reflection of that group's life, but thorough 'creating on the imaginary plane a universe whose content may differ entirely from that of collective consciousness'.[31]

From Lukacs' theory of the novel Goldman borrowed the concept of literary form as central to a work's meaning. The notion of form in Goldman differed from that of Lukacs'. In Goldman's "For a Sociology of the Novel", form refers variously to plot structure or literary style (e.g., the nouveau roman). Thus, the characteristic novel of the emergent capitalist era takes the form of a 'degraded search' by a 'problematic hero' for authentic values.

Goldman concentrated on the 'consciousness, the mental reality which is not absolutely determined by material existence. Goldman's notion of 'world view' describes the comprehensive and far reaching form of group consciousness, which affects all kinds of relationships between people and between people and nature. He argued that major writers create an advanced version of a worldview by increasing the degree of structural coherence. For Goldman, says Raman Selden, 'it is the structure of the worldview and not the content which is important. The structure concerns the principles or underline categories by which it orders reality'.[32]

For Goldman, literary form is not, however, homologous with the consciousness of a particular social group; instead, it structurally reproduces a nature of every day life in the individualistic society created by market production. He thought that there is a rigorous homology between the literary form and the Novel. The hero is problematic since he cannot embody any authentic values, which are only present in the novel by implication. This according to Goldman is precisely homologous with the role of the use-value of a commodity in a capitalist society dominated by exchange-value. Its 'action assumes an implicit character, exactly like that of authentic values in the fictional world'.[33]

According to Goldman, during the second phase of the capitalist society, i.e., the economy of monopoly capitalism, there is a change in the novel, there is the dissolution of character for example the novels of Kafka, Joyce and Camus. In Goldman's view, the phase of capitalism is paralleled philosophically by existentialism. Since the Second World War, in his view, there is the capitalism of organization and a consumer society. The appearance of new novel in this face is centered on the absence and impossibility of communication. According to Goldman, the authentic values sought by the problematic hero in classic novel are precisely those values repressed by capitalism itself. That is why the novel form in the period is bound up with development of bourgeois but not with expression of the real consciousness of that class.

In the above context Goldman says, 'man conceives himself or feels himself as part of a developing whole and situates himself in a historical or transcendent transindividual dimension. But bourgeois ideology, bound up like bourgeois society itself with the existence of economic activity, is precisely the first ideology in history that is both radically profane and ahistorical.... [it] created the first radically non-aesthetic form of consciousness (rationalism)'.[34]

Adorno's Cultural Industry

During 1930s German Marxism was forced into complicated and anaesthetised responses to the Fascist takeover. A number of the orists and philosophers treated art and literature as privileged domain. The most important among them is Theodor W.Adorno. Adorno believed that serious art unlike the non-serious or popular art which tries to pollute with existing ideologies, was set apart from reality. This detachment allowed serious art to criticize reality. This criticism is not by direct reflection but by providing a negative image of the alienated and fragmented condition of modern society. In his view, one who is really interested in freedom cannot avoid the dimensions of art, the imagination and beauty. Art, for Adorno, offers social and conceptual imaginations. Art though routed in particular cultural context generates its own novel structures of meaning, independent of any worldly content. He cites music as the purest art, because it does not refer directly to the world, where as all other art forms like literature, painting, film are burdened by their representation value.

In his "Minima Moralia : Reflections from Damaged Life" he says;

1· The task of art today is to bring chaos into order.
2· Artistic productivity is the capacity for being voluntarily involuntary.
3· Art is magic delivered from the lie of being truth.
4· Since works of art are sprung, for better or worse, from fetishes ... are artists to be blamed if their attitude to their products is slightly fetishistic?
5· The art-form which has from earliest times laid the highest claims to spirituality, as representation of Ideas, Drama, depends equally, by its innermost presuppositions, on an audience.[35]

Adorno wrote extensively on culture, philosophy, literature and music. In the opinion of Gillian Rose, 'Adorno's sociology of literature and music is devoted mainly to examining genres and individual works of art in the light of the thesis that a contradiction has developed between the forces and the relations of production.'[36]

In "the Culture Industry : Enlightenment as mass Deception", which appeared as a long chapter in Adorno and Horkheimer's "The Dialectic of Enlightenment" (1947) Adorno argues that the administered modern word is sustained in part by technologically reproduced mass art. He contends that the cultural industry serves the totalitarian impulses of modern capitalist society. In his view, the cultural industry ultimately contributes to the liquidation of the individual and maintains status quo. The cultural industry transforms art into commodities and people into consumers. Though the culture industry helps to create a state of mind in which people's desires for pleasure and happiness are activated but deferred in endless entertainment.

Adorno disagreed with Lukacs on every count : with his ideas of form and style, with his notions of realism and of modernism, and with his interpretation of contemporary state of literature. In his view, Lukacs failed to understand the stylistic and technical features of the novel because he subordinates such features to the underlying perspective or view of the world, understood as the content of a work, in marked contrast to Lukacs' own earlier book, "The Theory of The Novel", in which he himself established the primacy of form. According to Leitch, 'For Adorno, modern art resists the self-evidence empirical reality, lends suffering a voice and acknowledges a better future to come.'[37]

Raymond Williams' Cultural Materialism

Raymond Williams was the leading figure among the Marxist literary intellectuals. Williams is best known for espousing the study of culture and society along with that of literature. He provided a model for those interested in investigating literature in terms of politics, ideology and social theory. Arguing against traditional views, that assume the autonomy of literature and its privileged cultural value, Williams analysed it as a specific, historical product, carrying class values.

'Culture' has always been, Williams major preoccupation. In fact his major works, "Culture and Society"(1954), "Long Revolution "(1961), and "Culture"(1981) are almost exclusively devoted to concept of the culture. There is a substantial discussion of culture in other writings like, "Marxism and Literature"(1977). Williams talks of three levels of culture-lived, recorded, and of the selective tradition connecting the two. Writing, for example, would be culture at the recorded level, while "literature", as we commonly understand it, would constitute the selective tradition. How some pieces of writing become literary works is something that involves one in the questions of valuation and evaluation. For Williams, cultural practice and cultural production, 'are not simply derived from an otherwise constituted social order but are themselves major elements in its constitution.'[38]

Williams considered artistic practice primarily a human activity, an important means of communication in which we create the common reality of our lives. By "creative", he means a particular selection from and appositive response to a body of experience. To him, it is in art primarily that the effect of a whole lived experience is expressed and embodied. The artist's success lies in making others live through the experience that is offered, while the distinction of value in art lies in the actual power to communicate.

Williams responds specifically to the state of English studies of his time, but he also raises the perennial problem in literary theory- the definition of literature. Modern literary theorists often look to formal artistic features intrinsic in works, discerning what Roman Jakobson terms their

"Literariness" or "poeticity". Williams sees literature instead as a shifting historical product-not a transcendent entity but a complex mutating human product linked with concepts such as literacy, imagination, taste, and beauty, all inflected by sociohistorical conditions. He also notes that criticism and its function have similarly muted to reflect changing social roles.

Williams calls his theoretical approach : "cultural materialism." at once invoking the Marxist focus on the economic means of production and emphasizing the role of culture. Stressing the complex interaction of culture and society, he investigates the material, historical factors that inform culture-part of society's "superstructure"-but he also shows how culture shapes society in an ongoing process, often contesting and resisting dominant modes of production.

Herbert Marcuse's Aesthetic Dimension

Herbert Marcuse another member of Frankfurt School gained prominence in 1960's because of his appeal for a biological-moral-aesthetic revolt for the militant student groups and intellectuals of the capitalist world. He builds on the work of Kant, Schiller, Marx and Freud. Marcuse emphasizes on the aesthetic dimension of life. For him the response of human beings to the beauty and excitement of artistic images is one of the most important motivating factors in their lives and, as such, a control of aesthetic sensibility means the control of the lives of the people. For him aesthetic form is the result of the transformation of a given content into a self contained whole. He says,' ' only in art has bourgeois society tolerated its own ideals and taken them seriously as a general demand.'[39]

In his view Utopia, fantasy and rebellion are allowed only in art. The real wonder of affirmative cultural is that human beings can feel happy without being so at all.

In his "Counterrevolution and Revolt" Marcuse shows how changes in structure of society are linked to changes in our sensory experience of reality. Specifically the essay "Nature and Revolution" is built upon the dynamic species relationship Marx constructs between nature and senses. In the essay he says, 'Aesthetics of liberation, beauty as a 'form' of freedom : it looks as if Marx has shied away from this anthropomorphist, idealistic conception. Or is this apparently idealistic notion rather the *enlargement of the materialistic base*? For 'man is directly a *natural being*; he is a corporeal, living, real, sensuous, objective being' who has 'real, sensuous objects' as the objects of his life. And his senses ("like those organs which are directly social in their form") are active, practical in the 'appropriation' of the object world; they express the social existence of man, his 'objectification.' This is no longer Feuerbach's 'naturalism' but, on the contrary, the extension of Historical Materialism to a dimension which is to play a vital role in the liberation of man.'[40]

The ideal society for Marcuse is modelled on the work of art itself. He considered form as the negation and mastery of the disorder, violence and suffering. The restoration of order within art is only an illusion. According to Marcuse, 'The aesthetic as the possible Form of a free society appears at the age of development where the intellectual and material resources for the conquest of scarcity are available.'[41]

The subversive effects of art literature are explained by Marcuse in his "Counterrevolution and Revolt" (1972). In this book Marcuse emphasises on the most important works of art and literature since the nineteenth century, in which a thoroughly anti-bourgeoisie stance is widespread.

In "The Aesthetic Dimension" (1977) Marcuse shows that art is committed to liberation of sensibility, imagination and reason. This reason is distinct from the rationality of the dominant institutions. By its association with Eros, instinctual repression, the aesthetic dimension protests against the established world and acts as a promise of liberation. In his view, all authentic works of art are subversive of perception and understanding, of dominant consciousness and the ordinary experience. The authentic works of art express a truth, an experience; necessity is an essential component of revolution. The 'inwardness' that art generates as a political value as it can act as a counter-force against aggressive socialization. Marcuse even says that there can be more subversive potential in the poetry of Baudelaire and Rimbaud than in the didactic plays of Brecht. In his sense, the art of the past still provides enjoyment, because it alters the existing reality into another dimension, one of liberation and it even appeals to repressed qualities of human sensibility through its aesthetic form.

In fact, Marcuse is concerned more with individuals than with society. He felt that community is an association of free individuals, not masses. In a way Marcuse wanted art to address the elite but not masses. He says, 'Art cannot change the world, but it can contribute to the changing consciousness and drives of the men and women who would change the world.'[42]

Caudwell's Materialist Poetics

The most important Marxist critic of the 1930s was Christopher Caudwell, whose Marxist writing was done in only two years, i.e., between 1934-36. He was killed in Spain a year later. Unlike the Oxford and Cambridge educated Marxist intellectuals who dominated communist cultural work in Britain, Caudwell was an autodidact. He therefore drew on a much wider range of sources for his ideas. Many of them are scientific and anthropological sources. He also proposed a more ambitious approach to the arts than other British Marxists. In addition to the interpretation of sociological equivalents, he wanted to define the specificity of art as a social practice, in his major work "Illusion and Reality" (1937).

"Illusion and Reality" was unusual in two respects : in contrast to the many Marxists who assumed literature more as the novel, Caudwell focused on poetry, and in order to determine the function of poetry, which he assumed to be constant, he saw its origins in primitive societies. His major forerunner in this respect had been Plekhanov, while later authors undertaking a similar task have included George Thomson (in his studies of Greek drama) and Lukacs, in his late aesthetic theory.

Like other writers, Caudwell argued that pre-class societies had a unity of social practice, which separated out into the division of labour as class societies developed. Tribal poetry is thus closely linked with the economic and social life of the tribe. In the view of Caudwell, ' It expresses the social relation of man's instincts to the un-gathered fruit. These instincts have generated these emotions (the emotions present in the poem) just because they have not blindly followed the necessities of the germ plasm, but have been moulded by the objective necessities of collective action to common economic end. The phantasy of poetry is a social image.'[43]

This linking of the biological, psychological, social and natural to form a poetics, is representative of Caudwell's method. The book goes on to trace the separation of poetry from religion, and of science from magic, as class differentiation develops. Nevertheless, poetry retains a necessary role in the relationship of the instincts to social life, and of man to nature. Only the content of the relationships change throughout history.

Poetry takes on a privileged status in relation to the other arts. Caudwell says, 'Poetry expresses the freedom which is here as in man's general timeless unity in society; it is interested in society as the sum and guardian of common instinctive tendencies; it speaks of love, death, hope, sorrow and despair as all men experience them. The novel is the expression of that freedom, which men seek, not in their unity in society but in their differences, of their search for freedom in the pores of society, and therefore of their repulsions from, clashes with, and concrete motions against other individuals different from themselves.'[44]

In Caudwell's view poetry preserves an essence of humanity, while the novel is product of class society and may die with it. Caudwell's hectic account of "capitalist poetry' introduces the single ideological theme which for him characterizes bourgeois civilization : an obsession with 'freedom'.

The important side of Caudwell's work is that it explores the work of poetry, its means and methods of effectively. Although dissociating his ideas from Freud, Caudwell entitled a chapter of "Illusion and Reality", 'Poetry's dream-Work', anticipating much later work on a materialist poetics.

Gramsci's Antagonistic Aesthetics

Antonio Gramsci, a leader of the Italian Communist Party, spent the last decade of his life in a Fascist prison, where he composed his "Prison Notebooks". Among these fragmentary writings there are numerous reflections on the character and place of what later Marxists were to call 'ideological struggle', in a capitalist society which continues to function primarily through the consent of the masses, with armed force to be used only when that consent crumbles.

Gramsci was sentenced to twenty years in prison. He was released from prison because of ill health in April 1937. He died in less than two weeks after gaining his freedom. For four years (1929-33) in prison, before his health collapsed, Gramsci was allowed to write. The result was the four volumes of the "The Prison Notebooks", on which most of Gramsci's reputation as a social and cultural theorist rests. The essay "The Formation of the Intellectuals" is one of his best writings. In his view, 'All, men are intellectuals… but not all men have in society the function of intellectuals.'[45]

Gramsci wanted to consider how the intellectual can be effective, especially in moving people to action. Gramsci identifies two types of intellectuals. Traditional intellectuals are the administrators and apologists for existing social and cultural institutions, such as schools, various religious denominations, corporations, the military, the press, political bureaucracies, and the judicial system. Writers, artists, and philosophers are traditional intellectuals insofar as they work within formal institutions. In contrast, organic intellectuals rise out of membership in social groups (or classes) that have an antagonistic relationship to established institutions and official power. They "articulate" those groups' needs and aspirations, which have frequently gone unexpressed. The organic intellectual does not simply parrot pre-existing group beliefs or demands but brings to the level of public speech what has not been officially recognized. While a given group does have certain tendencies, the process of articulation itself will shape it, giving it new identities and commitments-new ways of understanding itself and its desires.

Althusser's Aesthetics of Overdetermination.

The French structuralist Marxist Louis Althusser defined literature in terms of its capacity to reveal or rupture from within the terms of seeing proposed by the categories of dominant ideologies. That is why he believed that Marxist literary criticism should understand the formal process through which literary texts work upon and transform dominant ideological forms. Althusser starts rightly with the Kantian notion that the distinction between thought and reality is irreducible. According Anil Raina, in Althusser, we find an attempt to amalgamate the Gramcian notation of hegemony and an indigenous concept of Ideological State Apparatuses with theory of "Subject" derived from Freud and Lacan.

In the view of Raina, 'the crucial term in Althusser's work is 'ideology' which, to him, has a number of attributes. It has a material existence but no history, and is a 'representation' of imaginary relationships of individuals to their real conditions of existence, functioning in order to secure the reproduction of the relations of production. It 'hails' or 'interpolates' concrete individuals as concrete subjects, by function of the category of the subject and, as such, is organic of part of every social reality.'[46]

Althusser's major concepts-'ideological state apparatuses', "interpellation', imaginary relations', and 'overdetermination'- permeates the discourse of contemporary literary and cultural theory. His theory of ideology has influenced virtually all subsequent serious works on the topic. The problem Althusser wanted to solve in "Ideological State Apparatuses"- to determine how a society reproduces its basic social relations, there by ensuring its continuing existence – is an eternal one in social theory. Althusser, employs a structuralist account of the societal mechanisms that inculcate such a consent, as well as psychoanalyst account of how ideology makes individuals "subjects" of the dominant social order.

Althusser famously terms them as societal mechanisms for creating loyal or obedient citizens who practice dominant values. These apparatuses are complex and differing from one society to another. In fact they are civil institutions that have legal status. That is why they are designated as "state apparatuses". They include churches, schools, the family, courts, political parties, unions, the media, sports and the arts. The ideological state apparatuses (ISAs) differ from "repressive state apparatuses" (RSAs), such as the police, military, the prison system, and government. They are not unified. They operate basically in the private sphere, and they do not depend upon direct coercion but through indirect or implicit consent realized in accepted practices. One tacitly learns the practice of obedience to authority, for example in church, in school and at home. According to Althusser a dominant social order cannot survive if it simply depends on force. To prove this he traces the rising influence of schools as the dominant ISA in modern society.

According to Althusser, 'all ideological State apparatuses, whatever they are, contribute to the same result : the reproduction of the relations of production, i.e. of capitalist relations of exploitation.'[47]

Eagleton's Aesthetics of Sociology

Among the major Marxists literally critics, Terry Eagleton is very famous in the recent times. A student of Raymond Williams, Eagleton has been the foremost Marxist commentator on literary theory since the 1980s. In his "Function of Criticism : From the Spectator to post-Structuralism" (1984), Eagleton declares that contemporary criticism has lost its social purpose and became marginalized through the technocratic fetishizing of grand theory. Continuing the Althusserian tradition, Eagleton's "Criticism and Ideology" (1976) builds upon the notion of literature as "production". The book questions the attempts of liberal humanism to consider the "aesthetic" in isolation from its social and ideological meanings. Like Althusser, Eagleton argues the need for a science of the text. In his view, 'The task of Marxists criticism is to provide a materialist explanation of the bases of literary value.'[48]

Eagleton is concerned much with the materialist analysis of literary texts. In his view, 'The value of a text, then, is determined by its double mode of insertion into ideological formation and into the available lineages of literary discourse.'[49] For him the formal values are values only to the extent that they are allowed to perceive the working of an ideology. In fact, for him, the perception of ideology is a value in its self. 'The distinction between the "aesthetic" and "ideological" elements a text, then, is methodological than real.'[50]

Poststructuralist and postmodernist Aesthetics

The words 'Poststructuralism' and 'Postmodernism' are often used interchangeably. In recent times these two movements set the terms and agendas for many of the major developments and debates in the field of aesthetics. In fact, there are serious attempts to redefine the very concept of the aesthetics. Some times postmodernism has been called a movement that emphasizes the anti- aesthetic. And it played a significant role in shaping the direction of the other movements, particularly feminist, postcolonial, and cultural. It inspired even certain theories like queer theory.

Poststructuralist accounts of literature often stem from deconstructive theory. Especially its three concepts of textuality, rhetoricity because the signifier (word) is disconnected from the signified (concept) and the referent (thing), language floats or slides in relation to reality, a condition made more severe with the additional sliding introduced into language by figurative language, such as metaphors and metonymies. Such rhetoricity adds layers of substitutions and supplements to floating signifiers. Textuality and rhetoricity are conditioned by yet a third sliding or differential element, intertextuality-a text's dependence on prior words, concepts, connotations, codes, conventions, unconscious practices, and text. Every text is an intertext that borrows, knowingly or not, from the immense archive of previous culture.

The term 'inter' textuality, captures the sense of textuality as being conditioned by this inescapable historical intertext. According to Roland

Barthes, 'any text is a new tissue of past citations. Bits of codes, formulae, rhythmic modes, fragments of social languages, etc. pass into the text and are redistributed within it, for there is always language before and around the text.'[51]

Postmodernism is a wide-ranging cultural movement, which adopts a sceptical attitude to many of the principles and assumptions that have underpinned Western thought and social life for the last few centuries. These assumptions, constitute the core of what we call Modernism. It includes a faith in the inevitability of progress in all areas of human endeavour, and in the power of reason, as well as a commitment to originality in both thought and artistic expression.

As a cultural ethos, modernism is uncompromisingly forward–looking and, at least implicitly, makes the assumption that the present civilization is to be considered superior to the past in the extent of its knowledge and the sophistication of its techniques. As an aesthetic, modernism promotes the view that originality is the highest state of artistic endeavour, and that this can best be achieved by experimentation with form. Postmodernism has turned such ideas on their head, by calling into question modernism's commitment to progress, as well as the ideology under-pinning it, and encouraging a dialogue between past and present in thought and the arts. Postmodernism has therefore involved a rejection of the modernist commitment to experiment and originality, and a return to this use of older styles and artistic methods.

The characteristic postmodernist style is pastiche, with authors returning to a realist style of novel-writing, artists moving away from abstraction and back to figurative painting, and architects freely mixing old and new styles in building. Jean-Francois Lyotard understands postmodernism as a rejection of all-encompassing cultural theories, such as Marxism. He argued for a much more pragmatic attitude to political life and artistic expression that simply ignores the oppressive rules of the grand narrative. Postmodernism is therefore as much an attitude of mind as a specific theoretical position in its own right. In general, postmodernism can be regarded as part of a longer-running philosophical tradition of scepticism, which is intrinsically anti-authoritarian in outlook. It is more concerned with undermining the pretensions of other theories than putting anything positive in their place. Lyotard himself sees postmodernism and modernism as cyclical movements, which alternate throughout the course of history.

Poststructuralism is a generic term used to refer to all those theories that came to reject the principles of structuralism, which, form the 1950s through to the 1970s constituted the major paradigm of French intellectual enquiry. Among the theories that carne to challenge the stranglehold of the structuralist paradigm where deconstruction, feminism and postmodernism, all of which can be considered as poststructuralist in that they challenged the assumptions on which structuralism was based.

Structuralists had held that underlying all phenomena there are deep structures that dictated how those phenomena developed and that the world was organized into a series of interlocking systems, each with its own 'grammar' of operation. All systems were amenable to structuralist analysis, given that their grammars were seen to operate in similar ways. Structuralism became an exercise in classification whose goal was the comprehensive mapping of all systems.

Against this essentially orderly picture of the world, deconstructionists offered a far more 'anarchic' alternative. Difference, rather than similarity, was the defining characteristic. Jacques Derrida spoke of the 'innocence of becoming' rather than the predetermined working out of deep structural patterns, meaning that the future was always to be considered open and unknown. Postmodernists, too, have reacted against the rigidity and apparent authoritarianism of the structuralist model. The postmodernists and poststructuralists argued against theories that claim to offer universal explanations of any phenomena.

Let us now move to Poststructuralist and Postmodern thinkers like Georges Bataille, Roland Barthes, Michel Foucault, Jacques Derrida, Paul de Man, Jean Baudrillard, Jean-Francois Lyotard, Gilles Deleuze and Felix Guattari.

Bataille's Aesthetics of Transgression

Much of Georges Bataille work related to the concept of transgression. His major themes are the 'concept of boundary' and the way in which the moral political and epistemological bounders are constructed within society. Bataille work extended to various fields like fiction, autobiography, criticism and philosophy. Through transgression, Bataille seeks to disclose the conflicts and aporias, which define human values and institutions.

Bataille in the text, "Sanctity, Eroticism and Solitude" (1955) says, 'In the very first place eroticism differs from animal sexuality in that human sexuality is limited by taboos and the domain of eroticism is that of the transgression of these taboos. Desire in eroticism is the desire that triumphs over the taboo. It presupposes man in conflict with himself.'[52]

According to Clive Cazeaux Bataille's essay, 'is ahead of its time in anticipating the importance deconstruction will assign (fifteen or so years later) to the textual instabilities implicit in binary oppositions, such as '*within limits, without limits*'. The paper is also, in parts, a rejoinder to Hegel. Whereas Hegel's *Phenomenology of spirit* reduces materiality to opacity of thought which is eventually overcome by reason, Bataille insists that there is always a level of base, material existence which exceeds thought. The rigour and discipline which define philosophical method prevent it from embracing the extremes of human life. Consequently, although it might aspire to be 'the sum of *knowledge*', as Hegel envisages the subject, philosophy can never be 'the sum of experiences.'[53]

A great deal of Bataille's writing is concerned with 'material baseness' – manifest in obscenity. Bataille's concern to show how highly intellectual productions often conceal an inassimilable base element, led him to ethnographies of societies whose social bond seemed to be founded on practices quite horrific to a modern Western sensibility.

Barthes' 'Mythologies'

Roland Barthes is one of the most prominent intellectuals to have emerged from France in the post Second World war period. "Mythologies", is one of his earliest and most widely read works. This text debunks a number of the myths that envelop daily lives of the people. Most of the articles in the book are journalistic in style. The articles analyse the events and trends that took place in France during 1950s. The articles focus primarily on the multiple manifestations of mass culture, films, newspapers, photographs, toys and cars. Barthes considered that trivial things in life can be read full of meanings.

In fact, Barthes was fascinated by the meanings of the things that encircle the every day lives of the people. Barthes never saw the cultural objects 'innocent' or 'natural'. They are capable of producing all kinds of meanings. The objects do not simply have utilitarian function, they involve in some symbolic function also. Objects are not devoid of connotations. Even the same objects sharing the same functional utility won't mean the same to all the users. The objects connote different things about their users. Barthes tries to uncover these connotations in the objects in his work "Mythologies". Barthes never takes things granted, he rather concentrates on their function as signs, doubting the obvious in the process Barthes continuously involves. In his study, Barthes makes explicit the meanings of apparently neutral objects and exposes the social and historical conditions they obscure.

Barthes does not use myth as a story of supernatural being; he uses it to mean an unproven and false or illusory thing. Barthes aims at analysing the myths that surround the contemporary society. He concentrates on the myths that circulate day-to-day constructing a world for the people and their place in it. In the view of Barthes, myths construct mythological reality and make the people commit to its values, in a world where the myths support the existing power structures and claim that these power structures are but natural. The business of the mythologist is to expose these artificial constructions.

In the view of Barthes, myth today is not just a concept, or an idea but a message. Myth is 'neither a lie nor confession : it is an inflexion'. Barthes considers myth almost equivalent to ideology. Terry Eagleton defines ideology as, 'A dominant power may legitimate itself by promoting beliefs and values congenial to it; naturalizing and universalizing such beliefs so as to render them self-evident and apparently inevitable; denigrating ideas which might challenge it; excluding rival forms of thought, perhaps by some unspoken but systematic logic; and obscuring social reality in ways convenient to itself. Such `mystification', as it is commonly known, frequently takes the form of masking or suppressing social conflicts, from which arises the conception of ideology as an imaginary resolution of real contradictions.'[54]

Eagleton's definition of ideology is relevant to Barthes' "Mythologies". The commonality between the Eagleton's definition of ideology and Barthes' perception of myth is the notion of a socially constructed reality, and this reality is passed off as 'natural'.

Barthes' objective is to study how mass culture is saturated with ideological proportions, which he calls 'myths', offered as if they were natural and axiomatic. Barthes aims to expose or study the social life of signs and how signs naturalize the patriarchal and ethnocentric worldviews. He studies exhibitions, advertisements, photographs, articles, films, wrestling matches and exposes their covert functions. He was very critical of the myth- making function of the contemporary culture.

In the view of Barthes, myth is defined by the way it utters its message, hence it is an outcome of speech (parole) rather than language (langue). In ideology, what is said is vital, it conceals it, whereas in myth, how it says and what it says is crucial.

With his example of the 'Negro' soldier, Barthes makes his concept very clear. Barthes studies the Negro Soldier saluting the French flag on the front cover of 'Paris-Match'. This is an example to myth. According to Barthes, the Negro, for any reader, becomes the very presence of French imperialism. As myth conceals nothing its effectiveness is certain. Here myth is a kind of ignominy shown in the concrete terms. The reader of myth accepts the message completely at its face value. In myth, it is not possible to see the distinction between signifier, for example the Negro soldier, and the signified, the French imperialism. The message in the myth is self- explanatory, it need not be interpreted or demystified. The ideology of myth is not obvious, if it is so it does not function as myth. The myth works as a myth only when it seems completely natural. Barthes text addresses a number of issues like imperialism, sexual politics, cultural consumption, and technocratic symbols etc. Barthes believed that myths carry on the status quo and reinforce the ideology of the existing society.

Foucault's Aesthetic Discourses

Michel Foucault's philosophy and aesthetic ideas radically transformed numerous methods of literary and cultural disciplines. Though much of Michel Foucault work is in the other fields like philosophy, history, power and knowledge, he inspired the study of aesthetics in various ways. His essay "What is an Author" (1969) directly questions some of the most fundamental assumptions of literary criticism. Foucault starts off his essay by discussing criticisms of a previous book, "The Order of Things". In this book Foucault had started an investigation into the conditions of possibility under which human beings become the objects of knowledge in certain disciplines. He was working to discover and explain the rules and laws of formation of systems of thought in the human sciences, which emerged in the nineteenth century. His main method for looking at these disciplines, and how they constitute the objects of their study, was through examining discourses, or discursive practices.

Foucault makes a list of some questions about authorship, which he will not address directly. Rather, he wants to discuss the relationship between an author and a text, and the manner in which the text points to the author as a figure who is outside the text, and who precedes the text. Eventually, Foucault will talk about the author as a centre of the text, the place which originates the text yet remains outside it.

But before he does that, Foucault talks about Samuel Beckett, and particularly about a line from Beckett, “what matter who’s speaking? Foucault sees this sentence as an expression of some of the major principles of contemporary writing. Foucault calls it ecriture .One of the hallmarks of ecriture writing is the interplay of signifiers; language in this kind of writing is not about reference to a signified, but rather it is about the play among signifiers. The ecriture that Foucault is discussing tends toward the monologic, rather than the dialogic. As such, this writing is always working against the grammatical rules and structures within which meaning (or sense) is made. Because of this, Foucault concludes, such ecriture is not about the exalted emotions related to the act of composition. Writing is not the vehicle for the author’s expression of emotions or ideas, since writing isn’t meant to communicate from author to reader, but rather writing is the circulation of language itself, regardless of the individual existence of author or reader.

In the entire Western cultural history, writing has been a means of staving off death, of becoming. Foucault points to the Greek epic, where the hero can die young because his epic feats have guaranteed his immortality, and also to a non-Western text, "The Arabian Nights", where Scheherazade’s storytelling night after night kept her from being killed. In modern times, however, writing (ecriture) reverses the equation; rather than guaranteeing immortality, or keeping death away, writing kills the author. Why? Foucault says that a writer’s particular individuality is cancelled out by the text, by writing, because we now see ‘writer’, or ‘author’, as the function of language itself. In the humanist model, the categories of author, text, and reader seemed self-evident and separate. An author is someone who produces a text, which is then read by a reader.

The author was the source and origin of some creative power, which was unique to him or her, and out of which he/she created something entirely new. In the poststructuralist view, however, relations between author, text, and reader are replaced by an understanding of the relations between language (as a structure) and subjects (positions we inhabit within the structure of language.) Foucault says author, like reader is the name of a subject position within language, or, more specifically, within a text or textual ideology.

In this way the author is decentred. He is only a part of the structure, a subject position, and not the centre. In declaring the author dead, Foucault follows Nietzsche's declaration, at the end of the nineteenth century, that God is dead. By declaring the death of the author, Foucault is deconstructing the idea that the author is the origin of something original, and replacing it with the idea that the author is the product or function of writing, of the text.

An author only exists as the product of a text, or of writing. That is primarily what Foucault's article explores. What an author produces, according to Foucault, is a work. The task of humanist criticism used to be to trace the ties between an author and the work he created. Foucault says that, once we throw the idea of author as individual creator into question, what remains is the work.

Foucault takes up the question of author as product of work again, asking how the name of the author serves a function within literary-social relations. The name of the author is, first of all, a proper name, a signifier that designates a specific and historical individual. But an author's name does more than that. When we way Aristotle, or Shakespeare, we mean more than just the person with that name. In fact the person is attributed with the mode of thinking the objects of contemplation, the methodology, and the writings associated with that name.

The author's name, according to Foucault, characterizes a particular manner of existence of discourse; the texts attributed to an author are given more status, more attention, and more cultural value than texts, which have no author. In the very beginning of the essay "What is an Author?" Foucault says, 'the coming into being of the notion of "author" constitutes the privileged moment of individualization in the history of ideas, knowledge, literature, philosophy, and the sciences. Even today, when we reconstruct the history of a concept, literary genre, or school of philosophy, such categories seem relatively weak, secondary, and superimposed scansions in comparison with the solid and fundamental unit of the author and the work.'[55]

At the end of the article, Foucault talks about the idea of a transdiscursive position, people who are initiators of discursive practices, not just individual texts. Such figures as Marx and Freud radically shift an entire mode of thinking; the discourses they initiate make them more than just authors or author functions. At the end of the article Foucault declares that, "the author is not an indefinite source of significations that fill a work; the author does not precede the works; he is a certain functional principle by which, in our culture, one limits, excludes, and chooses; in short, by which one impedes the free circulation, the free manipulation, the free composition, decomposition, and recomposition of fiction. In fact, if we are accustomed to presenting the author as a genius, as a perpetual surging of invention, it is because, in reality, we make him function in exactly the opposite fashion. One can say that the author is an ideological product, since we represent him as the opposite of his historically real function. When a historically given function is represented in a figure that inverts it, one has an ideological production. The author is therefore the ideological figure by which one marks the manner in which we fear the proliferation of meaning.'[56]

In 1963 Foucault published a monograph on the French experimental novelist Raymond Roussel. In the essay he says about Raymond Roussel that, 'He was not in search of beauty : he was not an aesthetician but a student of what the ancient Greeks called aisthçsis, "feeling", "experience" "felt experience."'"[57]

Foucault, in the works of Roussel in the Surrealists in Georges Bataille and in Maurice Blanchot among others, finds an obscure but articulate engagement with experiences that many modern philosophers of aesthetics would ignore.

Derrida's Deconstructive Aesthetics

The most important contribution, in the second part of the twentieth century to the study of culture comes from the French philosopher Jacques Derrida. Derrida's deconstruction is one of the most prominent and distinctive strategies of critique within Poststructuralism. Deconstruction blurs the boundaries between literature and philosophy. Derrida made valuable contributions for the reformulation of cultural studies in the recent times. Literature and art has always been a fascination for Derrida. He once declared that, 'For I have to remind you, somewhat bluntly and simply, that my most constant interest, coming even before my philosophical interest I should say, if this is possible, has been directed towards literature, what is literature?'[58]

The word deconstruction is coined by Derrida to offer a mode of reading which is attend to a text's multiple meanings. Rather than attempting to find a true meaning, a consistent point of view or unified message in a given work. A deconstructive reading carefully teases out, 'the warring forces of signification' at play and waiting to be read in what might be called the textual unconscious. As a mode of reading, then, which exposes a text's internal differences and attends to its repressed contradictions or inherent vulnerabilities, its strategy is also interventionist. In this way deconstruction is political.

Deconstructors tend to seize on the inconsistencies, inequalities, hierarchies, which are expounded or glossed over either by a text, by a whole discourse, or even by an entire system of beliefs. For instance, the structure of hierarchy which Derrida sees implicit in 'binary oppositions' which have traditionally informed, organized and ranked Western thinking, and have therefore led us to value a concept such as 'order' more highly than its opposite. What the privileging of one term over and above the other such as good over evil, light over dark, reason over emotion, male over female, master over slave, model over copy, original over reproduction, literature over criticism, high culture over popular culture, etc. reveals is that the preference for one term always works at the expense or exclusion of the other.

In view of Allan Megill, 'Derrida's deconstruction of art... his deconstruction of a whole philosophy, of a whole ideology that has grown up around art : runs parallel to his deconstruction of tradition and crisis. Derrida is deeply engaged with questions of art and literature.'[59]

In fact, in his collections of essays "Writing and Difference", we see that five of its eleven essays deal with aesthetic as literary issues. The first essay, "Force and Significance" is a critique on structuralist and modernist literary criticism of Jean Rousset. Another two essays deal with the texts of Antonin Arttaud. In other writings like "Dissemination", "Margins of Philosophy", "Glas", and "Truth in Painting" we find Derrida discusing numerous authors ranging from Mallarme to Jean Genet. What we find in Derrida is a postmodernist polemic against modernism in art and criticism. Megill understands Derrida's reading of Jean Genet in "Glas"as paradigmatic of this polemic. Derrida reads Genet against the existentialist reading of Sartre.

In a way the whole of Derrida's critical work can be seen as an attack on aesthetic modernism carried out from the standpoint of aesthetic postmodernism. The aim of postmodern aesthetic is not only to break down the dualisms within art but also the fundamental dualisms upon which the notion of aesthetic realm depends. The postmodern aesthetic blurs the dichotomy between aesthetic and nonaesthetic. This blurring of dualisms in the field of art can be understood as philosophical complements to such aesthetic developments as Duchamp's 'urinal/fountain sculptures'.

Megill identifies four issues in the aesthetic ideas of Derrida. They are : "First, there is the question of the "other," raised in its most obvious and compelling form by the unorthodox French phenomenologist Emmanuel Levinas, Second, there is the question of "writing," or of secondariness, which we can link to the poet Edmond Jabes. Third, there is the question of "interpretation," for which Freud can serve as a convenient cipher. And fourth, there is the question of "art," linked to Kant".[60] These four issues are closely interrelated and refer the Romantic and Kantian aestheticism.

In the above context Megill says, "Writing and interpretation come to be valued not because they can reveal to us the light of truth but because they are themselves truth. Thus, they have a "purposiveness without purpose" analogous to that which Kant found in aesthetic objects. Derrida's move beyond Kant is to argue that "purposiveness without purpose" Pervades all we do. His move beyond Hegel and Heidegger is to substitute an explicit irony for their conviction that in one way or another art gives us access to the truth of Being.'[61]

In an interview Derrida's said, 'At any rate I wouldn't distinguish between "literature" and "literary criticism," but I wouldn't assimilate all forms of writing or reading. These new distinctions ought to give up on the purity and linearity of frontiers. They should have a form that is both rigorous and capable of taking account of the essential possibility of contamination between all these oppositions, those we encountered above and, here, the one between literature and criticism or reading or literary interpretation.'[62]

De man's Negation of Centres

Paul de Man as a deconstructionist contributed tremendously to the discipline of aesthetics. De Man thought that literary theory begins when the role of language is made problematic. Traditional literary history, which includes aesthetics, takes language for granted and interpreted the text either in terms of non-linguist effects or as pure verbalism. In contrast to this De Man argues that language is fiction. It is fiction not because, it refuses to accept reality but because it is not a priori certain that language functions according to principles which are those of the phenomenal world. De Man in his first collection of essays, "Blindness and Insight : Essay in the Rhetoric of Contemporary Criticism" (1971) shows the early development of his understanding of reading and explores related ideas of literature and language. In a way, this volume reveals de Man's early engagement with deconstruction.

Like a typical deconstructionist De Man declares that there is no authoritative centre in a text, no core of fixed meaning and there is no single point more important than any other. In his view, literature has a problem of reading, to be specific a misreading. In "Blindness and Insight".(1983) he says, 'The systematic avoidance of the problem of reading, of the interpretative or hermeneutic moment, is a general symptom shared by all methods of literary analysis, whether they be structural or thematic, formalist or referential, American or European, apolitical or socially committed.'[63] For De Man the task of reading is not all straightforward. The hypothesis of "Blindness and Insight "is that not only does a reading say something the text does not say but it even says something the reading did not mean to say. It is not just that critics unknowingly misinterpret texts but that the very nature of language makes reading impossible.

De Man's essay, "Literature and Language", gives us an opening into two of his most important concerns : reading and rhetoric. It also explains the main argument of "Blindness and Insight", namely, that all critical readings are misreadings. That is to say, all critical texts have, what de Man calls, a "critical blindness" to their subject matter. For example, he argues that while New Criticism insists that the study of literature should be based on a close attention to language – 'the words on the page' – it is blind to the obvious consequences of this. New Criticism resists anything like a linguistic vocabulary to describe literary language and has no interest in understanding the phenomenon of language beyond its appearance in literary rhetoric, despite demonstrating the importance to under-stand precisely this. In particular, it identifies literary language as innately ambiguous and paradoxical.

While discussing the background of de Man's "Allegories of Reading" (1979) Martin McQuillan explains, ' However, the stable appearance of such orders is the result of the privileging and exclusion of certain terms within the architecture of a text. The operation of logocentrism in philosophy is called metaphysics. Philosophy is an important topic for deconstruction because our understanding of all of the concepts that defines the enterprise of everyday life comes from philosophy. Ideas such as reading, writing, selfhood, politics, justice, the nation, friendship, sexual difference, drugs, truth, and so on, are all philosophical concepts. Far from being a marginal discourse within western culture, philosophy is rather the ordering principle around which western thought is organized. It is important; therefore, if the effects of logocentrism are to be under-stood that we examine the work of logocentrism in philosophy and philosophy as a system of logocentrism (metaphysics). That is, we interrogate the privileged or marginal status accorded to certain terms within the philosophical tradition.'[64]

De Man outlines his project for "Allegories of Reading" (1979) in the opening essay 'Semiology and Rhetoric'. He notes that the authors considered in the first-half of the book - Rainer Maria Rilke, Marcel Proust, and Friedrich Nietzsche - are concerned with a deconstruction of the rhetorical status of metaphysical concepts, such as the self, history, and knowledge. These writers, according to de Man, can be placed together to form a tradition of the critique of metaphysics, which runs from Romanticism to Modernism. The key to this critique, says de Man, "is the rhetorical model of the trope or, if one prefers to call it that, literature"[65]

According to de Man, philosophy is figural. This suggestion deconstructs the binary opposition between philosophy and literature, which pervades the tradition of western thought since ancient Greece. Philosophy has always been thought of as having a unique relation to truth, while literature is a form of fiction and so revels in its status as non-truth. In this scenario the non-truth of literature is clearly related to its use of figurative language, which is a form of deception. For example, while a poet may say 'flowers are gold' flowers are not actually

Traditionally, this has led to literary and philosophical texts being read in different ways : one as serious and one as 'non-serious'.

However, according de Man, philosophy uses the same language as literature and is therefore open to the same sort of rhetorical analysis as literature. If philosophical texts are equally aware of their rhetorical status they will also deconstruct themselves, demystifying the metaphysical concepts they contain. For de man 'literature' and 'philosophy' are not separate discourse. Rather 'literature' is de Man's word for the behaviour of tropes (so-called 'literary language') while all texts are 'philosophical' because they produce knowledge. On the one hand, de Man continues to read Literature - poetry, prose, and drama - because such texts provide an abundance of information about rhetoric and so are keys to understanding language in general.

Another important work of Paul de Man is "Aesthetic Ideology" (1996). Most of the essays in "Aesthetic Ideology" follow an argument through the philosophy of Kant and Hegel, who recognise that an understanding of aesthetics is a necessary condition of a philosophical inquiry into politics.

It can be argued that aesthetics, or representation, is the crucial link between real events and philosophical texts. De Man argues that far from formulating an adequate notion of aesthetics that will help them develop their philosophical systems, Kant and Hegel's texts succeed in undoing the aesthetic as a valid philosophical category.

For example, de Man suggests that while Hegel's "Aesthetics" "is dedicated to the preservation and the monumentalisation of classical art, it also contains all the elements which make such a preservation impossible from the start".[66] In de Man's reading of Hegel, the paradigm for art in the Aesthetics "is thought rather than perception, the sign rather than the symbol, writing rather than painting or music".[67]

However, de Man argues throughout these essays that the deconstruction of the category of the aesthetic comes about not as a weakness in Kant's and Hegel's argument but as a consequence of the rigour of their argument. Martin McQuillan classifies the arguments of de Man as:

1· Ideology is the confusion of Linguistic with natural reality, or reference with the objects referred to.

2· What we take to be an experience of the material world is in fact an experience of the materiality of language, which gives the world meaning and makes it knowable.

3· If language itself is material, our experience of the material is therefore open to all the undecideabilities and impossibilities of deconstruction, which de Man's work identifies.

4· There is no meaning that is outside of the effects of textuality.

5· The real is always rhetorical. The distinction between the literal and the figural is an effect of language not a given fact of the natural world.

6· Aesthetic ideology is the belief that the figural and the literal are separate realms.

7· Deconstruction cannot be a totalising way of reading. It is always caught up in the event that it reads, unable to escape the ideological conditions of that reading.

8· Deconstruction is a disarticulation of all totalitarianism(s).[68]

A pre-eminent postmodern theorist, Baudrillard is best known for his application of semiotics, the study of language as a system of signs, to Marxist concerns. The term "postmodernism," as applied to literature and other art forms, refers to a philosophical position that denies the existence of rational order in the universe beyond the random play of elements on the surface of reality. As applied to economic and social institutions, "postmodern" or "post-industrial" describes a technology-driven society dominated by white-collar and service-industry employment rather than manufacturing or agriculture. Baudrillard involves very much in the analyses of the contemporary society. Baudrillard is generally viewed as an important social critic. Helming commented, 'If culture-bashing must go on,… then Baudrillard is as satisfying a culture-basher as we presently have. To read his impassioned denunciations of advertising, consumerism…. TV, and the conduct of politics in a media age, is to see everything you most despise about our culture trashed in the manner that it deserves.'[69]

Baudrillard often making outrageous iconoclastic statements about contemporary society and technology in the course of his analyses, which have veered increasingly towards a full-blown postmodernism is frequently considered deeply nihilistic. Baudrillard's views emerge as a conglomeration of ideas derived from Marxism, cybernetics, social theory, psychoanalysis, communications theory and semiotics. Following in the anti-foundationalist line of Derrida and Lyotard, his work develops a narrative about the end of modernity as an era dominated by production, industrial capitalism and 'a political economy of the sign'.

According to Baudrillard, the society has ushered into the era of simulation, of undecidable, commutable values, where distinctions of the beautiful and the ugly in fashions of left and right in politics, of truth and falsehood are all erased. In the view of Baudrillard, 'The era of simulation is thus everywhere initiated by the interchangeability of previously contradictory or dialectically opposed terms. Everywhere the same "genesis of simulacra :" the interchange-ability of the beautiful and the ugly in fashion; of the right and the left in politics; of the true and false in every media message; of the useful and the useless at the level of objects; and of nature and culture at every level of meaning. All the great humanist criteria of value, all the values of a civilization of moral, aesthetic, and practical judgement, vanish in our system of images and signs. Everything becomes undecidable. This is the characteristic effect of the domination of the code, which is based everywhere on the principle of neutralization and indifference. This is the generalized brothel of capital : not the brothel of prostitution but the brothel of substitution and interchangeability.'[70]

Lyotard's Anti - universal Aesthetics

Jean-Francois Lyotard argues that the information generation becomes increasingly diverse and complex and knowledge can no longer be regarded as Universal body of ideas. His essay "The Sublime and the Avant-Garde" (1984) argues for the : 'Sublime as concept of privation, with implications for the political and epistemological status of art'.[71]

In his view the, 'Postmodern artworks show the impossibility of complicit knowledge through their form, rather than offering the idea as a subject practiced, stylised expression. However, he finds that the processes of revolution and renewal in modern art are worryingly consistent with capitalism, and observes that artists can be seduced by market-driven demand for the 'new'. The 'ambiguous, even perverse' correlation, which exists between capitalism and the sublime levels room for a reply though'.[72]

In another text, "Defining the Postmodern" (1986) Lyotard expresses his ideas of art in lucid terms. In fact this essay captures many of his major themes. According to him modernism in the arts partakes of the universal aims of modernity. Thus modernist architecture sought to make everything new, to transform the whole world, to effect a total revolution in how people live together by creating entirely new cities. But we have now-after Auschwitz and the Soviet gulags—come to recognize that such modern dreams of transforming humanity can be pursued only violently, and even then they will not succeed. Allegiance to one universal standard, by which all are judged generates murderous hostility to the different, to whatever resists or simply does not desire to go along with the program. Modernist architects and city planners who razed old neighbourhoods, confident that theory plans for "urban renewal" would make for better lives. Instead, they created inhospitable concrete wastelands, unconnected to how people interact in lived space.

In Lyotard's view, 'the development of techno-sciences has become a means of increasing disease, not of fighting it. We can no longer call this development by the old name of progress. This development seems to be taking place by itself, by an autonomous force or 'motricity'. It doesn't respond to a demand coming from human needs. On the contrary, human entities (individual or social) seem always to be destabilized by the results of this development. The intellectual results as much as the material ones. I would say that mankind is in the condition of running after the process of accumulating new objects of practice and thought. In my view is a real and obscure question to determine the reason of this process of complexification. It's something like a destiny towards a more and more complex condition'.[73]

In the "Postmodern Condition" and other works Lyotard links postmodernist art with the sublime. He suggests that, art is one place where that which resists being fully captured within any existing signifying system can make its existence felt. To avoid modernity's persistent tendency to reduce everything back into known terms we must cultivate an appreciation of the sublime, of that which exceeds calculation and understanding.

Deleuze and Guattari's Aesthetic Vision of the World

Gilles Deleuze and Felix Guattari are also exponents of French poststructuralist aesthetics. Deleuze and Guattari in collaboration produced monumental works. All most all of their works have significance in the field of aesthetics. Art and philosophy, they claim, 'intersect and intertwine but without synthesis or identification'.[74] In their view abstract art and conceptual art are two recent attempts to bring art and philosophy together. However they do not substitute the concept for sensation. Instead, they create sensations but not concepts. They say, 'Abstract art seeks only to refine sensation, to dematerialise it by setting out an architectonic plane of composition in which it would become a purely spiritual being, a radiant thinking and thought matter, no longer a sensation of sea or tree, but a sensation of the concept of sea or concept of tree. Conceptual art seeks an opposite dematerialization through generalization, by installing a sufficiently neutralized plane of composition ...'[75]

They distinguish art from technology. They distinguish it according to wehther they are governed by external or internal dynamisms. In their view technology is teleological. It is produced in order to serve extrinsic purposes. The product of technical machines decides in advance, where as the product of the work of art is a psychic effect on the viewer that cannot be predicated in advance. Art has its own economic. It can create new values and finalities for human relations and productive activities.

According to Goodchild, Deleuze and Guattari have an aesthetic rather than a technological vision of the world. Moreover, their thought becomes expressively oriented towards extending aesthetic relations throughout the fields of nature, history, and society. The ultimate goal of the revolution of desire is 'life as a work of art'. Deleuze regarded the three main modes of thinking—art, science and philosophy—as powers to transform life.

In the view of Deleuze, we can define the distinction between literature, art and philosophy not by cataloguing literary and philosophical texts and finding some shared feature, but by looking at what they do, and what they do when they are extended and stretched to their utmost. Philosophy, art and science need to be seen as distinct moments of the explosive force of life, a life that is in a process of constant 'becoming'. It is not that we have a world or life and that philosophers or writers then describe or interpret. Each act of art, science or philosophy is itself an event and transfiguration of life. And each transformation changes life in its own specific or singular way.

Literature is the power of fiction itself : not making a claim about what the world is, but about the imagination of a possible world. Art is not about representation, concepts of judgement; art is the power to think in terms that are not so much cognitive and intellectual as affective. We are not reading a work as artistic or literary if we read it for its representation of the world or its presentation of theories.

Throughout their major work, "A Thousand Plateaus", Deleuze and Guattari draw a distinction between minoritarian and majoritarian. Claire Colebrook explains, 'Literature, when it fully extends its power of being literature, is always minoritarian. Minor literature is great literature, not necessarily the literature of minorities, although this can be the case. Kafka was a great writer, not because he captured the unrepresented spirit of the Czech people, but because he wrote without a standard notion of 'the people'. He wrote, not as being with an identity, but as a voice of what is not given, a 'people to come'. But the same goes for all great writing. Shakespeare can be considered a 'minor' author precisely because his works do not offer a unified image of man, or even a unified image of Shakespeare. His texts are more like question marks, with each production or reading raising new questions'.[76]

In "Kafka : Toward a Minor Literature" (1975), Deleuze and Guattari claim that Franz Kafka, although writing in a dominant language, introduces into it elements of his own Jewish, minoritarian culture. He thus recombines dominant ways of thinking with elements of a minority culture to produce something entirely different—a minor literature—thereby undermining power. They say, 'A minor literature doesn't come from a minor language; it is rather that which a minority constructs within a major language. But the first characteristic of minor literature in any case is that in it language is affected with a high coefficient of deterritorialization. In this sense, Kafka marks the impasses that bars access to writing for the Jews of Prague and turns their literature into something impossible—the impossibility of not writing, the impossibility of writing in German, the impossibility of writing otherwise'.[77]

Aesthetics of Unconscious

In the twentieth century, Sigmund Freud radically altered the Western conceptions of the human being and human nature. This has its impact on the field of aesthetics too. The influence of Freud has been very wide spread. His theories like the 'Oedipus complex' have helped a lot to understand the inner dynamics of the literary and cultural texts. His theories of unconscious exposed to the world the hidden forces that are operating in human psyche. Freud's theories have been especially influential in literary criticism and instrumental in the development in some areas of literary theory. Freud himself acknowledged that art exercised considerable impact on him. He says, 'Nevertheless, works of art do exercise a powerful effect on me, especially those of literature and sculpture, less often of a painting. This has occasioned me, when I have been contemplating such things, to spend a long time before them trying to apprehend them in my own way, i.e., to explain to myself what their effect is due to'.[78]

Several reading strategies emerge from the psychoanalytic theories of Freud. A text might be read for the way unconscious material manifests itself through indirect means—images or descriptions that evoke psychological issues. The relations between characters might be studied for what they disclose about family dynamics and the way such dynamics shape selves. A psychoanalytic reading might also attend to such themes or issues as separation, loss, boundaries, fusion with others, and the struggle to form a coherent and functioning self out of a damaging context or a traumatic personal history. Finally, language itself can be studied, as in Jacques Lacan, as a means of instantiating unconscious processes and working through some of the issues and emerging self faces as it struggles for adult existence or as it seeks to come to terms with disturbing unconscious material.

In the field of literature and aesthetics the Freudian critics give central role to the distinguishing between conscious and unconscious mind. They associate the literary text's 'explicit' content with the conscious and the 'implicit' content with the unconscious. In their interpretation of artefacts they privilege the unconscious. They think that what the work really about can be understood by studying the text's implicit meaning. They study closely the unconscious motives and feelings of the author as well as the character. They identify the content of psyche for the literary work and privilege it at the cost of social or historical issues. The 'psycho drama' is more important than that of 'social drama' in the constructions of any text for them.

The French structuralist and poststructuralist psychoanalyst Jacques Lacan reinterpreted Freud. Lacan's ideas influenced the study of literature to some extent. Lacan in his "Ecrits" thought that unconsciousness is structured like a language. Because, language envelops every thing we do and say. We can apprehend the unconsciousness and dreams, jokes and slips of the tongue. Literature as a narration is language. It functions at a higher level where connotations dominate denotations. In narration form obscures meaning. In a way literature and unconsciousness enjoy a special affinity. This affinity is possible because of language. Language joins the two fields together. But this union functions only when a reader activates the circuit between them. By focussing on language and mechanism of language, that is found in topes, Lacan brings his analysis immediately in to the field of literary analysis. The literary work represents a reader's ego to itself through the language of the text-a text that exerts a "magnetic pull" on the reader "because it is an allegory of the psyche's fundamental structure".[79]

When Lacan stated that the unconscious is structured like a language, he opened a royal road between literature and the unconscious. Language not only structures our perception of reality, ' it is "the precondition for the act of becoming aware of oneself as a distinct entity'.[80]

We contain language; at the same time language also contains us. According to Ben Stoltzfus explanation,' in tropes there is neither an inside nor an outside and it is this reversibility that allows the unconscious, when veiled by figural language, to reveal itself...'

Lacan's analysis of narration begins with language and proceeds to rediscover the discourse of the Other that is embedded in speech and literature. The blockage of desire, along with its corollary, repression, produce a neurosis whose narrative symptoms are metaphorical. In the production of narrative, unconscious content is condensed as metaphor and displaced as metonymy. This narrative process embodies the same characteristics of Freud's dream work, and the function of the literary critic is to show how conscious discourse veils unconscious meaning, that is, how the signifiers resolve simultaneously into manifest signified (metaphor and metonymy) and latent referents (the repressed). Lacan's formula, S^1 over S^2, means that the signifier can have two signifieds. If the dream is the iconic, although masked mirror of the unconscious, fiction is its linguistic reflector'.[81]

Feminist Aesthetics

Feminist philosophy plays a vital role in Western aesthetics. It challenges traditional conceptual boundaries. It proposes new forms of thought within, and sometimes against, the horizons of experience and it opened up numerous theories like psychoanalysis, phenomenology and postmodernism.

Feminist aesthetic is a part of the broader feminist political movement that seeks to rectify sexist discrimination and inequalities. While there is no single feminist literary criticism, there are so many interrelated projects, which expose masculinist stereotypes, distortions, and omissions in male-dominated literature. They study female creativity, genres, styles, themes, careers, and literary traditions. They develop and evaluate the lost and neglected literary works by women. They develop feminist theoretical concepts and methods and examine the forces that shape women's lives, literature, and criticism, ranging across psychology and politics, biology and cultural history.

Feminist theory and criticism have brought revolutionary change in literary and cultural studies and expanded the canon, by critiquing sexist representations and values. It emphasized the importance of gender and sexuality. Among various Feminist writers who contributed and redefined the concept of aesthetics five major thinkers can be identified. They are : Simone de Beauvoir, Kate Millett, Helene Cixous, Luce Irigaray and Julia Kristeva.

In her text "The Second Sex "(1949) De Beauvoir argues that patriarchical cultural has made the man the norm and the women the deviation. She also explains how women in social political and cultural life have been made to internalise patriarchical culture. Throughout history women have been reduced to objects for men and have been constructed as man's Other. Kate Millett 's 'Sexual Politics' (1969) talks about the nature of power relations between sexes, the fate of feminist struggle and its opponents. And the sexual power–politics in the literary writings.

Helene Cixous made a valuable contribution is analysing literally text and understanding feminist aesthetics. Cixous developed a specific kind of writing called *ecriture feminine* . It is a form of writing that opposes the dominant patriarchical culture. It rejects patriarchical culture or writing that privileges a hierarchical way of thinking, based on a series of binary oppositions like, male/female, active/passive, day/night. She wants to regain the feminity in terms of plurality.

In her fictional writings Cixous explores many of the issues that also dominate her theoretical and critical works. Subjectivity, the corporeal roots of language, femininity, relations to the Other, and the possibilities of social and subjective transformation recur in her fictional texts as points of focus, or of tension, in texts whose radical deconstruction of linguistic and narrative structures enact the audacity of her cultural and political project.

Another French feminist theorist Julia Kristeva made significant contribution to the disciplines like Psychoanalysis, Linguistics and Literary Theory. In fact, she is one of the famous proponents of feminist theory. Her work has become an integral part of the structuralist and poststructuralist theories. She talks about the role of language in the construction of identity. She never considered language a fixed system. In her view, it is an ongoing process and the meaning emerges in the dynamic interplay between semiotic and symbolic. In their interplay one modality regulates the other. For example, the semiotic force allows a flexible and creative use of language to generate new meanings. However, in the absence of the ordering abilities of the symbolic it becomes understandable. In her view, the symbolic tries to create an exact correspondence between word and object. She thinks that in the unstable relation between symbolic and semiotic numerous modes of discourses emerge.

Kristeva shows a radical difference between scientific language and poetic language. As there is no slippage between word and the thing described, the semiotic is suppressed in the scientific language. But in poetic language the domination of semiotic can be seen in rhythm, syntactic and linguistic distortions such as metaphor and metonymy.

Kristeva has never involved in any active feminist movement. She thought that an agenda or a programme that tries to achieve political power, within the existing order results in another master discourse. This master discourse, in her view, instead of challenging hierarchical disinclinations between centre and margins, consolidates them.

Luce Irigaray, a prominent French philosopher and psychoanalyst made remarkable contribution to feminist studies. She put a radical critique on Freudian psychoanalysis. Her work "Speculum of the Other Women" criticises Western philosophy from Plato onwards. She analysed how the woman as a subject is excluded from Western philosophy and how subjectivity is constructed based on one sex : male. In her view, the primacy accorded to the phallus resulted in women being characterised as absence, lack and negativity. Women have been understood from male perspective only. Even her other works like, "The Sex Which is not One"(1977),and "Ethics of Sexual Difference"(1984) reflect her quest for the women voice, a feminine symbolic order. In these texts she talks about the plurality of female sex.

Though Irigaray argues against the Western philosophy, and Freudian and Lacanian psychoanalysis, her primary intention is to suggest how women should construct their own subjectivity on their own terms. As the feminine is ignored and suspended in the masculine symbolic order, women have to liberate and reconstruct it in their own symbolic order. Ultimately she also proposes *ecriture feminine*.

Notes

1 Terry Eagleton. *The Ideology of the Aesthetics*. London : Blackwell, 1994, p. 13

2 Andrew Bowie. *Aesthetics and Subjectivity : From Kant to Nietzsche.* Manchester : Manchester University Press, 1990, p. 1.

3 Clive Cazeaux (Ed.) *The Continental Aesthetics Reader.* London : Routledge, 2000, p. 3

4 Clive Cazeaux *The Continental Aesthetics Reader Ibid.*, p. 3

5 Andrew Bowie. *Aesthetics and Subjectivity* : *From Kant to Nietzsche*, p. 3.

6 G.W.F.Hegel. Aesthetics : Lectures on Fine Art. Vol. I, Oxford : Clarendon Press, p. 94.

7 Clive Cazeaux. *The Continental Aesthetics Reader*, p. 9

8 Andrew Bowie. *Aesthetics and Subjectivity : From Kant to Nietzsche*. p, p. 133-134.

9 G.W.F.Hegel. *Aesthetics : Lectures on Fine Art*, p. 20

10 Friedrich Nietzsche. The Will to Power. Quoted by R.J. Hollingdale in *Nietzsche.* London : Routledge & Kegan Paul. 1973 , p. 132.

11 Friedrich Nietzsche, "The Birth of Tragedy". in *The Birth of Tragedy and The Case of Wagner.* New York : Vintage Books 1967. p, p. 31-32.

12 Nietzsche. In The Gay Science. Quoted by R.J Hollingdale in *Nietzsche*, p. 152.

13 Nietzsche Quoted in *Ibid.* o. 152.

14 Allan Megill. *Prophets of Extremity : Nietzsche, Heidegger, Foucault, Derrida.* Berkley : University of California Press, 1985, p. 35.

15 Alan Bullock. *The Fontana Dictionary of Modern Thought.* London : Fontana Press, 1990, p. 645.

16 Clive Cazeaux (Ed.). *The Continental Aesthetics Reader* London : Routledge, 2000, p. 66.

17 Martine Heidegger. *Being and Time.* Oxford : Blackwell, 1995, p, p. 26-27.

18 Martine Heidegger. "The Origin of the Work of Art" in *The Continental Aesthetics Reader*,(Ed.) Clive Cazeaux p, p. 97-98.

19 Martine Heidegger. Language. In *Norton Anthology of Theory and Criticism.* (Ed.) Vincent B. Leitch. p, p. 1121-1134.

20 Clive Cazeaux. (Ed.) *The Continental Aesthetics Reader*, p. 70.

21 Clive Cazeaux. *Ibid.*, p. 71.

22 Emmanuel Levinas. Reality and its Shadow. In *The Continental Aesthetics Reader.* (Ed.) Clive Cazeaux, p. 123.

23 Hans-George Gadamer. Aesthetics and hermeneutics. In *The Continental Aesthetics Rader*. (Ed.) Clive Cazeaux., p. 181.

24 Clive Cazeaux. *Ibid.*, p. 77.

25 Gianni Vattimo. The Death or Decline of Art. In *The Continental Aesthetics Reader.*, p. 190.

26 Anil Raina. *Marxism and Literary Value.* New Delhi : Prestige Books 2002, p. 54,55

27 Clive Cazeaux. (Ed.) *The Continental Aesthetics Reader.* London : Routledge , p. 200.

28 Clive Cazeaux. *Ibid.*, p. 201.

29 George Lukacs. Specific Particularity as the Central Category of Aesthetics. In

The Continental Aesthetics Reader (Ed.) Clive Cazeaux , p. 231.

30 Coated by Dave Laing in *The Marxist Theory of Art.* Sussex : The Harvester Press, p. 84.

31 Coated by Dave Laing, *Ibid,* p. 84.

32 Raman Selden.(Ed) *The Theory of Criticism : From Plato to the Present,* London : Longman 1988 , p. 422

33 Dave Laing. *The Marxist Theory of Art* , p. 85

34 Lucien Goldman. *Towards a Sociology of Novel.* London : Tavistock, 1975 , p. 14-15.

35 Adorno Minima Moralia. in *The Continental Aesthetics Reader,* p. 250.

36 Gillian Rose *The Melancholy Science : An Introduction to the Thought of Theodor W.Adorno.* London : Macmillan, 1978, p. 120.

37 Veincent B.Leitch (Ed). *The Norton Anthology of Theory and Criticism,* p. 1222.

38 Raymond Williams. *Culture*, London : Fontana, 1981, p. 13.

39 Herbert Marcuse. *Negations*. London : Allen Lane, 1968, p. 114.

40 Herbert Marcuse. Nature and Revolution. In *The Continental Aesthetics Reader*. (Ed.) Clive Cazeaux, p. 261.

41 Herbert Marcuse. *An Essay on Liberation*. Boston : Beacon Press, 1969, p. 48.

42 Herbert Marcuse. *The Aesthetic Dimensions*. London : Macmillan, 1979, p. 12.

43 Christopher Caudwell. *Illusion and Reality.* London : Lawrence & Wishart, 1938, p. 32.

44 Christopher Caudwell. *Ibid.*, p. 206-207.

45 Antonio Gramsci. The Formation of the Intellectuals, in *The Norton Anthology of Theory and Criticism* (Ed.) Vincent B.Leitch New York W.W.Norton & Company, 2001,, p. 1140.

46 Anil Raina. *Marxism and Literary Value.*, p. 68.

47 Louis Althusser. *Ideology and Ideological State Apparatus* in *Ibid.,*, p. 1492.

48 Terry Eagleton. *Criticism and Literature*. London : NLB, 1976,, p. 162.

49 *Ibid.,*, p. 186

50 *Ibid.*, p. 178.

51 Roland Barthes. "Theory of the Text". in Robert Young (Ed.), *Untying the Text* London : Routledge 1981., p. 39.

52 Georges Bataille. "Sanctity, Eroticism and Solitude". In *The Continental Aesthetics Reader* (Ed.) .Clive Cazeaux, p. 386.

53 Clive Cazeaux. *Ibid.*, p. 371.

54 Terry Eagleton. *Ideology : An Introduction.* London : Verso. 1991, p p. 5-6

55 Michel Foucault. "What is an Author?". In *Michel Foucault : Aesthetics, Method, and Epistemology*. (Ed.) James Faubion. London: Penguin, 1998, p. 206.

56 Michel Foucault *Ibid.* p, p. 221-222.

57 James D.Faubion. (Ed.) *Aesthetics, Method, and Epistemology,* p. XIII.

58 Jacques Derrida. Quoted by J. Hills Miller in *Jacques Derrida and the Humanities : A Critical Reader*(Ed.)Tom Cohem.Cambridge: Cambridge University Press 2001., p. 58.

59 Allan Megill. *Prophets of Extremity : Nietzsche, Heidegger, Foucault, Derrida,* p. 299.

60 Allan Megill. *Ibid.*, p. 304.

61 Allan Megill *Ibid.*, p. 307.

62 Jacques Derrida. *Acts of Literature.* (Ed.) Derek Attridge. London : Routledge, 1992, p. 52.

63 Paul de, Man. *Blindness and Insight : Essays in the Rhetoric of Contemporary Criticism.* Minneapolis : University of Minnesota Press, 1979, p. 282.

64 Martin McQuillan. Paul de Man : London : Routledge 2001, p. 32.

65 Paul de Man. *Allegories of Reading : Figural Langue in Rousseau, Nietzsche, Rilke, and Proust.* New Haven and London : Yale University Press, 1983, p. 15.

66 Paul de Man. *Aesthetic Ideology,* (Ed.) Minneapolis : University of Minnesota Press, 1996, p. 102

67 Paul de Man. *Ibid,* p. 103.

68 Martin McQuillan. *Paul de Man,* p. 96.

69 Steven Helming. Quoted in *Contemporary Literary Criticism : Excerpts from criticism of the Works of Today's Novelists, Poets, Playwrights, Short Story Writers, Scriptwriters, and Other Creative Writers.*(Ed.) Roger Matuz. Detroit : Gale Research Inc. Vol.. 60, p. 8.

70 Jean Baudrillard. *Selected Writings* (Ed.) Mark Poster. Oxford : Polity Press, 1988., p. 128.

71 Clive Cazeaux. *The Continental Aesthetic Reader*, p. 378.

72 Clive Cazeaux. *Ibid.*, p. 378.

73 Jean Francoise Lyotard. "Defining the Postmodern". in *The Norton Anthology of Theory and Criticism.* (Ed.) Vincent B. Leitch., p. 1614.

74 Gilles Deleuze and Felix Guattari. *What is Philosophy*? London : Verso, 1996, p. 5.

75 Gilles Deleuze and Felix Guattari. *Ibid,* p. 198.

76 Claire Colebrook. *Gilles Deleuze.* London : Routledge, 2002, p. 104.

77 Gilles Deleuze and Felix Guattari. "Kafka : Toward a Minor Literature" in *The Norton Anthology of Theory and Criticism* , p. 1598.

78 Sigmund Freud. Quoted by Richard Wollheim in "Freud and the Understanding of Art" in Cambridge Companion to Freud. Cambridge : Cambridge University Press, (Ed.) Jerome Neu, 1996, p. 249.

79 Ben Stoltzfus. *Lacan and Literature : Purloined Pretexts*. New York : State Universe of New York Press, 1996, p. 1.

80 Anika Lemaire. *Jacques Lacan*, London : Routledge and Kegan Paul, 1977, p. 54

81 Ben Stoltzfus. *Lacan and Literature : Purloined Pretexts*, p. 2.

II

Modernism : a historical background

Any discussion on modernism begins with the discussion on Modernity. Modernity is generally held to have come into being with the Renaissance and was defined in relation to the Antiquity. The idea of modernity highlights a novelty of the present as a break or rupture from a rapidly approaching and uncertain future. In its broadest sense, it is associated with the ideas of 'innovation', 'progress', and fashion and counterposed to the ideas of 'antiquity', the 'classical', and tradition. as a way of differentiating the most 'up- to- date' element of the present. According to Madan Sarup, it 'implies a progressive and economic and administrative rationalization and differentiation of the social world'.[1]

Differentiation means the separation of fact from value, the ethical from the theoretical spheres. In fact, these were the processes, which are responsible for the emergence of the modern capitalist industrial state.

Rene Descartes was considered the founder of philosophical modernity. He was the architect of the idea that "method" is the road to knowledge and truth. He beatified Galileo's concept of objectivity and subjectivity for the modern world. One of the consequences of this view is the idea of value of freedom in the social sciences. Whatever may be the idea, it must be proven by a rational and objective method. As the value claims cannot be proven, they can never be considered knowledge. Hence, they have no space in the realm of science.

According to Descartes, the "objectivity" is essentially that part of the world that can be described in what he calls "nature's language", the language of mathematical physics. Values, interpretations, prescriptive and all the mental languages can never describe objective reality, because none of them are quantifiable or scientific data. 'Only the quantifiable data of physical reality are objective'[2]. To understand or discover the truth of this data we need a method and it must be founded on rationality and objectivity. In the view of Hollinger, 'Thinkers like Leibniz argued that someday all human problems will be solved by a mechanical algorithm'.[3]

This idea got a lot of importance in the modernity. According to this the human enquirer must become objective by shedding all subjective elements or qualities.

In spite of the fact that there were some attempts to reconcile science, religion and morality, modern philosophy sustained only with absolute dualisms like facts/values, objectivity, science/culture, and reason/emotion. With these philosophical dichotomies modernity evolved in sociology and philosophy as a distinct category. In fact, the very notion of modernity was based on the notion of traditional societies in contrast with the industrial societies. That is why modernity was considered as a synonym name for the process whereby a society is transformed from traditional to modern. In the general sense of the term, modernity is marked with the rise of industry, cities, market capitalism, increasing secularisation, democratisation and social legislation.

To be brief, modernity is an umbrella term referring to a cluster of social, economic and political systems that came into existence around the eighteenth century in the West. In the view of Jan Nedeveen Pieterse, 'Modernity is a keynote in reflections on globalisation in sociology… Globalisation is the corollary of modernity… In conjunction with globalisation, modernity provides a structure and periodisation. … Together globalisation and modernity make up a ready-made package'.[4]

The idea of modernity found one of its first expressions in the seventeenth and eighteenth century debates between ancients and moderns, concerning literary style and the status of classics as represented in, for example, William Temple's "Essay on Ancient and Modern Learning (1690), and William Wotton's "Reflections up on Ancient and Modern Learning (1696). The moderns had rejected classical style, such as the idea of timeless beauty or the reverence for the Augustan Age, in favour of the contemporary, which was characterized by a strong belief in science and progress. From the beginning, modernity was closely associated with the rise of the modern science, and is best exemplified in Francis Bacon's opposition to the wisdom of antiquity. The modern was defined by an orientation to the present and postulated an origin from which the present was a deviation. Modernity was also defined in opposition to the Pagan period, which had been overcome. To be modern was to be contemporary, to witness the present.

From the beginning, modernity had been designating a particular kind of consciousness. The idea of 'the moment' is central to the time consciousness of modernity. This consciousness expresses a tension between present and past. The moment of modernity exists in the space between present and past, for the modern is not only an epoch that lives for the future, but is one that is formed out of a concept of history. According to Gerard Delanty, 'the critical appropriation of the past provides the modern spirit with its central driving thrust. The overcoming of an origin is part of this way of thinking, which ties the moment of the present to an act of historical appreciation'.[5]

In a way, the idea of modernity is a projection backwards as much as forwards. It is for this reason that many of its formulations embodied nostalgia as much as utopianism. The Christian thinkers of the late Roman period were able to define their age as modern in opposition to the pagan world of antiquity, a term that was associated with the opposition of civilization to the pagan culture of the 'barbarians'. In a way the temporary dimension to modernity has been closely associated with logic of exclusion and inclusion. Modernity simultaneously emerged as category, a way of making 'now' versus 'then'. This began to happen when the 'now' came to be understood as something other than a continuation of the ancient ways, and instead, as marking an age of novelty.

This shift begins to be visible in the idea of a new beginning, prominent in the Renaissance. Robert B.Pippin says, 'It is to the early Renaissance that we owe the formation periodisation of history into antiquity, the Middle Ages, and Modernity, and to thinkers Petrarch in the fourteenth century that we owe the notion of modernity as a kind of awakening from a long, "dark sleep".[6]

Rene Descartes has been considered one of the proponents of this radical break. In fact, modernity's early philosophical self-understanding is manifested in Descartes famous radical doubt, an extreme rejection of everything accepted on trust, authority, tradition, and common sense. Medieval notion of divine omnipotence, common sense, trusted world of appearance was thought as a kind of dream. According to Pippin, 'Once so much is put in doubt (once the world is "lost") on what basis can the human subject "re-establish" a connection with the actual world?" On what basis or foundation can a true "science" of reality be built?'[7]

Descartes gave an answer to this question. The answer is in one word : Method. If we can discuss the right method, if we can construct a procedure, whose 'rules' can in general be argued to produce safe or "certain" results, repeatable in other experiments, at other times and places, we will have the weapon we need to master the deceptive nature. Descartes argued that the thinking subject's certainty of his own existence, his existence, as thinking or mental being was the foundation of this method. Whatever may be doubtable, the subject cannot be deceived that he is thinking what he is thinking. Self-certainty became the 'measure' for the method.

As already seen, modernity is also an awareness of the 'moment', is an epoch stretching forward as well as backwards in time. The future is emanating not from the present as such, but from an event which preceded the present and from which the present also derives its strength. That is why in the age of Enlightenment, the epoch of modernity was seen as the period stretching from the sixteenth to eighteenth century, when, as a result of the scientific revolution, the Renaissance, the Reformation and the age of discoveries, the old certainties of the Middle Ages were shattered.

Delanty says,' The notion that the future has already begun is central to the time consciousness of the modern, which derives its legitimation from its own self-projection back on history'.[8] Jurgen Habermas thinks that, 'the secular concept of modernity expresses the conviction that the future has already begun : It is the epoch that lives for the future. In this way, the caesura defined by the new beginning has shifted into the past, precisely to the start of modern times'.[9]

The early modern idea of revolution, for example, has not signified a radical break from the past and an embrace of the future, but signalled a cyclical conception of history by which the future was returning as an appropriation of the past. The problem of the modernity was always the problem of justifying itself by means of criteria that could be derived neither from what had been rejected nor from its own self-legitimation.

Modernity has been seen as an idea, a cultural impulse, a time consciousness, an historical event, a social condition, and an epoch in historical time. However, it is primarily understood as an idea. A particular striking example of modernity as an idea can be seen in Kant's " An Answer to the Question : What is Enlightenment". This essay published in 1784, had been the subject of much of the subsequent discourse of modernity from Hegel to Foucault and Habermas. Kant's answer to the question, "Do we live in an 'enlightened age?" "No", but we do live in an age of enlightenment". By this, he meant that the age itself was not coeval with the culture of the enlightenment. To be specific, there was disparity between form and reality : the forces of enlightenment had not fully penetrated the age. Kant clearly equated enlightenment with a particular way of thinking and one, which exemplifies the spirit of modernity.

Kant firmly believed that Enlightenment is humankind's exit from its self-incurred immaturity. Immaturity, in Kantian sense, is the inability to make use of one's own understanding without the guidance of another and it is self-incurred when there is a lack of resolution and courage to use it without the guidance of another. Thus *Sapere aude!* ' Have courage' to use your own understanding is the motto of Enlightenment. This statement captures the central idea of Kant as well as Enlightenment. It revolves round the themes of autonomy, critique and publicity.

According to Delanty, 'Kant's whole ethical philosophy was a defence of the autonomy of morality, for him it cannot be derived from anything other than the moral law, in other words from itself. Morality is autonomous of all worldviews that postulate conceptions of a unified worldview, for under the conditions of modernity the principle of differentiation and decentring is irreversible: the cognitive, the aesthetic and the moral are differentiated from each other and from religion'.[10]

Hence, the project of autonomy and the principle of cultural differentiation constitute the foundations of the Kantian idea of modernity.

The second important aspect of Kantian philosophy and conception of modernity is the idea of critique. Kant in his preface to the "Critique of Pure Reason" argued for the need to institute a tribunal. This tribunal is none other than the critique of pure reason. In this work, Kant staunchly defended critique as a form of cultural suspicion. In fact, Kant was the first major thinker who formulated the idea of critique. He considered the critique of reason a critique of false claims of reason. Kant called his method transcendental critique. For him, the critique meant a search for conditions of the possibility of knowledge or self-knowledge. The thought that all knowledge is mediated knowledge, because it is conditioned by the cognitive structures of the mind, hence, reason always cannot always be used in pure form.

Kant rejected the claims of rationalism, particularly in its Cartesian form, which claimed that pure and objective knowledge is possible. Ultimately, it was a scepticism, which found its expression in the form of critique. In his writings, Kant had a deep understanding of the nascent culture of critique that had arisen with modernity. In the view of Kant, enlightenment is possible only when a certain kind of freedom exists. The essence of this freedom is the freedom to make a public use of one's own reason; the public use of reason must be free. It can bring about enlightenment. He thought that public reason is essentially reflective, intellectual discourse, contrary to it, private reason is primarily institutionalised, specific to particular non-public contexts. Kant says,'I understand, however, under the public use of his own reason , that use which anyone makes of it as a scholar before the entire public of the reading world. The private use I designate as that use which one makes of his reason in a certain civil post or office which is entrusted to him'.[11]

The public use of reason pertains to academic discourse. Its chief characteristic is argumentation. Private reason, in contrast, does not require argumentation. Kant feels this would be disruptive for the smooth functioning of society. The public reason could be used to justify authority, as it is institutionalised in a public order. Hence, Delanty says,'Kant's vision of modernity was one of both political and conservativism and intellectual radicalness, of ever expanding horizons of cognitive experience'.[12]

Delanty makes valid observations in this context. He says," The target of critical argument for Kant was religious and ecclesiastical dogma, since he believed this was the only remaining obstacle to enlightenment, for the arts and science had emancipated themselves from the prince's consciousness. Kant like many of the moderns did not reject Christianity but believed that its cognitive and institutional jurisdiction must be restricted. Thus the idea of the critique of tradition enters the discourse of modernity, whose self- consciousness is one of argumentative renewal and rejection of fundamental acts, other than that of the "tribunal reason".[13]

In another essay "The Conflict of Faculties" (1798) Kant defends the autonomy of philosophy as the foundational faculty. Philosophy, for him, unlike law, medicine and theology-which expresses the private use of reason- is based on the vocation of free thinking and does not serve any institutional function. He believed that it is the ultimate trustee of public reason. To be brief, modernity, according to Kant is associated with the spirit of Enlightenment.

With the advent of Hegel on the scene, modernity is wedded to the philosophy of history. Hegel, in his "Lectures on the Philosophy of History", sees modernity as the emergence of the new and it entails a reflective consciousness of history and this consciousness sees the future as already having begun in the recent past. For Hegel, modernity expresses the unity of past and present. It is an amalgamation of Greek civilization, Christianity, the French Revolution and the modern state.

In his "Phenomenology of Mind", Hegel says, "'Besides it is not difficult to see that our time is a birth-time and a period of transition to a new era. Spirit has broken with the world it has hitherto inhabited and imagined, and is of a mind to submerge it in the past, and in the labour of its own transformation. Spirit is indeed never at rest but always engaged in moving forward. But just as the first breath drawn by child after its long, quite nourishment breaks its gradualness of merely quantitative growth-there is a qualitative leap and child is born-so likewise with the Spirit in its formation matures slowly and quietly into its new shape, dissolving bit by bit the structure of its previous world, whose tottering state is only hinted at by isolated symptoms. The frivolity and boredom which unsettle the established order, the voyage foreboding of something unknown, there are the heralds of approaching change. The gradual crumbling that left unaltered the face of the whale is cut by a sunburst which, in one flash illuminates the features of the new world'.[14]

In Hegel, we find that the consciousness of the present moment is much stronger than in Kant. Hegel saw modernity not just as enlightenment, but also as a relationship to history. In a way Hegel historicized Kant's critique. The morality that Kant talked about can be created in society and articulated in human history. In this way Hegel's epistemology transforms itself into a social theory and ceases to be a mere theory of knowledge. Hence, the constitution of knowledge in history becomes an independent question to Hegel. This is because Hegel thought that reality is constituted by knowledge and knowledge is always a critique. Critique is a form of knowledge that transforms its object. In this way, knowledge and reality are dialectically shaped. According to Hegel critical knowledge is a form of consciousness raising and the highest form of knowledge is consciousness as self-consciousness. Hegel considered critique a kind of constructive activity.

The social theory of Hegel was, basically, idealistic. According to him, the evolution of forms of knowledge corresponds to phases in the development or the progression of the society. The 'general' or 'universal' and the 'specific' are unified in the formation of even higher-forms of knowledge and these eventually transcend society. This process is a process of 'displacement' or 'overcoming'. Like Kant, Hegel also believed that knowledge was always self-limiting, always comes too late, unable to be realized in political practice, for social actors cannot conceive of their age in pure thought. Historical self-consciousness can ultimately, by means of 'cunning of reason', be available only to the philosopher, who can go beyond it by being its principle expression.

Hegel in his "Philosophy of Right" outlined a theory of civil society, which gave expression to a vision of modernity as a process of negation. Ethical life is constituted in the private realm, the public realm and the state. In his view state is higher expression of community than civil society. The function of state is to compensate the shortcomings of civil society. Delanty says,'In sum, the theme of Hegel's social theory is that of the fragmentation/alienation of consciousness in civil society and the search for a political solution for the realization of community. Modernity is the motif which gives expression to this struggle'.[15]

Two attitudes shaped much of the subsequent understanding of modernity : On the one side, a great faith in the process of reason to bring about freedom, on the other a nostalgia and sadness for the passing of an irretrievable organic unity. The first one had its inspiration in the promise of reason and the other reconciled the promise of freedom with a melancholic pessimism about modernity. The first tradition is represented by revolutionary romanticism, nationalism, Fascism, Marxism and Liberalism and the other can be seen in Nietzsche, Heidegger, Freud and Wittgenstein.

With the advent of Marx or Marxism on the scene, modernity is seen at odds with its own project. In place of historical constitution, self-constitution became the driving force of the modernity. The self is a collective social actor who must be historically constituted. There is a radical variation in the conception of the subject. It is radically different from that of Kant. After Marx, the focus of critique shifted from epistemological issues as in Kant, or philosophical issues as in Hegel, to the social relations of capitalism and its domination. However, the act of historical overcoming is strongly present in Marx. His orientation is more to future than to the past. For Marx, modernity is neither exclusively an idea, as with Kant nor an epoch in history in which an idea is realized, as with Hegel, but a radical project of action. According to Marshall Berman, 'Marx looked forward to communism as the fulfilment of modernity'.[16]

After the advent of Marx on the scene, there was an increasing recognition that cultural idea and social reality are contradictory. Because of that, modernity as project expressed less in overcoming of an origin than in the struggle to overcome alienation and exploitation.

Delanty understands this change or development as an anticipation of modernism. Modernism can be used to designate the radical turn in the culture of modernity. In fact, it refers to a radical breakthrough or change in aesthetics. While exploring the reasons for the above change, Delanty makes valid observations. In his view, 'The early discourse of modernity, epitomized in the writings of Kant took the central characteristic of modernity to the differentiation of cognitive spheres from each other in the wake of fragmentation of unified worldview of medieval Christiandom and the doctrine of the divine right of kinship. By the end of nineteenth century all this change. The aesthetic dimension undergoes an increasing formalization of style, which can be seen as an immanent development of the autonomous institution of art as a professional activity by which art ceases to be the representation of orders (social or religious) other than those of art itself'.[17]

Therbon says that there are four passes of entry into modernity. Taking the Globe as an arena of comparative empirical research, he distinguishes four major entries into modernity. One is the European gate of revolution or reform....The French Revolution and the British process from the mid-seventeenth century to 1832 constituted the first major unlocking of this gate. The second pass was located in the New Worlds of Americans, it is a product of transcontinental migration and genocide, it was through independence, first a major part of North America, soon followed by that of the South Central parts of hemisphere'. Third modernity could appear as a sudden external threat... This is a pattern of imposed or *externally induced modernization*. Finally, there is a vast area from North-western Africa via the Indian subcontinent route to the archipelago of Southeast Asia, where modernity arrived by *conquest, subjection and appropriation,* the gate of the colonial zone. In another sense, modernity means an opening in the mould of the traditional identity and a way to escape from the given identity of the family, the locality and social positions.

Modernity got tremendous thrust in progress, uncompromising belief in the human reason and unending desire for freedom. These ideas were strongly given a systematic shape with the development of sociology during nineteenth century. In this century, modernity was considered the whole assemblage of the characteristics of modern societies and there was an implicit desire to export it to other countries. One should not forget the fact that modernity was just not an economic, political and technological affair; it stretched its wings even to the fields of culture and religion.

The writings of Marx, Weber, Durkheim and Simmel prove this. Their writings very systematically analyze the importance of religion and culture in understanding modernity and the situation before the advent of modernity. These thinkers explained in concrete terms how modernity scoured tradition and how it replaced the community rules with the new ones akin to the routines of factory life or the regulations of the bureaucracy. The observations of David Lyon in this context are not out of place. He says,

'Modernity is all about the massive changes that took place at many levels from the mid-sixteenth century onwards, changes signalled by the shifts that uprooted agricultural workers and transformed them into mobile industrial urbanities. Modernity questions all conventional ways of doing things, substituting authorities of its own, based in science, economic growth, democracy or law'.[18]

Within a few decades, modernity that began in Europe could transform society radically and irrevocably. The everyday life of the people had been altered unimaginably. Machine became the metaphor of social life. The routine life of the people always resembled machine. The seasons, sunrise and sunset, dawn and dusk are symbolically replaced by timetables, clocks and electric bulbs, continuous quest for new raw materials, new sources of labour, and of late, new technological aids to replace human power. The driving force behind all the changes is nothing but capitalism in Marxian terms.

Heidegger defined modernity as the "Age of the World Picture". He says, 'The expression "world picture of the modern age" and "modern world picture" ...assumes something that never could have been before, namely, a medieval world picture and an ancient world picture. The world picture does not change from an earlier medieval one into a modern one, but rather the fact that the world becomes a picture at all is what distinguishes the essence of the modern age'.[19]

The following are the basic features of modernity :

Owing to the increasing division of labour, tasks became more sophisticated and specialized. The unavoidable division of labour is the result of the industrialization. The immediate outcome of this is differentiation. Thinkers like Emile Durkheim called this differentiation a new principle of social integration. There was a clear demarcation between public and private life. The roles of the church and family were taken over by schools, mass media and welfare departments.

Urbanity is another crucial phenomenon in Modernity. Modern life is indisputably urban life. The very structure of the city is based on rationality. Urban life affected the thinking of the people of all shades. George Simmel says, 'Punctuality, calculability, exactness are forced upon life by the complexity and extension of metropolitan existence'.[20]

Urbanism cannot be seen just by the statistics of the urban growth. It is a state of specific cultural consciousness also. Thinkers like George Simmel saw urbanism as a way of life. Urbanism pushes playful and fleeting trends and fashions. It can isolate people from their conventional and communal roots.

It keeps people in a dreamy world. It forces people raise blockades to guard their isolation. They live almost a secluded and alienated life without being aware of it.

The modern nation state necessitated the formation of special military force. The hierarchy in the military and its functioning became the model for social discipline.

The military way of discipline had tremendous impact on the structuring of the workers in the factories. It spread even to the schools and hospitals. Michel Foucault in his monumental work 'The Discipline and Punish : The Birth of the Prison" felt that the panopticon plan is the epitome of modern discipline.

Secularisation of the world is one of the aims of the modernity project. The church that was almost dictating the lives of the people before the advent of modernity was put out of place by the industrialization. The French Revolution declared the arrival of secular state. In fact, the theories of medieval philosophers were challenged in the fifteenth and sixteenth centuries. Thinkers like Niccolo Machiavelli pushed aside Christian idealism in favour of realistic power politics. Thomas Hobbes universalised Machiavelli's ideas. Both of them separated politics from religion. This approach was known as secularism.

There won't be any space for superhuman or supernatural forces. Scientific temperament dominates every sphere of the society. Modernization process systematically displaces religious practices and institutions. Reason and science are established in their place. The entire religious phenomenon loses its centrality in the social life of the people. In fact, religion has no legitimating power in modern society. This doesn't mean that religion will disappear altogether from the scene. It does survive on the margins of social life. Secularisation is a cultural process. In its process, it will influence all most all the artistic practices. The bureaucracy that naturally emerges in the modernity is nothing but rationalization of the existing social norms in accordance with a scientific method.

In the pre-modern or pre-industrial societies, family was the essential unit of production. All the members participated in an obliging set of survival activities... The family was a combined project; all its members considered themselves part of that whole. Each member used to contribute something to a common store. The family resembled a world in miniature. Modernity through industrialization radically alters or destroys the autonomous status of the family and its economy and reduces it to a small unit of consumption.

Production shifts from house to factory. People are placed in the hands of national and international markets. Family for its survival depends on structures that are external to it. The simultaneous disintegration of family because of the industrialization leads to the individualization in the society.

Reason or rationality occupied the status of divinity or God in modernity. Rationalism is the philosophical view that regards 'reason' as the chief source and test of knowledge. Rationalists assert that reality has an inherent logical structure and the intellect can grasp this.

Scientific method or laboratory method was conspicuous in every choice of the society. Machine like precision became the motive of every act in the society. This precision spread even to artefacts. From music to military, rationality was the criterion. Rationalism is another important feature of modernity : It's a way of inquiry that views reason as the primary source and investigation of knowledge. Rationalism believes reason to be a faculty, which grasps truths beyond the reach of sense perception, both in certainty and generality. The guiding principle to rationalism has always been mathematics. All the rationalists emphasized the superiority of the deductive method over all other methods in point of certainty. The first modern rationalist was Rene Descartes. Descartes ambition was to introduce the mathematical rigor into the philosophy. He wanted to doubt everything to arrive at something indubitable. In his famous *cogito ergo sum*, (I think, therefore I am) is an example . His aim was to achieve an absolute certainty. He desired to produce a philosophical system on which men could agree as fully as they do on the geometry of Euclid.

Alienation is the constant feeling in the modernity. It is a feeling of being isolated from certain aspects of one's own surroundings. Alienation may crop up when one's emotional ties with another person, group, institution, or belief are disrupted. Sometimes, entire groups become alienated. The very existence of modernity is depending upon the continuous upgrading of technology, unending spread of capital at the global level. More than these, the gulf between the capitalists and the labourers widens. Simultaneously the workers are alienated from their own humanity and work. The lust for profit among the owners increases the sense of alienation among the workers. So alienation and modernity go together.

Conventional regulation of individual and social life disappears. Traditional bonds of the family are cut off. The earlier moral order that was dictating the lives of people will crumble. Hence, a sense of loss and uncertainty will be looming large on the individuals. Professional judgements on anything gain momentum, whereas the institutional opinions lose their credibility. The intellectuals with scientific temperament will be providing guidance in the legislation of the modern world. Their ultimate promise is rational organisation of society.

Globalisation is one of the primary aims of Modernity. The global system, in the view of Jonathan Friedman, 'involves the articulation between expanding/contracting central 'sectors' and their emergent/disappearing peripheries. This articulation is one of decisive transformation of life forms in the broadest sense of the word. It is moreover long-term historical that can only be adequately understood as such. The historical processes of global system have specific properties, such as expansion/contraction, hagemonisation/fragmentation, that inform and limit the conditions of existence, reactions and cultural strategies of those who participate in them'.[21]

The Emergence of Modernism

The spirit of modernity is inseparable from the idea of scientific progress. The idea of scientific progress was instituted in the seventeenth century by Francis Bacon, Rene Descartes and Blaise Pascal. According to Bacon inventions and discoveries in the realm of mechanical arts like gunpowder, the compass and the printing had brought about many changes. These changes kept moderns in a superior position when compared to ancients; hence, the authority of the tradition was suspended. The spirit of modernity implied a strong expression of self–manifestation against the overwhelming authority of the ancients. However, this self-assurance of moderns succeeded first and most easily in science. Art and other aesthetic experiences as parts of the ontological changes brought in by the 'modernity' are called 'modernism'. The artists, writers, composers and architects who attempted to accommodate the dynamics of modernity are called modernists or modern artists.

Scientists like Pascal believed that scientific knowledge was susceptible to constant growth and infinite perfection. Pascal's idea of progress and perfectibility articulated in his treatise on empty space in 1647, relates to the science in the strict sense of the term as they are based on reason and experiment. These sciences are geometry, arithmetic, physics and medicine. He did not base his treatise on those investigations or observations of the disciplines like history, jurisprudence, linguistics and theology. He believed knowledge of the latter type of investigation is limited, whereas in the earlier type it is continuously augmented and perfected without limit. Pascal assured his contemporaries by declaring 'Our view is more extended ...we see more than they'.[22]

The restriction of progress and modernity was even more pronounced with regard to the arts. Progress and perfectibility remained the privilege of the philosophy and sciences. These two were excluded from the realm of arts. Behler says, 'With regard to the historical status of sciences and the arts, the realms of reasoned imagination, European classicism and enlightenment show a characteristic antagonism. The sciences appeared to be involved in an interminable progression, whereas the arts were thought always returning in cyclical motion to the position of correct standards and appropriate norms from which they had departed in periods of decay and barbarism'.[23]

The concrete philosophical thought for the above assumption was the belief that philosophy and sciences are infinite as thought and nature, whereas art has only certain point of perfection, and it is determined by man's inevitable nature. Hence, these philosophers and scientists believed that,'the fundamental rules of the taste are the same in all ages because they derive from invariable attributes of the human mind'.[24]

Arts like sciences were included in a process of infinite progress only at the end of the eighteenth century. This inclusion, in fact, is the most decisive suspension of the classical doctrine and the most impressive manifestation of the modern consciousness. This decisive step took place in various nations of Europe at about the same time. The new struggle between the ancients and the moderns appeared to have been won in art, poetry, and other literary fields, in favour of the moderns, and the age of modernity seemed to have truly begun.

Many events in human history contributed to the above change and break. The most important contribution is of the French Revolution of 1789. The French Revolution constituted a crucial turning point in Europe's political life. There is a close relation between the French Revolution and the Romantic Movement in literature. Romanticism brought a fundamental change in literature and arts by breaking with the classical tradition. Philosophy also added another dimension to its new orientation at the time. Behler says, 'Kant, in the preface to the second edition of his "Critique of Pure Reason" characterised the new manner of philosophical speculation introduced by him as a Copernican turn in philosophy, namely, as a switch of perspective form the objects of perception to the perceiving subject. Students of his doctrine soon declared Kant's innovation a revolution in philosophy and saw his thought a correspondence to the French Revolution, a different expression of a general upheaval characterizing their time. The late eighteenth century thus appears to be marked by at least three revolutions, that is, in politics, in literature and in philosophy, which in each case overcame an old order, an ancient regime, a modern state of affairs'.[25]

However, there is a fundamental resistance on the part of the artists and writers to take the position unreservedly on the side of modernity. We find the same kind of reluctance on the part of historians to come to a clear-cut period of designation of modernism.

The first signs of reversal in the enormous preponderance of the classical Greeks and Romans over the modern Europeans in the realms of literature and artistic creation can be noticed in the so called quarrel between the ancients and the moderns, i.e., between the proponents of classical art and the advocates of modern style. This critical debate, conducted mostly in seventeenth and eighteenth centuries in Europe, specifically in England, France and Germany are fundamental for the formation of modernity. Critics and writers like Saint-Evermond and Perrault, Dryden, Pope, and Johnson attempted to shake off the overwhelming weight of the Classical Greek and Roman models and gave the modern age self-confidence and the right to have its distinct style. The new author demonstrated that the modern age has not only grown beyond Aristotle's 'Physics' but also created artistic beauties unknown to the "Poetics".

The best example of the struggle between ancients and the moderns can be seen in Dryden's "Essay on Dramatic Poesy" (1668). In this writing, four witty interlocutors discuss the difference between the ancients and the moderns in the field of drama. In the view of Behler, the feeling of superiority of the moderns can be seen in the writings of the two French authors, Charles Perrault and Saint-Evermond. In the field of tragedy, Perrault gave unreserved preference to the tragedies of Corneille and Racine over those of the Greeks. Saint- Evermond was the most outspoken partisan of the moderns. He declared in his "Of Ancient and the Modern Tragedy" (1672) that Aristotle's "Poetics" was as outdated as his "Physics". Just as modern philosophers discovered truths that were unknown to Aristotle, the modern writers had created beauties on the stage that were not known to Aristotle. Fontenelle in his "Digression on the Ancient and the Moderns" (1688) maintained that the best works of Sophocles, Euripides or Aristophanes would not stand up to the tragedies and comedies of the Age of Louis xiv. Even Voltaire in his "Dissertation on Ancient and Modern Tragedy" (1748) stated that the French stage surpassed the Greek by virtue of the art of performance, by invention, and by countless particular beauties.

However, the writers who claimed the superiority of the moderns over the ancients in literature refused to apply the ideas of progress and perfectibility to this realm. This reluctance was simply because they no longer saw themselves as part of great flowering of literature. Therefore, an entirely new concept of literature and fundamentally new sense of modernity had to emerge, when classical model of literary creation was overcome and replaced by a notion of literature involved in a process in various European nations at about the same time and marks the beginning of new Romanticism.

The Romantics, by applying infinite perfectibility to the arts, created an entirely new concept of literature. These writers stood in the liveliest exchange with the social life in which literature also participated. To be specific, the hallmark of the eighteenth century Romanticism was the readiness to assume for art and literature an unlimited change and mutability. Infinite perfection is also an expression of the reaction to the French Revolution of those early romantics. However, an apologetic and bewildered exclamation was uttered by the writers when the French Revolution took an unforeseen course. Though they considered the French Revolution a lost cause, they wanted to rescue its treasures like, the liberation of humanity, through other means than political ones. The transformation of revolution into a universal and philosophical emancipation is a dominant attempt by the romantics all over the Europe of the time.

The early representatives of English romanticism, the members of the Lake School, responded to the French Revolution with great enthusiasm. In his book "The Prelude" Wordsworth rejoices on the first anniversary of the French Revolution. He was drawn into general emotion of fraternity. There was a feeling among many that France was catching up with England's "glorious revolution" of 1688 and heading for a constitutional monarchy. There are several books, which were influenced by this 'spirit of the age'.

Romanticism is usually held to have originated in France and the German thought had shaped or affected all Europe in varying degrees at different times. The movement is clearly a dislocation in thought and social structure consequent on three revolutions, the French, the American and the Industrial and it dominates three literary generations from 1790s to the1840s.

The literature and art that was produced in Europe and the United States from about 1840 until the 1890s, is defined as Realist. This form of realism began in France in the novels of Gustave Flaubert and the short stories of Guy de Maupassant. In Russia, realism was represented in the plays and short stories of Anton Chekhov. The novelist George Eliot introduced realism into English fiction; as she declared in *Adam Bede* (1859), her purpose was to give a "faithful representation of commonplace things". Mark Twain and William Dean Howells were the pioneers of realism in the United States. One of the greatest realists of all, the Anglo-American novelist Henry James, drew much inspiration from his mentors, Eliot and Howells. James's concern with character motivation and behaviour led to the development of a sub-genre, the psychological novel. In general, the work of these writers illustrates the main tenet of realism, that writers must not select facts in accord with preconceived aesthetic or ethical views but must set down their observations objectively. Concerned with the faithful representation of life, which frequently lacks form, the realists tended to downplay plot in favour of character and to concentrate on middle-class life and preoccupations, avoiding larger, more dramatic issues.

In art and literature, modernism began in the first decade of the twentieth century, as a reaction to the realism. The roots of Modernism are European rather than British, and indeed the determination to take European culture as a model was one of the hallmarks of the Modernist movement. As we have seen already, Realism, according to many thinkers and critics, is characterized by its attempt to offer up a mirror to the world objectively. It is also modelled on prose forms such as history and journalism, general features, characters, language and a spatial and temporal setting. The setting is very much familiar to the contemporary readers and presents itself as transparently representative of writer's world. Modernism challenged the hegemony of Realism and instituted itself as an alternative way of representing reality and the world. Peter Childs says, 'Very broadly speaking, the vast majority of attempts to offer alternative modes representation from the middle of the nineteenth century to the middle of the twentieth century have at one time or another been termed Modernist, and this applies to literature, music, painting, film and architecture (and to some works before and after this period)'.[26]

From 1920s on wards the term Modernism began to move from general sense and acquire a specific association with the experimentation in the arts and literature. Modernism strove to render human subjectivity in ways more real than realism. It even tried to represent consciousness, perception, meaning, emotion and the individual's relation to society through interior monologue, stream of consciousness, defamiliarisation, rhythm, and irresolution. Modernist writers tried to modify or even to overturn existing modes of representation and to express the new sensibilities, in a compressed, complex literature of the city, of industry and technology, war, machinery and speed, mass markets and communication, and of Internationalism, the New Woman, the aesthete, the nihilist and the flâneur.[27]

Modernism has been variously squabbled as a period, genre, style, or combination of these; but it is first a word; one which exists along side equivalent words. Its stem, 'Modern', is from the Latin *modo,* which means 'current', and hence has a far wider currency and range of meanings than 'Modernism' would offer. Historically the meaning of the world has been changing and acquiring new meanings from time to time. However, there was no radical change in the spirit it connotes. In the late fifteenth century, the Latin word *modernus* suggests the Christian present, which was quite opposite to the Roman past. Like wise, we distinguish the modern English from the Middle English. It is observed that the modern period in western literature begins with the sixteenth century, whereas our common sense states that the modern literature is the literature of twentieth century.

Notes

1 Madan Saru, *p. An Introductory Guide to Post-structuralism and Post-modernism.* Athens : The University of Georgia Press, p. 130

2 Robert Hollinger. *Postmodernism and the Social Sciences : A Thematic Approach.* London :Sage,1994, p. 24

3 Robert Hollinger, p. 24.

4 Jan Nedeveen Pieterse. In *Global Modernities.* (Ed.) : Mike Featherstone, Scott Lash and Ronald Robertson. London : Sage, 1995, p. 46.

5 Gerard Delanty. *Modernity and Postmodernity : Knowledge, Power and the Self.* London : Sage, 2000, p-9.

6 Robert B.Pippin. *Modernism as a Philosophical Problem*, Massachusetts : Basil Blackwell, 1991, p-17.

7 Robert B.Pippin. *Ibid.*, p. 23.

8 Gerard Delanty. *Modernity and Postmodernity : Knowledge, Power and the Self,* p. 10

9 Jurgen Habermas. Quoted in *Modernity and Postmodernity : Knowledge, Power and the Self,* p. 10

10 Gerard Delanty. *Modernity and Postmodernity : Knowledge, Power and the Self,* p. 11

11 Immanuel Kant. Quoted by Delanty, in *Ibid.*, p. 13

12 Gerard Delanty. *Ibid.*, p. 13.

13 Gerard Delanty. *Ibid.*, p. 13.

14 Georg Wilhelm Friedrich Hegel. *Phenomenology of Mind.* London : Routledge Kegan Paul, 1977, p. 6-7

15 Gerard Delanty.*Modernity and Postmodernity : Knowledge, Power and the Self Ibid.*, p. 15

16 Marshal Berman. *All That is Solid Melts into Air*, London : Penguin, 1988, p104.

17 Gerard Delanty. *Modernity and Postmodernity : Knowledge, Power and the Self Ibid.*, p. 17

18 David Lyons. *Postmodernity*. New Delhi : Viva Books, 2002, p. 27.

19 Martin Heidegger. quoted in *The Cambridge Companion to Modernism*, (Ed.) Michael Levenson, Cambridge University Press, 1999, p. 13.

20 David Lyons. *Postmodernity*, p. 31.

21 Jonathan Friedman. *Cultural Identity& Global Process*, London : Sage, 1994, p. 201.

22 Blaise Pascal. quoted by Ernst Behler in *Irony and the Discourse of Modernity*,. Seattle : University of Washington Press, p. 38

23 Ernst Behler . *Irony and the Discourse of Modernity*, p. 38

24 Ernst Behler *Ibid.*, p. 39.

25 Ernst Behler. *Ibid.*, p. 40.

26 Peter Childs. *Modernism*. London : Routledge, 2000, p. 3.

27 Peter Childs *Ibid.*, p. 4.

III

Modern aesthetics and its manifestation in various art forms

Modernism is an offshoot of modern philosophy. Any discussion on modernism can be developed only by tracing the philosophical and the historical lineages of modern Philosophy. Modern philosophy, a cultural movement in Europe popularly known as the Renaissance, overlapped the end of the middle Ages and formed a transition between medieval and modern periods. The period between 1300-1600 is considered the Renaissance. It was a time of intellectual resurgence stemming from the rediscovery of ancient Greek and Roman cultures. During the Renaissance, various radical changes occurred in sciences such as - astronomy, physics, and mathematics.

Renaissance humanists laid emphasis on the importance of human beings and the study of classical literature, which was thought as a guide to understanding life. The emphasis on science and on humanism directed changes in the aims and methods of philosophical inquiry. Scholasticism went into oblivion, and philosophy was free from of its ties to medieval theology. In the view of Clive Cazeaux ' There are a number of different aspects to the 'modern'. Principally, the term denotes the period in the history of ideas characterized by the development man's self-image as an autonomous rational being, distinct from God who, through reason and sensory knowledge, is able to know and manipulate the world. The work of the French rationalist philosopher Rene Descartes (1596-1650) is often cited as the threshold of modern thought. His *cogito* argument 'I think, therefore I am'—identifies the essence of the human being with reason and makes the material aspects of human life, that is, the body, sensory experience, and the natural world, subordinates to rational enquiry".[1]

In the view of Peter Barry, 'Modernism was that earth- quake in the arts which brought down much of the structure of pre-twentieth century practice in music, painting, literature, and architecture. One of the major epicenters of this earthquake seems to have been in Vienna, during the period 1890-1910, but the effects were felt in France, Germany, Italy and eventually even in Britain, in art movements like Cubism, Dadaism, Surrealism, and Futurism'.[2]

Basically Modernism was a literary and cultural movement, which flourished, in the first decades of the twentieth century. The roots of Modernism are European. There was an intense desire to propagate European culture as a model to the rest of the world. In fact, it was one of the basic characteristics of the Modernist movement. The terms "Modernist" and "Modernism" were not used by the proponents of the movement themselves. They rather referred to their works and aesthetic theories.

Modernism as a movement was not confined only to literature; it had spread to the disciplines like painting, music, sculpture, and architecture, as well as to theology, aesthetics, and anthropology. Modernism was related to both the content and form of work. In a sense, Modernism was a sign of cultural crisis and the crisis was both exhilarating and disturbing at once. It questioned all most all the earlier notions of the literary and cultural domains and opened up new possibilities. Modernism is discernible by experimentation.

According to Schulte Sasse, 'modernism 'should be seen as the cultural precipitate of the modernity'.[3]

In fact, Marx, Freud and Darwin had upset the human subject from its earlier protected place at the centre of the universe. They had exposed its unconscious reliance on laws and structures outside its control and even beyond its knowledge. Theories like Marx's Historical Materialism and its deterministic tendency, Freud's psychoanalytic theories that reveal the self as a hock in a course subjugated by unconscious, and Darwin's ideas of evolution and heredity which positions humanity as the most recent result of natural selection, combine to intimidate humanist self-confidence and to incite a feeling of ideological ambiguity and doubt.

The theories of these thinkers had tremendous influence over modernist writing. Specifically, in the field of arts the modernist ambiguity resulted in an enormously fruitful way. It formed the aesthetics of experimentation, fragmentation, and ambiguity. Modernism was erected on a sense of loss of community and civilization. It personified a succession of negations and paradoxes. As it has no established center it could embrace multiple features. The feeling of the loss of tradition was a general theme for the Modernist writer. Quite interestingly, some writers lamented this loss of tradition, whereas some others celebrated it. The co-existence of revolution and conservatism under the Modernist umbrella is an indication of its paradoxical nature. Another paradox is that we can see both the predominance of technological preoccupation and its condemnation in the modernist writings.

Science is the driving force behind modern philosophy. Francis Bacon of England was one of the earliest philosophers to propagate science. Bacon and Rene Descartes are considered the originators of modern philosophy. In his two influential works, "The Advance-ment of Learning" (1605), and "Novum Organum" (1620), Bacon proclaimed or stated that knowledge was power and that knowledge could be attained only by the inductive method of investigation. He anticipated a new world of culture and leisure that could be gained by inquiry into the laws and processes of nature. In recounting the world, he projected the effects of development in science, engineering, and technology.

The development in science and technology shaped the emergence of Rationalism as the philosophical outlook in the 1600's. The basic thought of rationalism is that the reason is superior and higher to experience as a source of knowledge and that the legitimacy or validity of perceptions of the senses must be established from more assured or concrete principles. The rationalists tried to determine the nature of the world and of reality by deduction from premises themselves established as certain a *priori*. They also accentuated the importance of mathematical procedures. Descartes, Baruch Spinoza, and Gottfried Leibniz were the leading rationalists of the times.

Descartes who invented analytical geometry was a mathematician as well as a philosopher. His crucial idea was to establish a sheltered foundation for the sciences, a foundation that resembles the foundation he had found for mathematics. Thus he was very much concerned with the fundamentals or foundations of knowledge. He executed philosophy on its unrelenting deliberation of epistemological questions. Descartes viewed all physical phenomena as connected mechanically by laws of cause and effect. He tried to probe the problem of how mind and matter are related.

Spinoza's system of philosophy was based on the model of geometry. He tried to develop philosophic conclusions from a few central axioms or truisms, which are supposedly self-evident truths and definitions. Spinoza identified God with the universe. As a mechanist he believed that everything in the universe is determined. His ultimate aim was ethical and to show how people could be free and could lead reasonable and thus satisfying lives. To be specific, his world is deterministic.

Leibniz thought that the tangible world is only one of many possible worlds. He considered the actual world is the best of all possible worlds. He developed a complex philosophical system and believed that the ultimate elements of reality are indivisible, mind like substances called monads. He identified the changing states of monads as "perceptions." But Leibniz thought only those monads that are true minds—divine, angelic, human, or animal—could perceive consciously. Leibniz said monads are "windowless"—that is, their states are generated from within the monad itself rather than being caused from without. Leibniz's work in mathematics predicted the development of symbolic logic i.e., the use of mathematical symbols and operations to solve the problems in logic.

After rationalism it was Empiricism, which was given much importance. Empiricism emphasizes the significance of experience and sense perception and considers them as the source and basis of knowledge. The great empiricists were John Locke of England, George Berkeley of Ireland and David Hume of Scotland.

Locke in his "An Essay Concerning Human Understanding" (1690), attempted to determine the origin, extent, and certainty of human knowledge. He argued that there are no innate ideas—that is, ideas people are born with. He believed that when a person is born, the mind is *tabula rasa* i.e., like a blank paper. Hence, experience is the source of all ideas and all knowledge.

Berkeley dealt with the question that "If whatever a human being knows is only an idea, how can one be sure that there is anything in the world corresponding to that idea?" His answer was "to be is to be perceived." Berkeley thought that no object exists unless it is perceived by some mind. He could see no independent existence to material objects, as they are ideas in the mind.

Hume further extended the ideas of Locke and Berkeley to a consistent skepticism. Hume thought that everything in the mind consists of impressions and ideas and the ideas come from impressions. Ideas can be traced to and tested by previous impressions. He disbelieved philosophical speculation. He held that all knowledge is the result of experience and all experiences existed only in the mind as individual units of experience. The personal experiences are nothing more than the contents of his or her own consciousness, or mind. In his view the lively and forceful units of experience as perceptions and less lively and forceful units as beliefs or thoughts. Words and ideas were meaningful only in relation to these units of experience. Every unit of experience was separate and distinct, but usually we experience them as being connected.

The towering personality in modern philosophy was Immanuel Kant. In the late 1700's he became the base for almost all later developments in philosophy. His philosophy is critical or transcendental philosophy. In fact, Kant was inspired by the skeptical philosophy of Hume. In his 'Critique of Pure Reason' (1781), he aimed to present a critical explanation of the power and limit of human reason, and to resolve what is knowable and what is unknowable. He concluded that reason could offer an understanding only of things as they come into view to us, by no means of things as they are in themselves.

Kant thought that the mind plays and a dynamic role in knowing and it is not mere recorder of facts offered by senses. The mind performs this through the basic categories of understanding, and these categories are independent of experience. In the absence of these categories or forms of understanding experience doesn't make any sense. Knowledge is possible only through these categories and this knowledge is limited only to things that can be experienced. Andrew Bowie says, 'For Kant it is clear that we can only know the world as it *appears* to us via the constitutive categories of subjectivity, which synthesize sense data. The world as an object of truth is located in the structure of the consciousness we have of it. This means that we cannot know how the world is 'in itself'. Knowledge's warrantability, the mechanical necessity of the law of causality, for instance, is dependent upon the subject, not upon the empirical data given to the subject or upon the inherent relatedness of one part of nature to another'[4]

Kant's philosophy motivated numerous philosophical systems. German thinkers like G.H.F.Hegel and Karl Marx drew inspiration ether directly or indirectly from Kant. Hegel's theory of historical change, which is known, as dialectic in which the conflict of irreconcilable opposites results in the creation of a new unity and then its opposite. Marx transformed Hegel's theory into dialectical materialism. In the view of Marx, only material things are real and all the ideas are built on an economic base. He thought that the dialect of conflict between capitalists and industrial workers would lead to the establishment of socialism, a political system.

Friedrich Nietzsche, another German philosopher proclaimed in his 'Thus Spake Zarathustra" (1883-1885) that "God is dead." He intended that the idea of God had lost its power to induce and regulate large masses of people. He held that people would have to look to some other idea to direct their lives. Nietzsche forecast the evolution of the superman and thought that the superman would be beyond the weakness of human beings and beyond the merely human appeals to morality. According to him such appeals are the appeals of the weak. Nietzsche's ideal person is the *overman* or superman. The super man is a passionate personality who learns to control passions and use them in an imaginative or creative manner.

The thought of the two British philosophers Jeremy Bentham and John Stuart Mills was an integral part of modern philosophy. The philosophy of these two is popularly known as utilitarianism. According to utilitarianism, the utmost happiness to the great number of people is the test of right or wrong. They proposed that all existing social institutions, especially law and government, must be transformed to satisfy the test of the greatest happiness.

From 1900 to the end of World War II there were a few more philosophical movements which were considered essential parts of modern thought, they are; existentialism, phenomenology, pragmatism and logical positivism. In fact, Existentialism developed out of the works of Soren Kierkegaard, a Danish philosopher Nietzsche. The other major thinkers in the existential movement include the French writers Albert Camus,

Jean-Paul Sartre, and Gabriel Marcel; the German philosophers Karl Jaspers and Martin Heidegger.

As a movement, existentialism rebelled against European philosophy of the times, which reached its zenith in the philosophical systems of Kant and Hegel. They rejected the domination of science over philosophy. In the view of existentialists the objectivity, certainty and universality are unfeasible or unattainable goals. They understood life as being a succession of choices that must be made with no method of knowing decisively what the correct choices are. Hence, the individual must decide to himself, which standards are to be accepted, and which is to be rejected. The human choice is subjective. There are no external standards, laws, ethics or traditions. As the individual makes his own choice, he is free. Since he chose freely, he is solely responsible for his choices or decisions and he is "condemned to be free". For an existentialist, responsibility is the negative side of freedom.

Edmund Husserl, another German philosopher developed phenomenology. He wanted to understand how consciousness works in order to better the understanding of human experience. The power of the mind to be aware of acts, sensations, and emotions is referred by consciousness. According to Husserl, our knowledge of reality got its source in the consciousness. In view of the phenomenologists, experience has two parts; the first part consists of objects of consciousness (the things which we are conscious of). The second is of experience of acts of consciousness like perceiving, believing, thinking, and desiring. They maintain that all acts of consciousness are related to objects of consciousness. Hence, it must be considered a phenomenon. This relationship is known as intentionality.

Husserl strongly believed that the task of phenomenology i.e., philosophy is to describe a phenomenon-the objects and this task must be independent of scientific assumptions. Husserl firmly believed this method would provide philosophical knowledge of reality. Later, William James and John Dewey of America developed Pragmatism. In their view knowledge is subordinate to practice and their relation to practice determines the meaning and the truth of ideas.

Philosophers believe that Descartes was the originator of philosophical modernity. But Francis Bacon, Thomas Hobbes and Machiavelli also contributed to the formation of modernity as a philosophical category. For example Hobbes discussed the nature of knowledge and modern methodology, Bacon considered science and other forms of knowledge as forms of power, Hobbes talked about the political individualism, newly emerging state and science of human nature, Machiavelli on the other side probed the nature of modern power politics.

In fact, it is Bacon's notion of power that marks a significant point of departure from the ancients; for the ancients the knowledge of nature consisted of passive understanding of a world, which cannot be changed. Following the footprints of Machiavelli Hobbes developed a concept of human nature. Simultaneously, modern political individualism, and modern liberal political theory emerged with Hobbes. According to Hobbes, People are selfish. People are often moved or motivated by their desire for power and by fear of others. Hence, he thought there was a great need of a some sovereign power to rule them. His idea that the human beings are complex physical systems had a deep impact on the social sciences. He was also the first to address the question of "social order".

In addition to the above mentioned historical development of modernist thought, one should remember that the European Enlightenment of the eighteenth century symbolizes a high point is Western history. As we have seen already, the roots of the Enlightenment go much back to the Western history and it continued long after that; the fact is that it formed itself as a project in the eighteenth century. The Enlightenment set to its self a goal of eradicating ignorance, because it believed ignorance is the source of all misery. Elimination of ignorance and establishing scientific knowledge was the ultimate aim of the Enlightenment. The thinkers of the Enlightenment firmly believed that scientific knowledge could lead society and people to endless progress; hence they almost deified science and reason.

They depended heavily on scientific method, emphasized on experimentation and meticulous observation. They even assumed that the scientific method could be applied to the study of human nature as well. They surveyed issues in education, law, philosophy, and politics and criticized sharply tyranny, social injustice, superstition, and ignorance. Many of their ideas contributed directly to the eruption of the American and French revolutions in the late eighteenth century. Galileo and Isaac Newton influenced the thinkers of Enlightenment to the core. They had considered that mathematics was the model that all other sciences should follow because they felt that mathematics yielded absolutely certain conclusions. This yielding is because mathematical process started with simple axioms i.e., the self-evident truths and moved from self-evident step to another. With the help of this method scholars discovered laws of nature that otherwise would have remained mysterious.

The philosophers of the Enlightenment assumed that each person has a rational will and it makes possible to carry out plans. They thought people do not always plan ahead but often act on impulse, and it is an inadequate education. All people are born with capacity to reason. In the view of Locke reason is the candle of the God set by the God himself in the human mind and it is the ultimate judge of every thing.

However, the writings of Marx, Darwin and Freud had influenced the modernist writings tremendously. Hence, it demands an examination of these authors in any discussion on Modernism or modernist writing. Marx in his Eleventh theses on Feuerbach declared 'The Philosophers have only interpreted the world in various ways : the point, however, is to change it'. This declaration of Marx was considered a battle cry for the later part of the nineteenth century. This slogan reflected the spirit of modernism and its untiring thrust for change.

There is a strong bond between modernism and Marxism. Marshal Berman made an excellent attempt to establish the relation between the two in his monumental work "All That is Solid Melts into Air : The Experience of Modernity" He says, 'In the first part of the *Manifeso,* Marx lays out the polarities that will shape and animate the culture of Modernism in the century to come : the theme of the insatiable desires and drives, permanent revolution, infinite development, perpetual creation and renewal in every sphere of life; its radical anti-thesis, the theme of nihilism, insatiable destruction, the shattering and swallowing up of life, the heart of darkness, the horror." In the later pages of his book Berman states "Marxism, modernism, and bourgeois in a strange dialectical dance...".[5]

After Marx a number of Marxists exerted tremendous influence in conceptualizing the modernism. Thinkers from George Lukacs to Frederic Jameson saw modernism as an alienation from capitalism. It has even been seen as culture of crisis. Marx himself placed this crisis at the center of capitalist development. In the Marxian perspective much of the modernist writing emerged out of a European loss of communal identity and alienating capitalism and regular industrial development.

Peter Childs brilliantly explains the view of the Marxist critic Frederic Jameson, on modernity. He says, 'According to Frederic Jameson, Modernism is the middle part in the triad of cultural periods that begins with realism and ends with postmodernism and parallels social and economic upheavals precipitated by technological innovations, such as the shift from steam to electric motors to electronic machines, and the development of a mass commodity of culture'.[6]

In fact, the "Communist Manifesto" may be seen as one of the early texts that demarcated the modernity from tradition. The radical break from tradition, shown by Marxism has an extensive impact the modernist writers. They began to represent the life of alienated urban living in their works. As we have seen, for Marx, modernity is an invariable urge for regeneration caused by the dynamics and crises of capitalism. Marx saw capitalism as a dynamic movement of creation, destruction, innovation and constant change. In this regard, it has a close resemblance with Modernism. In fact, the very terminology Marx uses is that of modernism. Though there are certain critical attitudes towards modernism among a few Marxist theorists like George Lukacs, most of them are in favour of modernist literature.

Frederic Jameson's monumental work "The Political Unconscious" is a milestone in the Marxist writings on modernism. According to Jameson, the modernist writers were dealing with history and making efforts to transcend it. Their criticism of the old world and expression of the possibilities of new world itself is an indication to the fact that they are trying to change the world. If we read the statement of Jameson between the lines, it amounts to saying that the modern writers not only interpreted the world, they tried their best to change it also as desired by Marx.

Besides Marxist critique of capitalism, the influence of Darwin's evolutionary theory can also be seen in the modernist writings. Darwin's propositions brought forth the fact that natural selection was at the source of human development and human beings were closer to animals than to God. Darwin even proposed that human beings are in evolving state and not static. Within a short span of time Darwin's theories began to construct a narrative of human history that was very different from the existing one. The new one did not believe that there was a single progression to humanity and that it was aiming to reach a final judgment day. It found a cyclical movement in nature.

Darwin laid the foundation of modern evolutionary theory with his concept of the development of all forms of life through the slow-working process of natural selection. By discarding the spiritual belief reproduction and the survival of the fittest were recognized as the forces behind all endeavors of human beings.

Darwin's theory has been a major influence on the life and earth sciences and on modern thought in general. In fact, all most all the disciplines ranging from botany to zoology had under gone a sea change. Darwin's theories made an assault on traditional thinking relating to God, the universe and the place of man in the world. Simultaneously, Darwin's ideas took a sociological turn and social Darwinism evolved.

Social Darwinism, in sociology was formulated in the late nineteenth century. It believed or proposed that the development of societies and individuals follow the pattern described by Darwin in his theory of evolution by natural selection. Some as the philosophical foundation for imperialism, racism, and rampant capitalism employed the assumption. The view of Peter Childs is significant here. He says, 'Social Darwinism argued that human societies can improve and evolve in the same way that species do, but societies too therefore have their origins and their antecedents. Just as apes are considered to be related but under-evolved humans, so then in the 1890s are non-European societies perceived as related but underdeveloped or degenerate civilizations. Many of these theories, such as those of the Scottish anatomist Robert Knox (1791-1862) and the French orientalist Comte de Gobineau (1816-1883), have been grouped together with social Darwinism as kinds of scientific racism'.[7]

The conscious feeling of supremacy among European civilization simultaneously led them to be fascinated by the notions like 'evolution', 'progress', and 'reform', For them evolution was meant to turn the 'primitive' into 'civilized',. All other non-European civilizations were seen as uncivilized, hence they must be transformed. In the quest for the Europeanisation of non-European world modernist literature served as a vehicle. The moral justification for colonialism in way was provided by the modernist literature. However, it was Darwinism that shattered the faith of the people in some Divine power.

The crisis of belief may be the starting point of modernism. This crisis was wide spread in the entire Western culture of the twentieth century. Loss of faith, 'degeneration of values' shattering of cultural symbols and other ethical norms, codes may be the pointers of this crisis. New technology, epistemological dilemma and the deeper understanding of the unconscious are the major aspects of the philosophical perspective that Frued embodied.

Freud is one of the major figures who influenced the formation of the modernist culture. Besides Freud we have a few more figures like Carl Jung, Henri Bergson, William James and C.S.Pierce. In fact, it was Darwin who emphasized instincts for survival and reproduction. Freud's ideas can be seen in the same way. Freud too confronted with the philosophical and religious thoughts by proposing that the human beings were rather less in control of their own thoughts and actions. His contention was that the unconscious thoughts and actions had to come up from within the self rather than from god was in radical conflict with the contemporary notions of soul. Ever since Freud came on to the scene, we find the disciplines of philosophy and psychology developing independently. Freud was an influential thinker of his age. Freud's psychoanalysis is a theory of human psyche and a way of interpreting or seeing culture and society. Freud's theory replaced the earlier ideas of man as political, religious and economic being.

In his "The Interpretations of Dreams" Freud offered his observations on psychoanalysis. Freud argued that dreams played a primary role in the 'psychic economy'. The psychic energy—which Freud called libido was identified with the sexual drive. It was a fluid and flexible force and capable of extreme and distressing power. The libido can find any kind of outlet to discharge and ensure pleasure and avoid pain. According to Freud, a wish can be satisfied by an imaginary wish fulfillment. Freud stated that all dreams are marked with visible anxiety, are the fulfillment of such wishes. Freud's greatest contribution is that of explaining the unconscious and to hypothesize that it obeys the principle of psychic determinism. In his view human thoughts, feelings, and impulses are not chaotic, they are related in a system of causally related phenomena. Behind this phenomenon there is some reason or meaning. Freud proposed that unconscious processes could be examined and understood basing on this phenomenon. The experiences, which are inaccessible to consciousness, can be brought into the consciousness by the process of recollection. Freud called these as the preconscious. Still deeper feelings or thoughts cannot be remembered because they are aggressively repressed in the unconscious. The logic that is applicable to conscious experiences cannot be applicable to unconscious the. The ideas, images, thoughts of the unconscious can be condensed to abstract forms and concepts. Often the connection between the original experience and the unconscious symbolic representation can appear obscure.

Another important figure in the modernist writing is the French philosopher Henri Bergson, who proposed a theory of evolution. His theory was founded on the spiritual dimension of human life. It had an extensive influence in a variety of disciplines. The influence of Bergson's writings on artists, and writers of the twentieth century is vast. Bergson's book "Time and Free Will", stimulated great interest among philosophers and fiction writers. This work brings forth his theories on the freedom of the mind. Another one of Bergson titled "Matter and Memory", highlights the selectivity of the human brain. However it is "Laughter", an essay on the mechanistic foundation of comedy. Which is his most quoted work. According to Peter Childs, 'Bergson believed that reality was characterized by the different experience of time in the mind from the linear, regular beats clock time which measures all experience by the same gradations'.[8]

Bergson held that time is the great reality. His concept of time is totally different from that of the commonsensical understanding of time. In his view time does not exist in the ordinary sense of yesterday, today, and tomorrow. He believed in a concept of time, which he identified as duration. Duration was not a mere succession of instants. It was a regular flow from the past into the future. According to Bergson creative evolution is possible because reality is a past. It is continuously becoming new, and constantly emerging into the future. Intuition was the most dependable guide on the way to understanding. Unlike the intellect, it did not misrepresent things in the process of analyzing them.

Nietzsche exerted tremendous influence on the art and literature of the twentieth century. He had profoundly influenced many writers, philosophers, and psychologists of the early twentieth. Nietzsche got great admiration for Greek culture. One of Nietzsche's important works "The Birth of Tragedy" presents a radical theory regarding the nature of Greek tragedy and culture. He said they could best be understood as the results of a conflict between two basic human tendencies : The Apollonian and Dionysian. The Apollonian tendency was a desire for clarity and order, represented by the Greek sun god, Apollo. The Dionysian tendency, which was a wild and irrational drive toward disorder, represented Dionysus, the god of wine. The Dionysian and Apollonian were the two categories of experience : The first one was of aesthetic pleasure and the second was of rational discourse.

Nietzsche in his "The Birth of Tragedy" explained that the order of the day was dominated by the rational Apollonian way of thinking or mentality and the aesthetic Dionysian sprit was suppressed. According to him, the modern man had lost contact with tragic myth, with sensuality and intuition. Nietzsche's declaration 'God is dead' in his "Thus Spake Zarathustra" created a furore among the creative writers. He supposed that religion had lost its sense and power over people. It was thought that religion could no more serve as the foundation for moral values. He held that it was time to critically examine their established values and their origins. Nietzsche himself tried to revalue the existing values of the times.

Nietzsche believed that all human behavior is motivated by the will to power. The will to power in not just power over others, rather it is on oneself. In creativity, the power over oneself is essential for creativity. Such a kind of power, he believed will be there with 'overman'. Though there was no 'overman', Nietzsche thought some individuals like Socrates, Jesus Christ, Leonardo da Vinci, Michelangelo, Shakespeare, Goethe, Julius Caesar, and Napoleon would serve as models. Though Nietzsche's concept of 'overman' had been misinterpreted and used by totalitarian philosophers, he wielded much power on modern German and French literatures. The great modern philosophers like Karl Jaspers and Martin Heidegger and the French writers Albert Camus and Jean-Paul Sartre were influenced by Nietzsche's announcement : "God is dead".

There has been a tremendous influence of science on modernism. The influence of natural science is very clear on literature produced in the nineteenth century. The towering personality in the naturalist writing is Emili Zola. Simultaneously literature had attempted to achieve the status of science. The thinkers and the artists of Renaissance thought strongly believed that science should come out of its contemplative role and concentrate on the conquest of nature.

Humanism is another characteristic of modernism. It has been very flexibly applied to various fields and methods, which emphasize the key place of the human dominion. Humanism was also seen as a method applicable to nonhumanistic issues. The general spirit of humanism was based on the scientific spirit. Terms that are related to humanism are frequently applied to modern treatises and methods, which are based on the centrality of human experience. In modernity, the word humanism in anthropocentric. In fact, humanism was responsible for the rise of social sciences in the modernity. Humanism provided the medium for the rise of modern philosophy. A number of disciplines like philosophy and art were nourished by humanism. Humanism showed great concern for change.

The culture, specifically the pre-modern European culture was inseparable from religious institutions. Since eighteenth century, the influence of theology on social life was replaced by history, economics, sociology and natural science. Instead of churches and religious monuments dominating the life of the people, museums, libraries and other public places began to influence. To be brief, the culture of modernity was the culture of secularism. Secular values directed the social life. The world has been disenchanted and exhausted of supernatural meanings. This does not mean that religion and supernatural beliefs disappeared from the modernist scene altogether. There was only the relative disappearance of these two.

Many an intellectual saw religion as a relic of the past and it was an obstruction to progress and knowledge. Some saw the end of religion as the end of morality and tradition. Some even feared that the loss of religion results in remorselessness in the world. However, the modernist thought replaced religion with secularism. In this context the opinion of T.C.W.Blanning is worth quoting, 'Most of them (the intellectuals) thought that there could a secular substitute for religion, as an alternative source of comfort and order, another way of understanding and mastering human existence'.[9]

History and myth were also integral parts of modernist writing. The modern writers are concerned with history in two senses. They were concerned with what was happening in the world and with the nature of understanding. Their understanding of history includes the mythopoeic one. For the modernists, myth, besides being an affirmation value was also a motivating force. They even saw myth as transhistorical or to borrow from Nietzsche "Trans-historical"[10]. The works of the great modernist writers like James Joyce, W.B.Yeats, Thomas Mann, and

T.S.Eliot are good examples. Michel Bell says, 'And it was with in this sense of the greater, transindividual "mind of Europe" that he (Eliot) was able to project his truly mythopoeic imagination....Its essentially mythopoeic status is reflected in the fact that his evidence for dissociation was not an historical argument so much a close reading of language understood as itself the embodiment of a quality of life. But, that leads to another major theme for the modernist generation'.[11]

Various literary and art movements were also served as vehicles of modernist project. Modernist ideals were consciously or unconsciously reflected in the writings and artifacts of the movements like Aestheticism, Dadaism, Surrealism, Cubism, Expressionism, Futurism, Impressionism, and Symbolism.

The following are the major pointers to Modernism

1. Everything in the universe that is worth knowing can be unified into as set of beliefs. All human beings can rationally agree to and rationally think on the basis of a universally applicable or valid set of methodological assumptions. This can be classified as the epistemological unity of humankind, which was claimed by the Enlightenment.

2. Universal rational moral principles are binding on all rational beings everywhere and offer guides and values or standards for conduct and judgment. This is the claim relating to the moral unity of mankind.

3. Any beliefs, values, claims, factors or issues that contradict, hamper or impede these two goals above are an obstacle to human progress and happiness.

4. In a society, which is based on science and universal values, the humans will have be free and have rational values.

5. The truth can only make us free. The more people know about themselves and their world the better their life will be, because ignorance is the root of grief and immorality.

6. Since 'knowledge is power', as Bacon would put it, the thinkers of the Enlightenment concentrated their efforts on the advancement of knowledge.

7. The Enlightenment very strongly proclaimed to go beyond illusions and mystery.
8. A new stress is on impressionism and subjectivity, that is, on how we see rather than what we see.
9. A movement away from the obvious objectivity endowed with the features like omniscient external narration, unchanging narrative points of view and straightforward moral positions.
10. A blurring of the differences or distinctions between genres. For example in this state novels become more lyrical and poetic and poems are like documentary or prose-like.
11. A new linkage for fragmented forms, discontinuous narrative, and hazardous collages of incongruent materials.
12. "A Tendency towards 'reflexivity', so that poems, plays and novels raise issues concerning their own nature, status and role"[12]
13. It is a commitment to finding new forms to explore how we see rather than what we see.
14. It is a new faith in quasi-scientific modes of conceptualization and organization.
15. It is a clear demarcation between popular and elite forms of culture.

Literature

History provides many contexts for the emergence of Modernism as a literary counterpart to the social and economic upheavals at the turn of the twentieth century. The roots of Modernism are European rather than British, and indeed the determination to take European culture as a model was one of the hallmarks of the Modernist movement. The term "Modernist" was not generally used by the exponents of the movement themselves, who rather referred to their works and aesthetic theories as "modern". Modernism as a movement can be recognized not only in literature but also in painting, music, sculpture, and architecture, as well as in the sciences and in theology, aesthetics, and anthropology.

Historical and material determinism, psychoanalytic theories which reveal the self as a pawn in a process dominated by an inaccessible unconscious play of forces, and a conception of evolution and heredity which situates humanity as no more than the latest product of natural selection—these theories conspired to threaten humanist self-confidence and to provoke a feeling of ideological uncertainty. In so far as the Arts were concerned, such insecurity proved immensely productive. It engendered an aesthetic of experimentation, ambiguity, and nihilism. Modernism was built on a sense of lost community and civilization. It embodied a series of contradictions and paradoxes. Since it had no stable centre it could embrace a multiplicity of features of the modern sensibility, which might have appeared, in a logical sense, mutually exclusive.

The loss of a sense of tradition, for example, was a theme common to Modernist writers, but it was lamented by some in an extreme form of reactionary conservatism, and celebrated by others as a means of liberation from the stranglehold of past practices. Revolution and conservatism coexisted, not necessarily peaceably, under the Modernist umbrella. The increasing dominance of technology was another prevalent Modernist preoccupation, but some condemned it as vehemently as others, who saw it as the flagship of 20th-century progress embraced it.

Not surprisingly, the diversity of Modernist theory is matched by the variety of Modernist practice. Poets like T. S. Eliot in his *Waste Land* (1922), and Ezra Pound in his *Cantos* (1917-1970) express the concerns of Modernism in a form which itself breaks radically with previous poetic tradition. Similarly, Virginia Woolf's *Mrs. Dalloway* (1925) and James Joyce's *Ulysses* (1922) explore the disintegration and fragmentation of conscious control in their protagonists, adopting a style which itself mirrors the fragmentation, disconnectedness of experience and the triumph of the random and contingent over the structured and unified. In works such as these it is impossible to separate form from content in any meaningful way. The dissolution of meaning, the incoherence of character, the lack of recognizable "plot" are features which not only transmit but actually constitute the "theme" of the art-work. Modernist novelists as well as poets viewed the work of art more as an aesthetic object than as a representation of reality. Their legacy survives in both contemporary theory and practice.

Modernist writing, particularly, the novel was seen as a reaction to the hegemony of realist fiction. Realism has been an issue in philosophy and in aesthetic representations since Aristotle, but in the discussions of the novel it is commonly used to denote a style of fiction, which came to prominence in the eighteenth century and stylistically shared much with historical, journalistic or biographical writing. Specifically in art and literature, Realism is an attempt to describe human behaviour and surroundings or to represent figures and objects exactly as they act or appear in life. Attempts at realism have been made periodically throughout history in all the arts; the term is, however, generally restricted to a movement that began in the mid-19th century, in reaction to the highly subjective approach of Romanticism.

The difference between realism and naturalism is hard to define. But, the two terms are often used interchangeably. The distinction lies in the fact that realism is concerned directly with what is absorbed by the senses; naturalism, a term properly applied to literature, attempts to apply scientific theories to art. The term Realism is used to describe the works of Balzac, Charles Dickens, Elizabeth Gaskell and George Eliot. The novels of these writers or the Realist writers deal with representative characters immersed in contemporary social problems.

The transition from realism to a Modernist style in fiction was accomplished not by one author, or even by one country, but by a range of writers and countries. According to Bradbury, "The French fathed the Modern Movement, which slowly moved beyond the Channel and then across the Irish Sea until the Americans finally took it over, bringing to it their own demonic energy, extremism and taste for the colossal'.[13]

The major authors of the movement are Flaubert, Baudelaire, Henry James, Mallarme, Yeats, Gide, Proust, Vallery, T.S.Eliot, Pound, Lawrence, Joyce, Woolf, Edith Sitwell, Marianne Moore, Hemingway, Cummings, Faulkner, Malraux and Graves.

According to Bradbury, the distinctive features of modernist writing are 'non-events'. The best example for this type of writing is 'Waiting for Godot', of Samuel Beckett. The events in this work never take place. K's trial in the novel "The Trial" by Kafka does not happen. The absences of the events reflect a contemporary sense of irony. In a way it is rooted in the modernist idea of time.

With the advent of Bergson there is a great shift in the concept of time and the shift has its influence on the modern fiction. According to Michael Hollington, 'We do not have to prove that Mann read him or Proust admitted him to detect his importance for their art. He exposed fallacies in our way of thinking of time as if it could be apprehended 'spatially' : events, he said, were imaginary spatial points in the uninterruptible, indistinguishable flow of time. In that scene I instanced in

The *Cherry Orchard*, Varya remarks that the thermometer is broken; it is the precursor of many other moments – the thermometers in *The Magic Mountain*, the compass like McCaslin lays aside in *The Bear*, the tilted clock on the mantelpiece in *The Great Gatsby* – where conventional instruments of measurement become useless, and the implication is essentially in accord with Bergson'.[14]

Stephen Spender in "The Struggle of the Modern" (1953) made two observations which, taken together, emphasize and clarify the point. First, 'Modern art is that in which the artist reflects awareness of an unprecedented modern situation in form and idiom', and second that 'the principle of reality in our time is peculiarly difficult to grasp, and the "realism" is not an adequate approach to it.' The same point emerges in Eric Auerbach's wide-ranging study of the representation of reality in western literature, "Mimesis" (1946). Auerbach considers a great variety of methods from Homer onwards, and his last chapter, entitled "The Brown Stocking",focuses on Mrs Ramsay in Virginia Woolf's "To the Lighthouse". Of this kind of novel, he notes that the author 'submits, much more than was done in earlier realistic works, to the random contingency of real phenomena.

It was not always easy to express this complexity in fiction, unless the writer goes beyond tradition. That is why the modernist writers felt that the traditional realistic methods were not sufficient to express the new experience. Because of the formalistic limitations of the traditional realistic writing, the modernist writers had to experiment with numerous styles. This was an attempt to go beyond simplistic accounts of experience. Instead of depending on simple narrative style, the modernists invented new methods of organisation in their writing. In place of simple narrative they used juxtaposition, irony instead of narrative unity.

Joseph Frank's important article 'Spatial Form in Modern Literature' in 1945 discussed the decline of chronological narrative structures in modern literature, and its replacement by what he called 'spatial form', the presentation of the unity of a work in the entire pattern of internal references', or 'the principle of reflexive reference'. This method, Frank found common to *The Waste Land, The Cantos, and Ulysses*

The influence of Nietzsche on modern literature is conspicuous. In his view, beneath the surface of the modern life, dominated by knowledge and science, there are vital energies, which were wild, primitive and merciless. Nietzsche believed that these abnormal forces at one time or the other would provoke man to rise to abnormal proportions and conquer the civilization. The primitive force will come out and will appear as a new barbarism.

One of the major writers that was influenced by Nietzschean tradition is Joseph Conrad. From about 1897 onward that tradition provided the foundation on which all his major work is built ; perhaps the most distinctive treatment of what has generally become a major theme in modern literature.

Taking into account the diversity of changes wrought upon literature by modernists, Peter Childs in his book "Modernism"[15] divided the key areas and aspects of many stylistic and thematic shifts into four sections and considers twelve authors (most of them British and American). These twelve authors (Charlotte Mew, Katherine Mansfield, D.H. Lawrence, Joseph Conrad, Henry James, Ford Madox Ford, Virginia Woolf, Rebecca West, T.S.Eliot, E.M. Forster, W.B. Yeats, James Joyce, represent modernists' central preoccupation with questions of form on the one hand, their concern with issues of subjectivity in relation to gender, history, language and perceptions of reality on the other.The themes Childs pointed out are:

1· The Struggle of Becoming; Freedom and Gender.

2· Epistemology and Narration.

3· Identity and War.

4· Symbolism and Language.

However, modernism is not simply confined to British and Àmerican literatures. In fact, much of the great modernist literature came from French, Russian, and German languages.

The difference between realism and modernism is of the style and underlying ideology. Preoccupation with style was one of the symptoms of modernist writings. Realism is committed to view man as an essentially social and political being, formed by his society and striving to attain understanding of its contradictions in order to act on it. Hence, the texts written in this tradition portray the lives of the individuals firmly rooted in specified and identifiable space and time. Realism in this way aims at a faithful reflection of reality. Modernist writing, on the other hand, was based on a view that man is by nature alone, anti-social, a social and unable to enter into relationships with the other human beings. The modern fiction portrays individuals 'thrown into the world'. They concentrate on the abstract potentialities of the individual's life. Hence, the modern fiction is intensely subjective and conveys subjective experience.

The best example for modernist writing is Kafka's fiction. George Lukacs and others thought Kafka's work is a prototype of modernist writing. It presents the man terrified in the presence of utterly strange, absurd and hostile reality. Kafka used a wealth of naturalistic details to convey a fragmented world and personal horror or 'angst'. Kafka's texts are studied in ways, which undermine conventional habits of reading and modes of communication. He frequently pits gestures against dialogue so as to undermine the intention of the words spoken.

Franz Kafka explored the paradoxes of modern life. For Kafka the modern life was balanced on razor-edge between a moral imperative and an irrepressible spiritual urge to transcend the world. Kafka once declared "in the struggle between yourself and the world you must take the side of the world".[16] Kafka's stories like "Metamorphosis" and "The Hunger Artist" reveal the two facets of human life, which are of equal importance. Just as the slow deaths of Gregor Samsa and of the hunger-artist symbolize the human urge to transcend life in the one case, the 'increasing vivacity' and the 'young body' of Gregor's sister and, the panther which replace the hunger-artist in the cage symbolize the unrestrained commitment to the vitality, the energy and the sheer animal aspects of life in the other. No hint is given as to which of the two constitutes the more positive commitment. Instead, there is offered a parable about the dual nature of existence; and one's sense of paradox rather than one's moral sense is appealed to.

Modern Painting

The term modernism is used in art, generally used to describe an international trend, which developed in the last years of the 19th century and went on to affect much of the twentieth century art. In painting also modernists wanted to disassociate themselves from the conventions of realism. In fact, they rejected realism. Modernists assert that the painting is an artifice and a constitution. They place great emphasis on the devices and techniques employed to a produce a particular work, and on the roie played by form-rather than content. Almost all modernist artists confronted a basic phenomenon : The radical transformation of western experience brought about by industrialization, and the devastating effects of First World War. In the early decades of twentieth century economic, political and technological changes threatened to deprive the individual of nay autonomy. Artists responded to this threat in innumerable ways.

The fundamental questioning, rejection, and revision of artistic principles that began in the late nineteenth century were to have a profound effect on the formation of modern art in the twentieth. This aesthetic revolution resulted in a profusion of styles and movements. Many of the movements were short-lived and most of them expressed an underlying restlessness in the search for new directions and novel principles. The modern art or painting is characterized by many movements and styles. They include Fauvism, Expressionism, Cubism, Futurism, Constructivism, Dada, and Surrealism.

Fauvism

Fauvism was a relatively short-lived movement in French painting (from about 1898 to about 1908) that revolutionized the concept of colour in modern art. The Fauves rejected the Impressionist palette of soft, shimmering tones in favour of the violent.At the turn of the century, artists in both France and Germany became interested in the art of non-Western societies. Fauves redetection of tradition shocked many people. Hence, they were nicknamed 'fauves' (wild beasts). Their leader was Henri Matisse. Other Fauves were André Derain, Georges Braque, and Maurice de Vlaminck.

Futurism

Futurism was an early twentieth century movement in art that pointedly rejected all traditions and attempted instead to glorify contemporary life, mainly by emphasizing its two dominant themes, the machine and motion. The principles of Futurism were laid down by the Italian poet Filippo Tommaso Marinetti and published by him in a manifesto in 1909. The following year the Italian artists Giacomo Balla, Umberto Boccioni, Carlo Carrà, Luigi Russolo, and Gino Severini were leading members of the movement.

Constructivism

Constructivism was a Russian art movement of the early twentieth century that had an important influence on later schools of art. The Russian sculptor and painter Vladimir Tatlin founded constructivism. Its name is derived from the "construction" of abstract sculptures from miscellaneous industrial materials, such as metal, wire, and pieces of plastic. Tatlin's relief constructions of 1913 to 1917 were the first works of the movement. By 1920 he had been joined by the artists Aleksandr Rodchenko, El Lissitzky, Naum Gabo, and Antoine Pevsner, among others.

Expressionism

Expressionism was a movement or tendency that strove to express subjective feelings and emotions rather than to depict reality or nature objectively. The movement developed during the late 19th and early 20th centuries. This movement is a reaction against the academic standards that had prevailed in Europe since the Renaissance, particularly in French and German art academies.

The Expressionist artist tries to present an emotional experience in its most compelling form. The artist is not concerned with reality as it appears but with its inner nature and with the emotions aroused by the subject. To achieve these ends, the subject is frequently caricatured, exaggerated, distorted, or otherwise altered in order to stress the emotional experience in its most intense and concentrated form. In the view of Grouchy, 'The Expressionist is always the artist who is completely engaged, both with his work, and with his own time. He never practices art for art's sake. Rather he reacts with intense love or hate or anger to his environment and to other human beings in it. His art is thus always self-revelatory and autobiographical'.[17]

The work of Expressionist artists was more concerned with recording subjective feelings and responses, via distortions of line and colour, than with the faithful representation of external reality. Members of the group included Ernst Ludwig Kirchner, Karl Schmidt-Rottluff, Erich Heckel, and Emil Nolde. Portraying the sufferings of humanity, they worked in a style somewhat resembling Fauvism, but with the added ingredient of angst (anxiety). The early, emotionally charged work of the Norwegian painter Edvard Munch was well known in Germany.

Somewhat later, in 1911, Franz Marc and the Russian-born Wassily Kandinsky led the other phase of German Expressionism.

Cubism

Cubism was also a movement in twentieth century art, especially in painting. It was primarily concerned with the depiction of subject-matter by breaking its form down into basic geometric shapes; by overlapping or interlocking these shapes, Cubist painters also attempted to depict objects from many angles not simultaneously visible in reality but arranged so as to form a unified composition. Cubism had profound and far-reaching effects on the development of art in the twentieth century. Indeed, it stands as the precursor to abstract and non-objective art. It was a revolt both against the sentimentality and realism of traditional painting of the late nineteenth and early twentieth centuries.

Pablo Picasso and Georges Braque developed Cubism in Paris between 1907 and 1914. Cubism, which became the most influential of all twentieth century art styles, emphasizes the flatness of the picture plane, or surface, and rejects traditional perspective. Another artist who accelerated the cubist movement was Paul Cezanne. Cezanne said that : everything in nature takes its form from the sphere, the cone, and the cylinder. According to Peter Childs, 'Cubist paintings were nearly all still lifes even though the Cubists rarely used nature, perfecting to paint humans or constructed objects. Previous to Cubism, virtually all paintings had obeyed the principle of 'one point perspective' seeing and painting an object from one position....the founding Cubists, Pablo Picasso and Georges Barque took this another step further by trying to depict the three dimensionality of the object in two dimensions of the canvass'.[18]

Dadaism

Dada as an artistic and literary movement reflects a widespread nihilistic protest against all aspects of Western culture, especially against militarism during and after World War I. The term dada, the French word for hobbyhorse, is said to have been selected at random from a dictionary by the Romanian-born poet, essayist, and editor Tristan Tzara. Tzara, the German writer Hugo Ball, the Alsatian-born artist Jean Arp, and other intellectuals living in Zurich, Switzerland started Dada in 1916. Tristan Tzara says, 'I am agaisnt system, the most acceptable system is on principle to have none'.

'Art is going to sleep for a new world to be born, 'ART'-parrot word- replaced by DADA...Art is a PRETENSION warned by the TIMIDITY of the urinary basin, the hysteria born in THE STUDIO'.

'Do not trust Dada. Dada is everything. Dada doubts everything. But the real Dadas are against Dada'.19

In their efforts to express the negation of all current aesthetic and social values, the Dadaists frequently used artistic and literary methods that were deliberately incomprehensible. Their theatrical performances and manifestos were often designed to shock or bewilder, with the aim of startling the public into a reconsideration of accepted aesthetic values. To this end, the Dadaists used novel materials, including discarded objects found in the streets, and new methods, such as allowing chance to determine the elements of their works

To describe their protest activities and the art they created in defiance of established aesthetic criteria. Best known of the Dada artists was the French painter Marcel Duchamp. One expression of his disapproval of "pleasing and attractive art" was a reproduction of Leonardo da Vinci's portrait of the Mona Lisa, to which he added a moustache. Duchamp's iconoclastic nature also found expression in what he called ready-mades—everyday objects that Duchamp presented as works of art. Other Dadaists were Francis Picabia, George Grosz, and Max Ernst.

Surrealism

Dada artists employed accident and chance to create works, and these methods were adopted by their successors, the Surrealists. In 1924 André Breton gave Surrealism its name and manifesto, asserting the superiority of the unconscious and the role of dreams in artistic creation. The most important Surrealists were Ernst, Salvador Dalí and Joan Miró, René Magritte, Jean Arp, and André Masson. There are two types of Surrealist pictures; the first type depicts dream-like images by using conventional techniques. The best example for this is the paintings of Dali. The second experiments with innovative techniques. For example, the paintings of Max Ernst. The irrational and the unconscious play significant role in the surrealist art. The Surrealists rejected reason and conventional ideas of morality. In fact, they rejected the very division of reality and unreality.

Modern Architecture

Architecture is a term with multiple meanings; all of them are associated with buildings. Architecture is the art and technique of designing and building. It is also art or science of designing and constructing buildings with long-lasting materials. Architecture follows certain canons to produce structures that are visually inspiring and aesthetically pleasing. The practioners of this art are called architects. Sometimes the word architecture may mean the buildings themselves. The term has a historical meaning also. For example, when we speak of Greek architecture or Gothic architecture it is indicating a specific kind of architecture practised in a specific period. Architecture also depends on technology and science of materials.

There is a concrete difference between architecture and other art forms. Like other art forms, architecture is not an independent activity. The artists must work with other people in preparing their arts/designs. The artistic contributions of the architects are always dictated by the needs and desires of the clients. Architecture is one of the ancient art forms. It has been there form prehistoric times. The architecture of a period reflects the values and ideals of the people of that period. For instance it is not difficult to imagine the harmony in the life of the ancient Greeks from their architecture, which is balanced and orderly. Likewise it in not impossible to understand the various religious ideals and intentions from the architecture of the periods, whcih is conspicuous of religious connotations.

The modern architecture began in eighteenth century. In fact, the 1800s had been considered the greatest productive and creative period in the annals of architecture. New building methods and materials were used in those years. Various styles that were quite unknown in the earlier centuries were introduced in those years. These styles had international consequences. Simultaneously the modern architecture began to reach a kind of climax with skyscrapers.

The skyscrapers were the most important symbols of the modern architecture. The unimaginable changes in architecture since the eighteenth and nineteenth centuries were the results of a number of theories and works by individuals and groups. Most of the masterpieces of modern architecture were designed or inspired by three architects. They are Walter Gropius and Ludwig Mies Van der Rohe (Germany), and Le Corbusier (France). These three formThe Bauhaus School.

The Bauhaus School was a school of design, architecture, and applied art that existed in Germany from 1919 to 1933. The Bauhaus was founded by combining two schools, the Weimar Academy of Arts and the Weimar schools of Arts and Crafts. The Bauhaus, or "house of building," a name derived by reversing the German word *Hausbau,* which means "building of a house." The Bauhaus wanted to end the split between art and technical expertise by training the students in the both areas. The Bauhaus school brought together architects, painters, and designers from various countries. Their common goal was to formulate goals for the visual arts in the modern age.

Le Corbusier (1887-1965) is considered the most prominent modern architect. In 1920's, Corbusier demonstrated his mastery of design in a series of residences near Paris. These constructions are examples of International Style in architecture. Corbusier was an architect, town planner and designer. He was one among the most able propagandists of the other International school of architecture. He put the functionalist aspirations of his generation with a strong sense of expressionism.

During the World War I period Corbusier was busy to understand and give shape to modernity in the streets of Paris. Simultaneously Corbusier came of f his nostalgia from pre-automobile days and began to celebrate modernity. He felt that the new people needed new type of streets. He described the new street as' Machine for producing traffic'.[20] In the view of David Lyons Corbusier tried to reconceptualize city. He says, 'The city could be reconceptualized from the vantage point of the car driver. No pedestrians or sidewalk cafes would obstruct the flow of traffic. The city would be built for cars. The elimination of the street would also eliminate crime and rebellion'.[21]

Corbusier developed the central doctrines of modernist architecture in a number of manifestos. Among his manifestos, the most popular one was "Towards a New Architecture" (1927). This Manifesto stated that utility and functionalism must be the controlling qualities of modernist architecture. Insistence on the low cost production, rationalized and standardized architecture for mass production, justification of functionalism, denial of nineteenth century's obsession with style were the basic architectural qualities of Corbusier. Corbusier says, 'A house is a machine for living in" and a curved street is a donkey track, a straight street, a road for man'.[22]

These declarations show his emphasis on simplicity. Most of the architectural ideas of Corbusier were emanated from the need of post-war housing regeneration in the West. Some of his buildings indicate that they were parts of a grand plan for a new society. The huge constructions by Corbusier aimed to incorporate private lodging spaces with collective activities. The collective activities include the shopping centres and gymnasium. These spaces provide a communal life with no sacrifice of individual space. The buildings were seen as alternatives to increasing spread out of suburban areas. There were utopian overtones in these grand plans. In one the Bauhaus Manifesto, Gropius said 'The ultimate aim of all visual art is the complete building!...Together let us desire, conceive, and create the new structure of the future, which will embrace architecture and sculpture and painting in one unity and which will one day rise toward heaven from the hands of a million workers like crystal symbol of a new faith'[23]

Simultaneously the International style popularised by Corbusier and other members of the Bauhaus school established itself, and by 1920s began to move ahead the cause of modernist architecture. White cubic shapes and the voidance of ornament recognized the International Style of the Bauhaus.

In the totalising impulse of modernist architecture, Tim Woods finds three important features : They are : reductionism, determinism and mechanism. According to him the significant characteristics of International style are :

1. "Style was removed from the vocabulary of form in favour of a new ascetic geometry. The tyranny of historicism in architecture was rejected, as 'ornament was Crime'.
2. A radically functional approach to architecture was taken, in which the imperative was Mies' notion that 'form follows function'.
3. Regularity, rationalization and standardization, and a clarity of outline and geometry, became the principal organizational features, as the architects sought a Universalist and abstract style."[24]

The International style of architecture propagated by aforementioned architecture almost became international. For a number of decades this style dominated the world over. This modernist architecture or international architecture banished all most the regional and local characteristics.

There was no space for regional flavour in modern architecture. It just propagated organized, recurring and modular designs. The international style dominated the modern architecture. It was technocratic in spirit.

Modern Music

In music the advent of modernism is usually dated from the breakdown of the underlying musical systems of tonality that had lasted for over three hundred years, and that formed the basis for baroque, classical and romantic music. According to Georgina Born, 'The late romantic composers, such as Wagner and Scriabin, had expanded the system so much that it was under great strain, its basic principles in question, and composers began a search for new organizing principles. First, around the turn of the century, came a period of atonality-the suspension and avoidance of all tonal reference and thematic form. But in the early 1920s a new compositional technique and philosophy called serialism was developed by Schoenberg and his pupils Webern and Berg (the Second Viennese School). Serialism, a stylistic revolution, became the most powerful development out of the crisis of tonality and was for some decades the organizing force of musical modernism'.[25]

In the west, the modern music placed much emphasis on the individuality and the personal expression. In fact, this is an extension of the high value placed on the individuality. The modern times provided the modern individual more time to study music and develop aptitude for musical composition. This resulted in the emergence of enormous range of styles, tastes and skills and simultaneously they became the features of modern composition. Radios and recordings decreased the space by transmitting music from one corner of the world to the other. The development in the communication systems further enhanced the speed of the spreading of music from one country to the other. The technological changes in the musical instruments also resulted in great innovations in the musical sphere. Diversity has become the prominent feature of the twentieth century music. Various styles that developed during the twentieth century, specifically up1950s have harmonic characteristics.

The hallmark of the music of the period is Chromaticism. The Greek word, *chroma,* means “colour” in a musical composition-the use of notes that do not belong to the musical scale on which the composition is based. As a result of extreme chromatism atonality or the complete absence of tonality, occurred in the music of a few composers. The most popular atonal composer was Arnold Schoenberg. Schoenberg was an Austrian composer and was one of the renowned composers of the twentieth century. In 1920s Sohenberg formulated his twelve-tone techniques. The twelve-tone techniques were also called “serialism“, as it was based on a series of pitches. The twelve- tone was introduced with an intention to find a substitute for the forms like sonata, on which tonal music had been based. In the beginning only the students of Schoenberg adopted his technique. Simultaneously all most all major composers of the twentieth century used the method. The other harmonic styles of the twentieth century include polytonality, or the simultaneous use of more than one tonality. Microtonality or microtonal music is another innovation of the twentieth century music. It is also based on a harmonic concept.

The other innovative music of the twentieth century was aleatory Music. Aleatory is a music in which the artist has allowed chance to play a role either in the work's creation or its performance. It specifically indicates a compositional aesthetics that was prevalent in 1950s and 1960s. The role of chance in the aleatoric music takes different forms. For example, the composer, in the process of composition may write numerous pages of music and allow the performer to choose pages to play and order them. Most of the composers in the late twentieth century freely drew on serial, electronic, aleatoric, and other techniques.

Modern Dance

Modernism in dance was a style of those artists, who, at the end of the 19th and beginning of the 20th centuries, broke with previous traditions to forge new techniques, theories, and aesthetics for dance. Modernism is a term in use throughout the arts and covers a great diversity of theory and practice. An emphasis on individualism, abstraction, and commitment to art of the present were common features. The pioneers of modern dance have, in some cases, little in common beyond a rejection of existing traditions and a desire to re-examine the fundamental principles of dance as a medium. The movement's origins were international with simultaneous developments throughout the Western world.

Americans such as Loie Fuller, Ruth St Denis, and Isadora Duncan were extremely influential in Europe while the influence of Europeans such as Rudolf von Laban and Mary Wigman was widely felt in America. Fuller exploited the capacity of new technology, dancing in a cloud of silk illuminated by the new electrical systems of theatrical lighting. Duncan's aim was to use the ideals of ancient Greek art to inspire more natural forms of dance. Duncan celebrated the human body as an instrument of emotional expression.

Rudolf von Laban's work as a theoretician and teacher was far more influential than his work as a performer and choreographer. Working in Europe, his analysis of human movement and his system of dance notation provided a theoretical basis for the study of dance and its teaching. His work with large amateur groups of dancers forming movement choirs reached beyond the bounds of conventional theatrical presentation, taking dance into the community at large, often in open-air venues.

One of his teaching assistants during World War I in Switzerland, Mary Wigman, was to become one of the most celebrated dancers of the modernist movement. She asserted the autonomy of dance as an art form, working often in silence and with minimal props. She created a powerful form of emotional expression often exploring the darker side of human nature in the grip of universal forces.

Martha Graham, another American, also wished to express emotion through the dancing body and developed a coherent system of technical training to achieve her choreographic aims. Distinctive features of Graham's technique were her use of muscular contraction and its release to produce motive energy, and her use of weight, sinking into and thrusting up from the floor.

Notes

1 Clive Cazeaux. *The Continental Aesthetics Reader*, London : Rouledge, 2000, p. 297.

2 Peter Barry. *Beginning Theory : An Introduction to Literary and Cultural Theory.* Manchester : Manchester University Press, 1995, p. 81.

3 Schulte Sasse. Quoted in *Postmodernism and the Social Sciences : A Thematic Approach,* by Robert Hollinger, London : Sage, 1994, p. 40.

4 Andrew Bowie.*Aesthetics and Subjectivity : From Kant to Nietzsche.* Manchester, Manchester University Press, p. 16.

5 Marshal Berman. *All that is Solid Melts into the Air : The Experience of Modernity.* London : Penguin, 1988, p. 90.

6 Peter Childs. *Modernism.* London : Routledge, 2000, p. 29.

7 Peter Childs. *Ibid.*, p. 39.

8 Peter Childs *Ibid.*,P-49

9 T.C.W.Blanning. *Short Oxford History of Europe : The Nineteenth Century,* Oxford : Oxford University Press, 2000, p. 134.

10 Frederich Nietzsche. Quoted in *Cambridge Companion to Modernism,* p. 15.

11 Michel Bell. "The Metaphysics of Modernism". *Cambridge Companion to Modernism,* p. 16.

12 Peter Barry Smart. *Beginning Theory : An Introduction to Literary and Cultural Theory,* p. 82.

13 Malcolm Bradbury and James McFarlane (Ed.) *Modernism : A Guide to European Literature, 1890-1930.* London : Penguin, 1991, p. 31.

14 Michael Hollington. Svevo, Joyce and Modernist Time. in *Ibid.*, p. 431.

15 Peter Childs. *Modernism* London : Routledge, 2000.

16 Franz Kafka. Quoted by Franz Kuna, "The Janus-faced Novel : Conard, Musil, Kafka,Mann" in Modernism (Ed.) Malcolm Bradbury and James McFarlane, p. 449.

17 P.J. de Grouchy. *Classics to Computer : A Study of Art in Revolution*; London :Longman,1970, 121.

18 Peter Childs. *Modernism*. London : Routledge, 2000.p, p. 111-112.

19 Tristan Tzara. Quoted C.W.E.Bigsby. In *Modernism*, London : Methuen,1972, p, p. 6-7.

20 Le Corbusier Quoted by David Lyon, in *Postmodernity*. New Delhi : Viva Books 2002, p. 32.

21 David Lyons, *Ibid.*, p. 32.

22 Le Corbusier .Quoted by Tim Woods, in *Beginning Postmodernism*, Manchester, Manchester University Press, 1999, p. 90.

23 Walter Gropius. Quoted in *Ibid.*, 91.

24 Tim Woods *Ibid.*, p. 92-93.

25 Georgina Born. Rationalizing Culture : IRCAM, Boulez, and the Institutionalization of the Musical Avant-Garde. Berkely : University of California Press. 1995, p. 48.

IV

The phase of transition : a socio-philosophical and historical compulsion

In spite of the commonality in phraseology to treat them as equivalents, postmodernity and postmodernism, do not mean the same thing. Postmodernity refers to a generalized change in social situation or conditions. The criteria of the change are multi-dimensional. There is a collapse of the division between elite and mass culture or high and low culture. In postmodernity, the teleological view of history has been replaced by a history with a view that emphasizes discontinuity and open- ended ness. The conventional model of knowledge which emphasizes myth and play has also replaced the scientific model which adhered to concepts like reality, truth and the ambition to discover the laws of nature.

In the view of Rosenau, postmodernism represents the coming together of elements from a number of different, often conflicting orientations. 'It appropriates, transforms, and transcends French structuralism, romanticism, phenomenology, nihilism, populism, existentialism, hermeneutics, Western Marxism, Critical theory, and anarchism'.[1]

According to Chris Rojek postmodernity is the, 'superimposition of local, community and national distinctions with a global, ever-changing sign-economy; and the practices of a political of impression instead of a politics of problem- solving '.[2]

Though, Terry Eagleton as a Marxist opposed postmodernism, he defined the terms postmodernity and postmodernism very succinctly. Inhis view, 'Postmodernity is a style of thought which is suspicious of the of classial notions of truth, reason, identity and objectivity, of the idea of universal progress or emancipation, of single frameworks, grand narratives or ultimate grounds of explanation'.[3]

In contrast to postmodernity, postmodernism refers to a change in social consciousness. Once again to quote Eagleton, 'Postmodernism is a style of culture which reflects something of this epochal change, in a depthless, decentred, ungrounded, self-reflexive, playful, derivative, eclectic, pluralistic art which blurs the boundaries between 'high' and 'popular' culture, as well as between art and everyday experience'.[4]

The distinctive feature of the change is a sense of uneasiness with the categories of thought and action associated with the modernity. The change is anticipated in the direction of postmodernity. Postmodernity can also be called a sensibility born between the collapse of one era and the birth of the new. In fact, it is a product of multiple events and developments which stimulated speculations in academic and popular culture when the modern culture was on the wane or when the modernist culture was breaking up.

Postmodernity indicates what came after modernity and the dissolution of those social forms that are associated with modernity. It describes the cultural situation in the wake of modernity's collapse as a cultural ethos. Modernity represented a culmination of numerous trends in the western world. These trends include the belief in economic and social development and in the inevitability of progress in the human affairs. It is believed that, in modernity, each generation would have greater knowledge and technological sophistication of the earlier generation. An absolute dedication to the progress was built into the politics of modernity. The progress was anticipated irrespective of the forms, the capitalist or the socialist. The modernists assumed that the quality of life would be improved and that science and technological development could guarantee this. An ideology of progress that embodied in grand narratives of one type or the other was an integral element in modernity.

Quite contrary to the above, postmodernity is the state where skepticism is expressed about notions like the progress. The decline of the belief in the universal theories is another important feature of postmodernity. There is a great commitment to pragmatism in political affairs. This commitment is accompanied by a deep suspension of authority and instrumental rationality and a concern for diversity and difference. The postmodernity emphasizes the diverse forms of individual and social identity.

The autonomous subject of modernity has been dispersed into a range of plural and polymorphous subject positions in postmodernity. In place of coercive totality and universalizing politics, postmodernity emphasizes a pluralistic society or democracy. In the opinion of Madan Sarup, in postmodernity, 'Instead of the certainty of progress, associated with the 'the Enlightenment project' (of which Marxism is a part), there is now an awareness of contingency and ambivalence. The productiveness of industrial technology which Marx so much admired, and which he hoped to tame by means of communism, has ceded place to universal consumerism. Puritan asceticism has given way to the pleasure principle'.[5]

In modernity it was believed that economic, cultural and political changes go together. Itwas believed so for the last two hundred years. From Karl Marx to Daniel Bell, the debate has been continuing in all these two hundred years. In fact, the idea that social and economic change go together on coherent trajectories has been attractive but controversial ever since it was proposed by Marx. In the long term, across many countries, once given processes are set in motion; certain important changes are likely to happen. Industrialization, for example, attempts to bring increasing urbanization, growing occupational specialization, and higher levels of formal education in any society that under takes it. These are core elements of the trajectory called modernization. However, this modernization trajectory is linked with a wide range of other cultural changes.Certain cultural values are conducive to the economic accumulation and investment that make industrialization possible.

But many thinkers in the second half of the twentieth century proved that social change is gradually replacing the outlook that has dominated the societies since industrial revolution. It reflects a shift in what people want out of life. It is transforming the fundamental norms governing politics, work, religion, family, and sexual behavior. Thus the process of economic development leads two successive trajectories, modernization and postmodernization. Both of them are linked to economic development. But postmodernization represents a later stage of development and is linked with very different beliefs from those that characterize modernization.

The modernization theory played a major role in sociology in the early decades of the twentieth century. But in the second part of the century, specifically after 1960s, modernization theory has been severely criticized. By 1970s the concept of Modernization has been widely discredited. One reason why modernization theory aroused such great interest among people was its promise of predictive power : it implied that once society entered the trajectory of industrialization, certain types of change were likely to take place. However, Modernization theory has been developed by numerous theorists. Most of them argued that technological and economic changes are linked with coherent and predictable patterns of cultural and political change. But there have been continuing linkages between these casual linkages.

While accepting the important role of cultural change, thinkers like Daniel Bell viewed the changes in the structure of the workforce as the leading cause of cultural change. Bell in his book "The Coming of Post-industrial Society" (1973) argued that the crucial milestone in the coming of post-industrial society is reached when majority of the workforce was producing neither raw material, nor manufacturing goods, but services. According to Bell the post-industrial society has three main components, 'a shift from manufacturing to services; the centrality of the new science-based industries; and 'the rise of new technical élites and the advent of new principle stratification'.[6]

In the postmodernity there has been a radical critique on modernization. Postmodernity does not see change as linear. It dóes not move in single continuous direction. The early versions of Modernization theory were deterministic with the Marxist version tending toward economic determinism and the Weberian version tending toward cultúral determinism. The fact is that all these determinisms, be they of economic, cultural or politics are mutually supportive. To divide them is nothing but oversimplification. Unless these systems are mutually supportive they cannot survive. However, the modernization is no longer at the cutting edge, and the social change is now moving in a fundamentally different direction.

According to Ronald Inglehart, 'the literature on postmodernism suggests some of the specific attributes of this new direction : it is moving way from the emphasis on economic efficiency, bureaucratic authority, and scientific rationality that characterize modernization, toward a more human society with more room for individual autonomy, diversity, and self-expression'.

In Inglehart's view, postmodern society is moving away from the homogenized functionalism and the enthusiasm for science and economic growth that dominated industrial society, to a society which gives weight to aesthetic and human consideration and incorporating elements of the past into a new context.

For many a postmodern writer reality is perceived through some kind of filter of culture. These cultural factors are becoming more important components of experience and allowing broader space for individual choices. But cultural factor is not the only factor that is shaping the reality. The postmodernists emphasize that one's perception of reality is shaped by one's subjective values and preconceptions.

According to postmodernism, social change after the Second World War has moved beyond the instrumental rationality that was central to modernization. It is now taking fundamentally different direction from that of modernity. Among various types of societies that ever exited, the greet majority of them disappeared in the process of modernization and a few are in the process. In fact at the beginning of twentieth century absolute monarchy was the most wide spread form of government. Today it has dwindled to handful of surviving cases. The Fascism that spread rapidly before the Second World War, simultaneously disappeared, but still a few loosely fascistic regimes are surviving. The most recent case of mass extinction is among societies is the collapse of communist regimes. Authoritarian economies is proved to be unworkable and uncompetitive in a high-technology government.

In the wake of the above experiences numerous cultural theories and approaches came on to the scene. The postulations of these new theories have crucial implications for social change. Cultural theory implies that culture cannot be changed overnight. One can change the rules and the laws. This resulted in a realization that deep-rooted values are not easily changed. For example Marxist left saw cultural factors as opiates of people and treated it as false consciousness that diverts the people from the real problems. The Marxists believed that proper indoctrination could speedily wash away all the previous orientations.

But, ultimately the Marxist program designed to bring swift and massive changes in the societies failed because, it never cared to understand deep-rooted values and habits of the people. As Inglehart says, 'The most ambitious programs of rapid social change required enormous coercion and failed nevertheless : Stalin's Forced Collectivization and Great purges and Mao's Great leap forward and Great Cultural Revolution not only failed to create a New Soviet Man, or new Chinese culture, but led to enormous human suffering and ultimately were immensely counterproductive'. [8]

The observation of Zygmunt Bauman is not out of context here. He says,'Modern utopias and revolutionary ideologies inspired their readers or followers to transgress; they painted an alluring image of a new order of things which will put paid to transgression, and all the discomforts that come with it, by banishing everything the humans might conceivably wish to be transgressed'. [9]

Frederic Jameson (1934-) the influential Marxist critic tried to understand the emergence of postmodernism in economic terms. Jameson not only sought to detect and understand the particular quality of the cultural experience designated postmodern, but also sought to locate them within social framework. Much of his theory derived from Marxism. That is why he located postmodernism as a cultural dominant of late capitalism in the post- Second World War period.

Jameson continuously refers postmodernism as the cultural logic of late capitalism and analyses the ways in which culture changes. Jameson, following E.Mandel's, considers postmodernism as the third stage of capitalism. His analysis is accompanied by a concrete cultural periodization. Thus for Jameson, realism corresponds to market capitalism, modernism to monopoly capitalism and postmodernism to late- capitalism or consumer -capitalism or multinational capitalism [10]. In this perspective he understands that culture is taking place on the superstructural levels.

Jameson's general characterization of culture can be understood from various angles. In a way Jameson designates the role of culture in late capitalism as one cultural profusion produced by the logic of the commodity form. Jameson says that the culture is the very element of consumer society itself. In his view no society has ever been saturated with signs and images like the present one. This opinion has been incorporated into his writing on postmodern culture when he refers to the destruction of 'the semi-autonomy of the cultural sphere' to be replaced by, 'a prodigious expansion of culture throughout the social realm, to the point at which everything in our social life ...can be said to have become "cultural" '. [11]

In fact, Jameson in his early text "Postmodernism and Consumer Society"(1984) anticipates his magisterial study of "Postmodernism or the Cultural Logic of Late Capitalism" (1991) . He expands his consideration of the ideology of form, moving beyond the literary canon to contemporary culture-including film, experimental poetry, popular fiction, art and architecture. He identifies two causal conditions for postmodernism across the arts : First its products which emerge as specific reactions against the established forms of high modernism; and second, its result from the erosion of the distinction between high culture and so called mass culture. However, he does not recognize them as the ultimate causes of postmodernism. In a typical Marxian fashion Jameson looks at the underlying economic formation. In that process he understands postmodernism as the inner truth of newly emergent social order of late capitalism. According to him, it emerged immediately after the Second World War and consolidated itself during the crisis of 1960s. For Jameson 'postmodernism' indicates a historical period, but not just a new aesthetic.

In fact, Jameson's "Postmodernism, or the Cultural Logic of Late Capitalism" has been regarded as one of the 'classic' texts in the debates on postmodernism. This text gives us the undeniable views on art. Jameson recognizes 'pastiche' as a significant characteristic of postmodern aesthetics. He says, 'Pastiche is, like parody, the imitation of a peculiar mask, speech in a dead language : but it is neutral practice of such mimicry, without any of parody's ulterior motives, amputated of the satiric impulse, devoid of laughter and of any conviction of that alongside the abnormal tongue you have momentarily borrowed, some healthy linguistic normality still exists'.[12]

Jameson's account of pastiche is presented in the discussion of architecture. Jameson's conception of postmodernism has its roots in architecture. He bestows a privilege upon architecture as the classic expression of postmodernist aesthetics. Jameson believes that "the practice of pastiche is a symptom of the 'linguistic fragmentation of social life itself to the point where the norm itself is eclipsed'.[13]

Quite against to the Marxian 'dominant ideology thesis' Jameson puts forward his ideas on pastiche. He says, ' If the ideas of a ruling class were once the dominant (or hegemonic) ideology of bourgeois society, the advanced capitalist countries today are now a field of stylistic and discursive heterogeneity without a norm. Faceless masters continue to inflect the economic strategies which constrain our existence, but no longer need to impose their speech (or are henceforth unable to)'.[14]

Jameson identifies three American novelists, namely William Burroughs, Thomas Pynchon, and Ishmael Reed, as postmodernist writers.

In the view of Jameson, in the era of globalised commodity fetishism, the culture of simulacra emerges. In simulacra the images of mass entertainment and commodity aesthetics, images of history, society, and nature do not have any relation with reality. The logic of commodity fetishism penetrates the human psyche and results in the production of artwork with depthlessness. Jameson shows the paintings of Andy Warhol as examples for the commodity aesthetics.

In Jameson's analysis, Warhol's paintings are devoid of expressiveness. The depthlessness is an indication of the neutralization of art in the late capitalism. The opinion of Paul Maltby, while he discussing Jameson's essay, is interesting here. Maltby says, 'His (Jameson's) logic of late capitalistic explanation of postmodernist art is a stronger version of a familiar argument about the neutralization of art in the late –capitalist society. According to the latter, transgression and scandal, once exploited by the *avant- garde* as weapons with which to offend bourgeois norms, are now 'economically' imperative; the sale of goods depends on innovations in commodity aesthetics (e.g., in advertising or product styling) which work precisely as sources of cultural shock. However, for Jameson, it is not simply a matter of the late-capitalist economy feeding off contemporary art. What, according to him, defines late capitalism is the globalisation of commodity fetishism, a process that has destroyed the "semi-'autonomy' of the cultural sphere"; a situation whereby the logic of exchange-value is understood to penetrate all cultural production, including aesthetic counter-practices'.[15]

As we have already seen, Jameson's reading of postmodernism as the "cultural logic of late-capitalism postmodernism is a new mode of production that realigns the economic and cultural according to the internal principle of recent state in the capitalist development in which the structures of co modification and representation have become indivisible. The cultural logic of 'postmodernism' in the sense of Jameson is much a schematic response to the global transmission of multinational capitalism as it is the superstructural expression of socio-economic conditions. In that way it is resistance. Such resistance to the late capitalism in the notion of Jameson is a 'cognitive mapping, which explores ways of redefining our relation to the built space our lived environment in response the 'penetration of capital into 'hitherto uncommodified' areas'.[16]

In the twentieth century electronic media are supporting an equally profound transformation of cultural identity. Telephone, radio, film, television, and now the computer and their integration as multimedia reconfigures words, sounds and images so as to cultivate new configurations of individuality. In a way, the postmodern society emerged in the process of tremendous mediaisation of society. Postmodern culture is often presented with as an alternative to the modernist society, which has been seen as often flawed and structurally limited. In addition to this, the discussion postmodern culture focuses, to a larger extent, on an emerging new individual identity or subjective position, one that abandons the narrow scope of the modern individual if modern society is said to foster an individual, who is rational, autonomous, centered, and stable, i.e. the 'reasonable man' of the law, the educated citizen of representative democracy, and the calculating 'economic man' of capitalism.

The most striking devolvement of the second half-twentieth century is the ascendance of postmodernism. The postmodernism's denunciation of meta-narratives, foundationalism, and essentialism attracted many a social scientist. Postmodernism revolted against the received epistemologies and challenged the universal knowledge. Though postmodernism had been described as a historical condition[17] and a stage of socio-economic development,[18] it derived its philosophical inspiration from Jean Françoise Lyotard, Michel Foucault, Jacques Derrida, Jean Baudrillard and Gilles Deleuze.

All most all these French philosophers have propagated anti-foundational agendas. These thinkers questioned the foundationalist agendas of the grand theories like Marxism and were skeptical about the single project of human emancipation. They questioned even the description of working class as the revolutionary subject of history and proposed plural projects of emancipation. These analysts pointed to the emerge of a new set of cultural and aesthetic categories and have effected a profound change in the intellectual climate and the language of the academic discourse. 'Indeed they have created an environment in which rationalist beliefs that characterize scientific enquiry since the time of Plato are being questioned and undermined'.[19]

However for any discussion relating to the emergence of postmodernism Lyotard's text "The Postmodern Condition" (1979) is the starting point. In fact, "The Postmodern Condition" is not so much a study about postmodernity, but rather a study about knowledge. In spite of the declaration of Lyotard that he intended to study the status of knowledge in the highly developed societies, the book traces the emergence of postmodernism. His observations relating to the late-twentieth century social development follow mostly the familiar scenario of the postindustrial society as sketched by Daniel Bell and others, the scenario in which information replaces the manufacturing of material goods as central concern in the most advanced countries.

The computerization of society ultimately affected knowledge and transformed knowledge into a commodity. Knowledge became 'an informational commodity; science has been forced to abandon its original goal of integrity and has become an instrument in the hands of the power.[20] Instrumental rationality has come to dominate other forms of reason. Lyotard's aim is to expose the legitimation of science and thus the transcendental status that the science has been enjoying. Lyotard negates any kind of legitimation. He says, 'Speculative philosophy is forced to relinquish its legitimation duties'.[21]

Lyotard argues that modernity is essentially a clash between grand narratives, which underpin life. Modernity sought to impose order on the basis the philosophy of liberal individualism and the market system. Modernity struggled to uproot the earlier regimes with scientific, quasi-scientific and inspirational blueprints. It wanted to suppress duality and difference, which was not possible to it. According to Bauman, 'Duality is the human fate, and human existence will stay dual, but bound to recognize itself simultaneously in two utterly dissimilar images of systemness and contingency. No monistic 'solutions', whether practical or theoretical, will either extirpate that duality from existence or theorizing it out and away. No selection, however wisely or cleverly made, will ever exhaust the infinity of possibilities which human 'underdetermination' opens up. Each order is in the end a selection, but each selection just it is a selection will therefore arouse anger and prompt rebellion, through against a selection can only be made in the name of another selection...'[22]

Lyotard exactly talked about the delegitimation of the grand narratives of this type. In Lyotard's view, individuals employed in the knowledge sector of society have shifted their interest from a concern with the ultimate ends of human life to pragmatic concerns relating to the optimal performance of means. According to Rojek, 'There has been a move from social engineering to performativity'.[23]

Lyotard's "incredulity towards metanarratives" led him to celebrate the plurality. In the view of Steve Best and Douglas Kellner, 'Lyotard's celebration of plurality replays the moves of liberal pluralism and empiricism. His 'justice of multiplicities' is similar to traditional liberal pluralism, which posits a plurality of political subjects with multiple interests and organizations. He replays tropes of liberal tolerance by valorizing diverse modes of multiplicity, refusing to privilege any subjects or positions, or to offer a standpoint from which one can choose between opposing political positions'.[24]

In a way, there is close relation between the emergence of postmodernism and the emergence of media society. The gigantic combinations of new technologies and the integration of old technologies, creation of new industries and expansion of older ones have their own implications in the political field. For example, the expansion of Internet. The Internet has tremendous political implications to the fate of nation state. The dominant use of English on the Internet indicates the extension of British and American power. In some ways the Internet undermines the nation state, as the messages in the cyber space are not easily delimited in Newtonian space, rendering borders ineffective. In this process culture is also becoming increasingly simulational. This is because the media often changes the things that treat, transforming the identity of originals and the things they refer. The reality became, to some extent, multiple.

In fact, reality itself became problematic in the postmodern societies. In some cultural activities reality has been substituted by 'virtual reality'. The term 'virtual' is used in computer jargon. Virtual Reality is a system that enables one or more users to look, move, and react in a computer-simulated world. Various types of interface devices allow users to have the illusory experiences of seeing, touching, picking up, and even manipulating virtual (simulated) objects. Virtual worlds and everything in them (including computer images of the participants) are represented by mathematical models and computer programmes.

The information technology and the other forms of communication media like virtual reality are increasing the forms of consumer culture.

In the electronic communications the human subject is constituted in ways other than that of the major modern institutions. In the modernity the human subject is autonomous, and rational. Whereas, in postmodernity the human subject is unstable, multiple and diffuse.

Post-Fordism is another feature of postmodern society. The model of post-Fordist entrepreneurship is said to be differentiated by a reversal of many of the characteristics of Fordism. New methods of production based on new technologies, such as biotechnology, and particularly microelectronics and information technology came onto the scene. The Post-Fordist work relations and practices are claimed to be characterised by "flexibility" in the work relations. Keynesianism was considered to degenerating into monetarism. Monetarism is generally corresponded to the analysis that changes in the money supply have little or temporary impact on the economy and that the economy will not mechanically progress towards full employment, and that economic policy can be successful in helping to achieve full employment.

A new individualism, brought by the new technological advancements shattered the earlier faith in the collectivist institutions of the Fordist era. Owing to these the role of trade unions decreased tremendously. In fact, there was radical fall in the membership of the trade unions. The state intervention in the industries also decreased. Privatization of the industries with rapid speed resulted in the quick development of free market economies. While discussing the end of Fordism Peter Wollen says, 'From being the symbol of instrumental reason in industry, the automobile had become a byword for waste and ornamentation. The economy and culture of the West entered a period of crisis, the decline of Fordism, as consumerism reached the limits possible within the old system. A long transitional period during the 1960s and 1970s finally led to the introduction of a new post-Fordist economy. The first signs of this were already visible in the 1950s, with the beginning of automation. At that time, automation was seen primarily as way of rationalizing still further the existing Fordist structures of industry. In reality, we can now see that it prefigured much more sweeping changes in the economy. The rationality of the computer and of robotics turned out to be significantly different from the rationality of the Highland Park assembly line'.[25]

Peter Wollen says Post-Fordism brought three main developments. The first was the rise of new industries because of the developments in the fields of electronics and information technology. Second, the use of these new technologies in the manufacture and design of old products and the upgrading of old industries. The third was the systemic shift from the objects as commodity to information, to information as commodity. In the beginning, these changes were associated with the shift from manufacturing to the service sector, and with the changes that took place in the international economic relations. The communication industry moved to the centre stage by pushing all other to the backdrop.

The electronic revolution that began with the sound recording picked up the pace with magnetic tape and extended into the technology of images with television and video. At present, the world is moving towards the digital age. The advent of computer on the scene radically altered the image production with the computer almost functioning as 'electronic brain'. All these changes brought in new theories of image and media in 1950s and 1960s. These theories reached their culmination in the writings of Marshal McLuhun. McLuhun (1911-1980), was Canadian writer on communications. McLuhun proposed a number of unorthodox theories on communications. His theories are the result of his firm belief that the electronic media—especially television—have an influence far bigger than that of the material they communicate. Peter Wollen considers McLuhun the theorist who put forward the theory of the end of Fordism.

In fact, McLuhun saw Fordism as a logical end of the 'Gutenberg era'. McLuhun thought that the new electronic technology and media would replace the pre-Fordist community with a new 'global village', which is referred by everybody. Peter Wollen says on McLuhun, 'The extraordinary achievement of McLuhun was to break out of the terms of the polemic for and against technology (Benjamin versus Huxley or Heidegger) by fusing romantic reaction with futurist technology. With McLuhun you get aspects of both Benjamin and Heidegger. Like Benjamin he privileges the tactile over the visual and dreams of the creation, through technology, of a radically new kind of human being. But like Heidegger he sees the new human being in a quasi-mystical way as a return to origins (back beyond mass production, beyond printing, even further, beyond the alphabet), to a world without separation, a world of perpetual now-ness'.[26]

The new media technologies are leading us to such a state where old divisions are blurring and losing their meaning as the technologies of image production and reproduction begin to amalgamate. The computer with its capacity to maneuver and simulate is becoming a part of an integrated system with both the old and new recording technologies. The socio-philosophical and historical compulsions resulted in the formation of postmodernity.

Notes

1 Pauline Marie Rosenau. *Post-Modernism and the Social Sciences : Insights, Inroads, and Intrusions*, Princeton : Princeton University Press, 1992, p. 13.

2 Chris Rojek. *Decentring Leisure : Rethinking Leisure Theory*. London : Sage, 1996, p. 129.

3 Terry Eagleton, *The Illusion of Postmodernim*. London : Sage, 1997, p. vii.

4 Terry Eagleton. *Ibid.*, p. vii.

5 Madan Sarup. *An Introduction to Post-structuralism and Postmodernism*. Athens : The University of Georgia Press, 1993, p. 130.

6 Stuart Sim. (ed.) *The Routledge Companion to Postmodernism*. London : Routledge, 20001, p. 196.

7 Ronald Inglehart. *Modernization and Postmodernization : Culture, Economic, and Political Change in 43 Societies*, p. 12.

8 Ronald Inglehart. *Ibid.*, p. 19.

9 Zygmunt Bauman, "Searching for a centre that holds" in *Global Modernities*. (Ed.) Mike Featherstone, Scott Lash and Ronald Robertson, London : Sage, p. 141.

10 Frederic Jameson. "Postmodernism : or the Cultural Logic of Late Capitalism". *New Left Review*, 146, p. 78.

11 Frederic Jameson. *Ibid.*, p. 87.

12 Frederic Jameson. *Ibid.*, p. 65.

13 Frederic Jameson. *Ibid.*, p. 65

14 Frederic Jameson. *Ibid.*, p. 65

15 Paul Maltby. *Dissident Postmodernists Barthelme, Coover, Pynchon*. Philadelphia : University of Pennsylvania Press,1991

16 Frederic Jameson. *Postmodernim; or the Cultural Logic of Late Capitalism*. London : Verso, 1996, p. 400.

17 Francoise Lyotard. *The Postmodern Condition : A Report on Knowledge*. Manchester : Manchester University Press, 1987.

18 David Harvey. *The Condition of Postmodernity*. Oxford : Basil Blackwell,1989.

19 Gurpreet Mahajan. *Explanation& Understanding in the Human Sciences.* Delhi : Oxford University Press, 1997, p. 104.

20 Jean Francoise Lyotard. *The Postmodern Condition.* Manchester: Manchester University Press, 1984, p.

21 Lyotard, *Ibid.*, p. 41.

22 Zygmunt Bauman, "Searching for a centre that holds", in *Global Modernities*. (Ed.) Mike Featherstone, Scott Lash and Ronald Robertson, p. 143.

23 Chris Rojek. *Decentring Leisure : Rethinking Leisure Theory*, p. 133.

24 Quoted by Hans Bertens in *The Idea of The Postmodern : A History.* London : 1995, p. 130.

25 Peter, Wollen. Raiding the Icebox : Reflections on Twentieth Century Culture. London : Verso, 1993, p. 63.

26 Peter Wollen. *Ibid.*, pp, 64-65.

V

The emergence of postmodernism and its philosophy

After the Second World War Philosophy and sociology have been increasingly fragmented into different approaches like Marxism, Feminism, Ethnography, Neo-Marxism, Structuralism and Semiotics. In the post 1960s scenario, there are some salient features of philosophy and sociology. Among them, the most important are the return of Marxism, the rise of Feminism and the emergence of the anti-colonial theory of development. Philosophy and sociology have been talking about Capitalism, industrial society, and modernization. But they seemed to have forgotten the fact that much of Capitalism and modernization was built on the back of an imperialism that subjugated the third world in order to pay for such development. The awareness of this fact is with the past colonies. A number of women movements emerged and Feminism as a large theoretical cannon blew up various forms of patriarchal myths.

Since 1960s, there has been a series of spectacular changes in culture and society throughout the world. The '60s was an era in which numerous social and political movements emerged and challenged the established forms of society and politics and even culture. These movements produced alternative thoughts. All most all the theories underwent many mutations during the twentieth century. Many new philosophers and theorists like Antonio Gramsci, Herbert Marcuse, Jean Paul Sartre and Louise Althusser came on to the scene from 1930s to 1960s and after. New concepts relating to the role of intellectuals, class and ideology gained momentum. Specifically, in sociology the concepts like 'the end of class' and 'end of ideology' were in vogue. The sociological approaches derived from the New Left Marxism deviated from the politics of the Communist countries and produced critiques of both Socialism and Capitalism.

Gramsci's concept of hegemony gave much impetus to cultural studies. Marxism had originally argued that Capitalist society would even more polarize workers and bourgeoisie. Since this did not happen in the West during the twentieth century, and rather the fairly opposite, the situation forced Marxists to rethink how Capitalist society functioned. It was increasingly recognized that society was becoming more complex. Gramsci was a key thinker in redefining the debate about class and power. His concept of hegemony has come to be central in the sociological discussions of the complexity of modern society. Gramsci pointed out that the ruling class did not rule by force alone but also by consent, forming political alliances with other groups and working ideologically to dominate society.

Gramsci replaced traditional Marxian notion of inevitable class struggle in society with more flexible, rather sociological, view of the conflicts between groups, parties, individuals and ideologies. The idea of hegemony draws attention to the fact that individuals are always reacting to and redefining the society and culture, they live in. Gramsci believed that ideologies are not simply injected into passive subjects who live them; In fact, there are areas of doubt and battle between dominant and subordinate groups in society. According to Gramsci, intellectuals play a key role in the ongoing formation and reformation of historical blocks. 'Historical block', is Gramsci's coinage. It expresses his sense that social groups are dynamically created in specific historical moment, or so called conjunctures. His ideas have had a lot of influence in cultural studies and discussions on popular culture. Gramsci's ideas have been crucial for British Marxists and for the version of cultural Studies that come from Britain.

The Frankfurt School of Germany has made an important contribution to the Marxian thought. It has influenced such radical movements as the New Left. The Frankfurt School, the persons and ideas associated with the institute for Social Research, founded and affiliated to the University of Frankfurt in 1923. This group of German critical theorists were mostly ignored when they wrote in the 1930s and '40s but began to be noticed in sociology in 1960s.They were concerning with the problem that society, although capitalist, did not seem to be displaying the simplistic revolutionary development that Marx had predicted. They believed that in addition to class conflict, the cultural and economic domination was taking on new forms. The failure of Marxism, both as a theory and in practice in Soviet Russia led them to develop a rational critical theory of the both.

To over come the limitations of Classical Marxism, the Frankfurt School set out a theoretical program. The program included five areas :

1. A critique of economic determinism.
2. A critique of mass society and its manipulation of culture.
3. The incorporation of Freudian theories, which would enable them to understand the subject in bourgeoisie society.
4. The development of a "Critical Theory" of capitalist society.
5. An analysis of instrumental reason.

The Frankfurt School, which was basically philosophical in its approach and analysis, emphasized the key roles that culture and ideology play in shaping the individual in mass society. They believed that mass culture was blinding everyone to the realities of life. The rise of Fascism and "culture Industry" seemed to them like similar signs of a new type of society that controlled its members through sophisticated cultural manipulation.

Herbert Marcuse (1889-1979) a member of Frankfurt School became famous during the 1960s for his support of radical and anti-authoritarian causes. His work "One Dimensional Man" (1964) brought together the arguments of the Frankfurt School. His unambiguous commitment to politics and social struggle led him to become a prominent spokesperson and theorist of the New Left in the 1960s and early '70s. In "One Dimensional Man", he discussed that capitalism generated false needs, false consciousness and mass culture, which enslaved the working classes. Marcuse argued for an authentic opposition and for liberation. Marcuse's "Eros and Civilization" (1955) is an important work in the debate about sexuality and society.

An awareness of culture and communication as significant factors in analysing society can be seen in the post-1960s scenario. Jurgen Habermas played an important role in these issues. Habermas combined these concerns with those of the Frankfurt School. His emphasis was rational communication and its possibilities in the existing society. He aims for the reconstruction of some of the central theses of classical Greek and German philosophy : the inseparatability of truth and virtue, of facts and values, of theory and practice. The ultimate objective of Habermas is to provide a framework within which a large number of apparently competing approaches to the social sciences can be targeted. The most important among them are the critique of ideology, action, theory, the analysis of social systems, and evolutionary theory.

The second wave of structuralist theory was also very much popular in the 1960s. The structuralist theory, which has its origins in the pioneering work "A Course in General Linguistics" by Ferdinand Saussure (1857-1913) once again, rewrote the ways in which the social determination and social agency were conceived. In the post-1960s shift into pluralistic theoretical approaches, Saussure's theory of semiotics or the study of signs filtered into sociology and culturology. Within a short span, the structuralist approach became popular with some sociologists and culturologists. It became very popular through the work of Roland Barthes and Claude Levi Strauss. Both of them made strong impact on many areas of culture, sociology and anthropology of the times.

Barthes and Strauss started from the axiom that language is a structured system. They then examined culture as a similar structured system. They applied the same, eventually, to the society as a whole. The most relevant part of structuralism can be seen in the discipline of cultural studies or in the analysis of culture. The Structuralists believed that we are all caught up in the language system and our understanding of things is also determined by that system. As we are all 'trapped' in language, we acquire culture through language. We are all speaking subjects. To understand culture one must understand the structures that function within it and the underlying patterns that shape it.

Roland Barthes exemplifies the best of structuralist readings of culture and society, specifically in his analysis of signs in a particular culture. The importance of the mass media in disseminating ideological views of the world is based on its ability to make signs, images, and signifiers to work in a particular way, and Barthes brilliantly shows the structures that make it work. He analyses the way in which 'signs' convey deeper, mythical meanings with popular culture than the surface images allude to.

Claude Levi-Strauss as a structuralist defined language as a system of signs and linguists as a branch of semiology. Lévi-Strauss has a pre-eminent place among those researchers who assert that the various cultures of human beings and their behaviours, language patterns, and myths demonstrate a common framework underlying all human life. In the path breaking work "Elementary Structures of Kinship (1962); his autobiography " Tristes Tropiques "(1964); and "The Savage Mind" (1966) he analysed social and cultural structures.

According to Strauss the objects of social anthropology –cultural phenomenon such as kinship systems and rituals – consist of communication, not just functions. Vincent B.Leitch says, 'Reforming anthropology as a study of culture rather than cultures, Levi-Strauss underscored the discipline's implications for history, politics, art, literature, economics and philosophy, dramatically transforming anthropology's profile in the academy'.[1]

There are two important aspects in the work of Levi-Strauss; the first one is the principle that social and cultural life cannot be uniquely explained by a version of functionalism. Cultural life is not explainable in terms of the intrinsic nature of the phenomenon in question. Nor can it be explained empirically by facts deemed to speak for themselves. The second one is that Strauss adopts a universalistic approach, by theorizing on the basis of both his own and other anthropologists data, whereas, other social researchers have limited their interpretations of social life to the specific society in which they have carried out fieldwork.

Strauss asserted that language preconditioned human culture as reflected in the symbolic order of aesthetics, religious and social life. He maintained that all cultural patterning depended on the vast reservoir of unconscious and universal structures of mind. The deep structures underlying surface manifestations of cultural significations could be analysed. According to Richard Kearney and Mara Rainwater, one of the most significant distinctions made by Levi-Strauss is in the course of difference between 'cold' and 'hot' societies. Culture in the Western Europe that changed rapidly and remained open to widely divergent influences he categorized as' hot', whereas those cultures that changed very little over time were 'cold'. Levi-Strauss found a prime example for 'cold' society in the Amazon Indians[2] ". In the view of Strauss, all aspects of culture, like sexual taboos, kinship laws, marriage rites, cookery, social hierarchies, religious rituals, mythic systems proved amenable to structural analysis. The rise of structuralist paradigm under Levi-Strauss was marked by his scathing critique of Sartre's existentialism.

Luis Althusser was also classified as a 'structuralist thinker. With his structuralist version of Marxism, Althusser shocked many inside as well as outside Marxism. Althusser' fame has its origins in his 'anti-humanism'. He provided an interesting counterpart to that of humanist Marxist thinkers like the members of Frankfurt School, Sartre and Gramsci.

However, Althusser did not see his work as being motivated by the French Structuralist movement of the 1950s and 60s. According to Althusser, the structuralist priority of system over individuals is already inherent in Marx's theoretical analysis, hence, his interrogation of whole-part relations proceeds in Marx's footsteps, but not Saussure's. The structuralist analysis revealed a complex set of relatively autonomous cultural, political and economic fields that function under the systemic pressures of dominating structure. Though the economic field is significant, it alone does not determine the activities within other fields. Althusser strongly opposed the economic determinism of base-superstructure model. He considered it a reductionist reading of Marx.

In the year 1966 Jacques Lacan published a legendary 900-page collection of his essays and conference papers, titled "Ecrits" (writings), the book was a sensation and changed the entire orientation of psychoanalysis in France and elsewhere. Lacan re-read Freud so as to clarify and reinvigorate a whole series of concepts. With the structuralist emphasis on language as system of differences without positive terms, Lacan highlighted the importance of language in Freud's work. The Saussurian theory of the arbitrary relation between signifier and signified together with the notion of language as a system of differences led Lacan to go on to say in the early 1960s that the subject is the subject of signifier.

Like Levi-Strauss, Lacan extended Saussure's system of structuralist linguists to the realm of anthropology. Lacan adopted it for a radical reinterpretation of Freudian psychoanalysis. He developed a new perspective on the 'unconscious', which did not assume to be the biologically determined field of libidinal instincts and drives postulated by Freud, but rather semiologically 'structured like language'. In 1950s itself Lacan challenged the orthodoxies in the field of psychoanalysis.

In the text "The Importance of the Letter', Lacan pays his allegiance to the intellectual dominance of language studies. In his view, what the psychoanalytic experience discovers in the unconscious is the whole structures of language. He declared, "unconscious is structured like language". In fact, Lacan rethought Freud in the wider framework of linguistic. For Lacan, 'The unconscious is comparable in structure to a language. In fact, Lacan argues that language is the condition for the unconscious...'[3].

Lacan became very popular during the May 1968 events in France. During that time, people were very concerned with the questions of self-expression, desire and sexuality. At that time Lacan's theory offered a way of thinking about social and the linguistic construction of the self. For Lacan there is no separation between self and society. Humans are becoming Social with the appropriation of language. The view of Richard Kearney and Mara Rainwater on Lacan's contribution to psychoanalysis was very interesting. They say, 'He (Lacan) deeply interrogated the fundamental praxis of psychoanalysis, which he claimed should avoid the illusions of a 'cure' or a belief in supposed infallibility of authority of the analyst. A medical doctor himself, Lacan was firmly convinced that to understand the language of unconscious desire in dreams or symptoms, a psychoanalyst needed less science and more art'.[4]

The above and a few other intense philosophical, political, cultural and social struggles in 1960s gave rise to many approaches to culture and society. The tumultuous struggles of the 1960s can be seen in a very concrete manner in the realm of theory. The political passions and energies, simultaneously, sublimated into the discourse theory. The new theories were appropriated. The most important theory that emerged in the 1960s is Post-structuralism, which rejected totalising, universalistic and scientific theories of structuralism, semiotics, psychoanalysis, Marxism and other master discourses.

The French intellectual scene since 1950s was dominated by the Structuralism. But in the 1960s, another movement, Poststructuralism replaced this domination. Structuralism emphasized order, structure, and rules, whereas Poststructuralism believes that language is subject to contingency, indeterminacy, and the generation of multiple meanings. Poststructuralism understands reason instead of being an instrument of understanding, serving as an instrument of mastery and social control.

Post-structuralism is neither a school nor a theory in the traditional sense of the term; rather it is a set of propositions. These propositions have at their core a self-reflexive discourse and are aware of their own tentativeness and ambiguity. Post-structuralism as the name suggests is a consequent upon the Structuralism. Without having a substantial knowledge of Structuralism, it is almost impossible to comprehend the precepts of Post-structuralism. Post-structuralism is marked by a denunciation of totalising, essentialist, and foundationalist concepts. Because, it believes that any totalising concept puts all phenomenon under one explanatory concept like the will of God. The essentialist concept proposes that there is a reality, which exists, independent of, beneath or beyond language and ideology-that there is such thing as 'the feminine', 'truth', or 'beauty'. The foundationalist concept advocates that signifying systems are stable and unproblematic representations of world of fact. Hence, any knowledge of Poststructuralism demands prior knowledge of Structuralism.

Structuralism was an intellectual movement that began in France in the 1950s and is first manifested in the work of the anthropologist Calaude Léve-Staruss and the French literary critic Roland Barthes. Léve-Staruss was famous for his role in the late 1950s the cross-disciplinary phenomenon called as Structuralism. In the beginning, the movement got its inspiration from Ferdinand de Saussure, a Swiss linguist. In fact, Saussure was responsible for the structuralist movement with his book "A Course in General Linguistics".According to Saussure, the meanings we give or attribute to words are arbitrary and that the meanings are retained by convention only. There is no intrinsic connection between words and the things they designate. In fact, Saussure distinguishes between two dimensions of language. The first one is how it is practiced or spoken; he called it 'parole' or 'speech'.Saussure asserted that language should be regarded as a social phenomenon and a structured system that can be viewed both synchronically and diachronically. In relation to the study of language 'diachronic' refers to the way of studying language taking into account the change and development through time. The synchronic takes into account the elements that are contemporary at a given point of time. In this way, Saussure formalized the fundamental approaches to language and asserted the principles and methods of each approach as distinctive and mutually exclusive.

In Saussure's view, the meanings of the words are relational. A word cannot give a meaning in isolation from other words. He isolated the study of language as a structured system of interconnected parts from the world of objects that words name. Language is not just a collection of names; rather it is an autonomous system of signs. The relation among the signs is arbitrary. The process of signification takes places not as a linkage between words and things but as the association of signifiers or sound images, and signifieds or concepts. Signifiers are constituted through their relations with other signifiers within the linguistic system and not by their relations to objects. Saussure argues that language does not have a direct relationship to reality but functions as a system differences. Words (signifiers) have no inherent relation with the concrete things that they describe (signifieds), but generate meaning as a result of their differential relationship with other signifiers. Saussure says that language is ordered in a specific way. Basically, it is a system or structure. Individual elements have no value outside this system. In his "A Course in General Linguistics", Saussure declares, 'in language there are only differences'.[5]

To be specific, Saussure proposed a number of divisions or distinctions between langue and parole, signifier and signified, semiology, semiotics, paradigmatic, and syntagmatic, synchronic and diachronic. All these distinctions form the basic method of structuralism. The Saussurian insights initially paved way for many a thinker like Lévi-Strauss, the psychoanalyst Jacques Lacan and the culturologist Roland Barthes. Saussure tried to provide a new linguistic theory with a scientific basis. He wanted to liberate linguistics from the positivist and empiricist methods. For this purpose, he depended much on his distinction between language and speech. This distinction, ultimately served as a cornerstone to the structuralism or structuralist linguistics.

Saussure's study of language emphasizes not on the empirical content of the words, as was the case in the traditional linguistics, but on the structural interrelationships that obtain between part and the whole. That is why Saussure thought the meaning of a sentence is found not in its structure but in its substance. Hence, Saussure gave priority to *langue* over *parole*. According to him individual understanding of a sentence cannot have meaning on its own, but it will have its meaning in the overall language system. Richard Kearney says, '*Langue*, as Saussure understands it, is not a formal system of signs which makes no claim to refer to anything outside of itself. *Langue* has no substantial existence either in an empirical sense (for language does not exist as some objective entity in the real world) or in an idealist sense (it does not exist as some subjective entity in the collective or individual mind)'.[6]

Traditionalist linguists propagated the referential models of language. The referential models constructed the sign as a name that is refereeing to a thing. Contrary to this, Saussure defined sign as a relation between a form or sound image expressed by the human voice and a concept or idea. Saussure called the first as signifier and the latter as signified. The basic aspect in Saussure model was its emphasis the arbitrariness of the structural relation between 'signified' and the 'signifier'. The relation between sign and that which it signifies is not natural, but a matter of social and cultural convention.

In the view of Richard Kearney,' The originality of Saussure's position was to argue that the meaning of language is generated *within* language itself that is not derived from some prior reality existing independently of language-be it God's metaphysical creation or man's subjective consciousness'.[7] In his view, the origin of meaning resides neither in God nor Man, but in language itself.

The notion, put forward by Saussure that language is a differential sign system represents Saussure's greatest break with the traditional views of language. From Plato to early Wittgenstein Western philosophy has agreed to the common premise that the signified (the concept or that to which the sign refers) could be defined in itself. Saussure castigated this approach by declaring that the essential aspect of language has nothing to do with the phonic nature of sign. As we have seen already the functioning of sign cannot be grasped through its material forms, but only through its opposition to other signs, whatever be the morphological embodiment of the sign. Saussure makes sharp distinction between the sign and the symbol. There is no arbitrariness in the symbol. The symbol has always has a degree of motivation to justify its symbolizing relationship. Language is never symbolic in this sense.

Allen Thiher says,'By radicalizing the principle of the arbitrary nature of the linguistic sign, Saussure demolished the underpinnings of aesthetic modernism. *The Course* can be read as something of an antimodernist manifesto, for it leaves no justification for a belief in the imagistic power of poetic revelation in language'.[8]

Saussure's "The Course in General Linguistics" is directed against belief in the natural bond between sign and signified. It rejects the naive metaphysics of representation. In fact, Saussure's definition of linguistic signs undermines the belief in the possibility of ironic or simultaneous representation.

Saussure is considered one of the forerunners of structuralism, as far as he uncovers the systematic codes that govern the workings of language. Saussure is less concerned with what meaning is, rather he paid much attention how meaning is produced by structural operation of sign system. Much of Saussure's concentration is on the structural dimension of language than on the empirical. This, according to Richard Kearney 'led to the revolutionary discovery that the linguistic system as a whole precedes the particular workings of signs and ultimately determines their capacity to generate meaning"... He (Saussure) suspended , as it were the complex problem of *reference* (i.e. of how words refer to empirical or ontological truths outside of language) in order to highlight what he deemed to be the more fundamental problem of how meaning originates within the formal operations of language itself'.[9]

Saussure's shift of attention resulted in a radical revision of traditional methods in linguistics. A number of theorists of Saussure combined the linguistic methodology of Saussure with other developments in the modern thought. They tried in multiple ways by explaining how cultural meanings relate to the hidden discourses. For example, Foucault in power and knowledge, Jacques Lacan in the psychic unconscious, Le'vi-Strauss in myth, kinship and symbol, Louis Althusser and Roland Barthes in literature and mass culture. Whatever may be the differences among them all the Structuralists agree upon that the language is a system of signifying operations that determine or predetermine our modes of experiencing of the world. They even believe that it is not possible to reduce the signifying operations to some 'subjective' references prior to language or to 'objective' empirical references beyond language. Simultaneously, Saussure's linguistic model has been extended to cultural and social codes. After 1960s, by rejecting a number of notions of structuralism Post-structuralism came on to the scene.

Post-structuralism saw the proliferation of new theories of language, the subject, politics and culture. It even provided a synthesis of Marxism, Psychoanalysis, Semiotics, and Feminism. Marxist discourse proliferated and an unimaginable variety of Neo-Marxist theories emerged. Feminism also became a new theoretical discourse throughout the world. Women revolted against the oppressive practices of both patriarchal societies and their male comrades in the radical movements. Many varieties of feminist theory found important tools in psychoanalysis and linguistics. As with Marxism, a tremendous range of feminist theories emerged.

In the above atmosphere, Douglas Keller says,' previously marginalized groups sought their voices in the United States : new African-American, Native-American, Mexican American, Asian-American, and other minority discourse and studies emerged. Gay and Lesbian studies problematized sexuality and provided new perspectives on gender and sexuality, culture and society. Theorists whose colonized countries generated new subaltern studies attacking the Western colonization, while the studies of the 'post-colonial subject' and voice from newly emerged nations produced some exciting theoretical innovations and greatly expanded the terrain of critical discourses'.[10]

The new discourse of race, class, ethnicity, sexuality and nationality, that emerged after1960s, challenged theoretical discourse to take account of phenomenon previously ignored or marginalized. The discourse of a Jean Françoise Lyotard, Jacques Derrida, Michel Foucault and Jean Baudrillard were enthusiastically taken up by their followers. These various strains of theories mutated into Postmodernism. According to Douglas Kellenr,'In sense, the postmodern theory exhibits the passions of the 1960s sublimated into theoretical discourse. The break or rupture desired in the 1960s a break then described in the discourse of revolution is projected onto history itself, or more limited domains of society and culture'.[11]

The breaks or rupture postulated in the 1960s as the goal of political struggle are now being described in the postmodern theory as breaks occurring as the result of new technologies and new form of political struggles. Postmodern theory, though laments the defeat and disappointment over the failure of 1960s movements to transform social and cultural life, translates some of the progressive tendencies and gains of the 1960s into theoretical discourse and cultural practice against more oppressive features and practices of the contemporary culture and society. Now let us discuss the key thinkers of the postmodernism.

Michel Foucault

Michel Foucault (1926-1984) the French philosopher, challenged the permanent truths about human nature and society, change in the course of history and offered new concepts that challenged people's assumptions about prisons, the police, insurance, care of people with mental illnesses, gay rights, and welfare.

Foucault's critique of modernity and humanism, his proclamation of the 'death of man', and his development of new perspectives on society, knowledge, discipline, and power, have made him a major source of Poststructural Postmodern philosophy. Mark Philip says, 'his work is above all iconoclastic in intent. His major concern is neither to offer new solutions to hoary philosophical problems, nor to provide a more adequate historical account of our current difficulties. He does both, but only in passing. His primary objective is to provide a critique of the way modern societies control and discipline their populations by sanctioning the knowledge claims and practices of the human sciences : medicine, psychiatry, psychology, criminology and so on'.[12]

Foucault is arguably the most influential European thinker and writer of the second half of the twentieth century. His unclassifiable work has attracted much criticism. However, the questions he raised, the issues he addressed, and the positions he took have become central features of today's intellectual landscape. Even in literary studies, Foucault stands as a major source for Poststructuralism, New Historicism, Cultural Studies and Queer theory.

Foucault examines the structures of organization at work in historical practices and institutions in order to show how knowledge and belief systems are constructed. He pays specific attention to the aspects of social life, which are normally marginalized or suppressed, e.g., sexuality, criminality, and madness. He argues that the sciences of man have subverted the classical order of political rule based on sovereignty, rights, and have instituted a new regime of power exercised through disciplinary mechanisms.

In fact, Foucault's critique draws much of its inspiration from anti-Enlightenment tradition that rejects equations of reason, emancipation and progress. Foucault's project had been to write a critique of the contemporary era. The constitution of preset had always been an obsession with him. In the seminal essay "What is Enlightenment?"

Foucault declares, 'I think that the Enlightenment, as a set of political, economic, social institutional, and cultural events on which we still depend in large part, constitute a privileged domain for analysis. I also think, that as an enterprise for linking the progress of truth and the history of liberty in a bond of direction, it formulated a philosophical question that remains for us to consider'.[13]

Foucault's interest in language and interpretation led him to write the book, "The Order of Things". Foucault intended to explore how man became the object of knowledge in Western culture. He did this by taking three periods in history-the Renaissance, the Classical and the modern unearthing each era's respective historical 'apriori'. In this unearthing he sought for the way in which human beings have historically become the subjects of political, scientific, economic, philosophical, legal and social discourses and practices.

"The Order of Things" is one of Foucault's early books, and one of the most important, for it deliberates on the problem of cultural ordering and raises the possibility of seeing ordering itself in operation. In the process of explaining the why and how this ordering or organization of particulars takes place, Foucault illustrates it with an example from the Argentinean writer Jorge Luis Borges. In fact, 'The Order of Things" begins with a quatation from Borges from a 'certain Chinese encyclopaedia'. The encyclopaedia divides animals into the following categories : a) belonging to the Emperor, b) embalmed, c) tame, d) sucking pings, e) sirens, f) fabulous, g) stray dogs, h) included in the present classification, I) innumerable, j) drawn with fine camelhair, k) drawn with fine camelhair brush, l) having Just broke the water pitcher, n) that from a long way off look like flies'.[14]

Mark Philip further clarifies this, 'As Foucault points out, what this fictitious classification suggests, by the stark impossibility of thinking, it is the limitation of our own system of thought. Because we are locked in our own discourse, we simply cannot see how the animal world could be mapped in this way. When we classify objects we operate within a system of possibility- and this system both enables to do certain things, and limits us to this system and these uses'.[15]

There have been various classificatory systems from animals to humans throughout history. Each system rooted in a different conception of the natural order of the world. However, we tend to assume that previous classifications are contaminated by religious and primitive forms of thinking and that only ours is truly free from error. Foucault will not accept precisely this move. In his view, truth is an effect of the rules of a discourse. However, we cannot say that our classificatory systems mirror certain enduring features of the natural world, which previous classifications distorted.

In the book "The Order of Things" Foucault identifies two eras in the history of human sciences : The first one is; the classical phase, that runs from 1660 to 1800, the second is the modern epoch, which begins with the nineteenth century and which was drawn to a close in 1950s. Foucault's major contention here is that during each of these periods, disciplines like linguistics, biology and economics shared a common 'well-defined regularity', and obeyed 'the laws of certain code of knowledge'.[16]

Foucault is very much concerned with this code. It can be called an *episteme*. An *episteme* is the underground grid of network, which allows thought to organize itself. Each historical period has its own *episteme*. This *episteme* limits the totality of experience, knowledge and truth, and governs each science in one period. Foucault's *episteme* can be compared to the idea of paradigm of Thomas Kuhn. According to Thomas Kuhn, science becomes normal when there is a broad consensus in the scientific community. This agreed upon, achivement model is called paradigm.

Foucault's observations of history are quite revelatory. He problematizes .While writing on Foucault's view of history Madan Sarup says,' Unlike the historian who traces a line of inevitability, Foucault breaks off the past from the present and, by demonstrating the foreignness of the past, relativizes and undercuts the legitimacy of the present'.[17]

As we have all ready seen in "The Order of Things" Foucault sets out a series of periodisation of knowledge. Paul Hamilton thinks,' Foucault defines history as much through its discontinuities as its continuities, as much through the differences between successive *epistems*, as he calls them, or each period's discursive regulation of what it is possible to know, as through their similarities'.[18]

Foucault opposes the 'anthropological' history and this opposition extends to any historical perspective. Foucault's thinking inaugurated an epistemological break in the study of history. This can best be seen in "The Order of Things. The book describes how the Renaissance mode of signification, which was found on the universal resemblance of things, gave way to classical episteme detaching language from the things it represented.

In "The Order of Things" Foucault argues that our "modern" conception "man " is only some hundred and fifty years old. This new "man" is a being that makes the world, but it is also a creature made from the world. This creature is subject as well as object of knowledge. The philosophical appearance of this being can be seen in Hegel's "Phenomenology of Spirit". It continued in the same central position in the subsequent philosophies, including the philosophy of Marx. In fact, it made its appearance in the early nineteenth century when, natural history becomes biology. Foucault says, 'When natural history becomes biology, when analysis of wealth becomes economic and Classical *discourse,* in which being and representation found their common locus is eclipsed then, in the profound upheaval of such an archaeological mutation, man appears in his ambiguous positions as an object of knowledge and as a subject that knows.'[19]

In all these 'new sciences' mentioned above "man" is essentially a finite being, an ephemeral expression of the laws of the various natural systems into which "man" is born and within which he has to die. In spite of all his finititude, "man" is somehow able to grasp his own nature to understand all that has even been and all that he ever might.

"Man" in short, a mystery. "Man" is a creature of paradoxes. This creature had its day. In this context Foucault says, 'For the entire modern episteme –that which was formed towards the end of eighteenth century and still serves as the positive ground of our knowledge, that which constituted man's particular mode of being and the possibility of knowing him empirically- that entire episteme was bound up with the disappearance of Discourse and its featureless reign, with the shift of language towards objectivity, and with its reappearance in multiple form. If this same language is now emerging with greater and greater insistence in a unity that we ought to think but cannot as yet do so, is this not the sign that the whole of this configuration is now about to topple, and that man is the process of perishing as the being of language continues to shine ever brighter upon our horizon?'[20]

At the end of the text, "The Order of Things" Foucault's observations are very interesting' He says, 'In fact, among all the mutations that have affected the knowledge of things and their order, the knowledge of identities, differences, characters, equivalences, words-in short, in the midst of all the episodes of that profound history of the *same*-only one, that which began a century and a half ago and is now perhaps drawing to a close, has made it possible for the figure of man to appear. And that appearance was not the liberation of an old anxiety, the transition into luminous consciousness of an age-old concern, the entry into objectivity of something that had long remained trapped within beliefs and philosophies : it was the effect of a change in the fundamental arrangements of knowledge. As the archaeology of our thought easily shows, man is an invention of recent date. And one perhaps nearing its end'.[21]

However, Foucault later regretted these type of pronouncements. James D. Faubion says, 'Foucault soon came to regret such grand and ephemeral pronouncements. He never, however, abandoned his suspicion of either phenomenology or Marxism'.[22]

The analysis of Richard Kearney, in this context, on Foucault's achievement is, ' Perhaps the most striking feature of Foucault's analysis was the claim that the revered Western notion of 'man' is itself a conditioned 'product' of a specific 'epistemic epoch'(i.e. the modern) which is now beginning to disappear. Far from being the creator of scientific codes of discourse, as humanism held, 'man' is now revealed as no more than a category created by these codes. We do not produce science, it produces us. And if it is true that science once served to objectively legitimate the construct of the human as an autonomous substance or individual consciousness, it is now in the process of dismantling this construct. And so Foucault announces that the famous era of the *death of God,* ushered in by Nietzsche and the existentialists, is now being superseded by new era whose single achievement is the *death of Man'*.[23]

Foucault's announcement of the *death of man* has far-reaching impact on humanities, including aesthetics. It radically alters our whole understanding of human sciences. Foucault tries to explain how what we have been considering as original or individual subject are mere surface 'effects' of an anonymous system of Language or thought. For example, works of art are not created by individual persons, but by the complex structures of interacting cultural codes, which prevail, in the 'epistemic' epoch during which these works emerged. The difference between one cultural epoch and the other is not because of the acts of some genius or creative imagination but because of an epistemological rupture in the system of relations, which govern them.

In an interview, given to Alessandro Fontana, Pasquale Pasquino, Foucault's says, "History has no 'meaning', though this is not to say that it is absurd or incoherent. On the contrary, it is intelligible and should be susceptible of analysis down to the smallest detail-but this in accordance with the intelligibility of struggles, of strategies and tactics. Neither the dialectic, as logic of contradiction, nor semiotics, as the structure of communication, can account for the intrinsic intelligibility of conflicts"[24]. Foucault opposed history as a retrospective projection on to the past of the coherence it needs to legitimate its own discipline.

All most all the texts of Foucault deal with history in one form or the other. He wrote definitive histories of madness, clinical medicine, the social sciences, the prison, and ancient and modern sexuality. According to Gary Gutting, 'Much of Foucault's historiography falls in the genre of "the history of concepts" as that has been understood by his friend Georges Canguilhem. This approach flows from an insistence on the distinction between the concepts of that interpret scientific data and theories that explain them'.[25]

As we have already seen many of Foucault's concepts of history fall under the category, he himself designated as 'history of the present'. Foucault begins with the perception that something is terribly wrong with the present. This view of history is totally opposite to the conventional one. His ultimate goal is not to understand the past but to study the present. In a way, Foucault tries to understand the present in terms of the past. To this extent, there is no difference between Foucault and other historians. But Foucault reverses this enterprise. Traditional history tries to show that where we are is inevitable, whereas Foucault tries to present the contingency of what history has given to us and the possibility of transcending it.

Historical practices and institutions project themselves as if they have no alternatives. As Garry Gutting views, 'Foucault's histories aim to remove this air of necessity by showing that the present ordered things quite differently and that the process leading to our present practices and institutions were by no means inevitable".[26]

Foucault questions this 'inevitability'. His history of madness, for example, is an attack on our concept of madness as mental illness and the practice of psychiatry based on this conception. Our commonsensical understanding is that mental illness requires the care and treatment of qualified medical professionals and psychiatric treatment is the only way of dealing with it. Foucault's history tries to show that there are alternative conceptions of madness. For example, during the Classical age, i.e., Europeans understood madness not as an illness that requires medical treatment but as a moral defect that reduced human beings to a level of animals. Hence, they never tried to cure the mad; rather they isolated and contained them.

In the view of the modern conception of madness as mental illness is constructed from the two key elements of the Classical conception of madness. The notion that the mad are animals was transformed into the modern conception of madness as a natural phenomenon. Biological and psychological laws govern this phenomenon. The Classical moral condemnation of madness was retained through asylum system of confinement. According to Garry Gutting the emergence of modern psychiatry is not a 'triumph of compassion that is based on scientific objectivity, but as the product of scientifically and morally suspect forces peculiar to the social and intellectual structures of the nineteenth and twentieth centuries'.[27]

In Foucault's view asylum is a key component of Modern madness. The structure of asylum life, for example, the moral and social authority of the doctor with the institution, i.e., the asylum, is the key to modern psychiatry and psychology. The medical gaze of the doctor is a covert moral judgment. The mad violate bourgeois morality and they are useless to the society. In this background, the ultimate aim of the modern psychiatry is to bring them back under the bourgeois values and make them 'useful'. In asylum, the doctor rules not by virtue of scientific objectivity but by virtue of moral authority.

In "The Order of Things", also we can see the same kind of analysis of the modern social sciences. Foucault thinks that all the modern scientific knowledge is based on a particular conception of human reality of man, i.e., the conception of man. Foucault considers that it is just one contingent understanding and that one will soon pass.

The role of power in society has always been a passionate theme to Foucault. During early 1970s, Foucault began to move away from philosophical themes, concentrate on the technologies of power. He took up the questions of power relations. In his view, we lacked an adequate understanding of power as something other than a reflection of economic structures. Patricia O'Brien says, 'At the heart of Foucault's history of Western civilization is the organizing principle of power. Culture is studied through technologies of power, not class, not progress, not the incommutability of the human spirit power cannot be apprehended through the study of conflict, struggle, and resistance except in the most limited manifestations. Power is not a characteristic of a class (the bourgeoisie) or ruling class elite, nor is it attributable to one. For Foucault, is a strategy attributable to functions (dispositions, manoeuvres, tactics, techniques). Power does not originate in either the economy or politics, and it is not grounded there. Power exists as "an infinitely complex network of 'micro powers', of power relations that permeate every aspect of social life." Power is not repress it also creates truth and hence its own legitimation. It is the job of the historian to recognize this truth production as a function of power'.[28]

Foucault never accepted that power is the power of the state. Time and again he argued that he had no theory of power. In his sense the state it self is an effect of multiplicity of movements. For Foucault the state, the body, the society, sex, the soul, the economy are not stable objects, they are discourses. Foucault says, 'My general theme is not society, it is true/ false discourse : let me say it is the correlative formations of domains, of objects, and of discourses verifiable and falsifiable which are assignable to them; it is not simply this formation which interests me but the effects of reality which are linked to it'.[29]

Foucault never thought power merely as a form of repression and did not reduce it to a consequence of legislation and social structure. In his view, no one is outside the power; there are no margins, no peripheries and no centre. Relations of power are interwoven with other kinds of relations like production, kinship, family and sexuality. Power relations historically serve economic interests but these interests cannot be accepted as primary. Foucault says, "There are no relations of power without resistances; the latter are all the more real and effective because they formed right at the point where relations are exercised : resistance to power does not have to come elsewhere to be real, nor is it inexorably frustrated through being the compatriot of power. It exists all the more by being in the same place as power; hence, like power, resistance is multiple and can be integrated in global strategies'.[30]

The "Archaeology of Knowledge" (1969) is Foucault's methodological reflection on his major works in the 1960s : "Madness and Civilization", "The Birth of the Clinic", and "The Order of Things". In these works, Foucault attempted a theory of historiography based on new developments in the studies of history. In the book "The Archaeology of Knowledge", he modified the key thesis of archaeology and made it a subordinate rather than an independent method. In the "Archaeology of Knowledge" Foucault argues against conventional history that emphasizes continuities or discontinuities. In his view within a specific period, within a culture, the same form of history is operative in the economic, political, social and religious spheres.

It is the change from one way of doing history to another that concerns Foucault. Foucault examines more directly the epistemological breaks that usher in every new era of knowledge. Knowledge is expressed through language. That is why Foucault studies each aspect of spoken and unspoken language in order to uncover 'endemic transformations systematically. He tried to define archaeology as an approach to the history of thought that eliminates the fundamental role of the human subject. In this context, Garry Gutting explains that, "Archaeology thus would operate as the historical counterpart of the structuralist counter sciences (psychoanalysis, ethnology, and linguistics) in the postmodern move away from a conception of man as the object that constitutes the world of objects.

Like any historical inquiry, Foucault begins with the documents, collections of statements that have been received from the past. Ordinary history or history in general considers the documents as clues to the intentional beliefs, thoughts, desires, and feelings of those who produced them. It aims to use the objective linguistic data of the statements to reconstruct the inner life of subjects. Foucault, in radical opposition to this method, proposes to take the statements as objects of study in their own right. There was no effort to use them as means to revive the thought of the dead in Foucault. He considers the documents simply as monuments.

In Foucault's view, history is no longer a collective consciousness that tries to refresh its memory. In other words, contemporary historiography rejects the handed down unities of anthropological historiography and endeavours to constitute its own unities, totalities, series and relations. In the view of Garry Gutting the methodology of 'Archaeology of Knowledge," "primarily, oriented toward the description of discursive formations ..."Archeology of Knowledge" thus appears as a methodological essay that both sums up Foucault's previous historical work and moves haltingly towards his later, genealogical work'.[31]

Foucault's major contribution to the world of thought comes from his three-volume study, "The History of Sexuality" also. When Foucault was writing "The History of Sexuality" in 1960s and 1970s there were going on a number of heated debates on sex, and sexuality. There were general talks of the importance of sexual liberation. Connections between workers struggle and women's liberation were shown and political programs and social liberation preoccupied the minds of the intellectuals. In such an atmosphere Foucault raised fundamental questions relating to sex and sexuality. How have we been led to speak endlessly of sex? Why has sexuality been so intensely pursued by western governance? Why has sex been the object of scrutiny, the key to so many disorders of the personality? How have we been led to experience our sexuality as the private experience of the individual? Foucault tried to answer the questions. Lawrence Barth says, 'The history of sexuality suggested to Foucault that it could be mapped at the intersection of a vast array of western techniques by which we know and govern ourselves'.[32]

Commenting on Foucault of sexuality Madan Sarup says, 'Foucault says that we have only had sexuality since the eighteenth century, and sex since the nineteenth century. What we had before that was, no doubt, the flesh'.[33]

Foucault presents a series of ideas and arguments against conventional notions of sex and sexuality.

In fact, "The History of Sexuality" is neither a history of sexuality nor of philosophical ideas about sexuality; rather it is a study of the formation and development of the experience of sexuality in modern Western societies. The first volume provides an analysis of sex as a historical construct rather than a biologically given property. The book locates sex and sexuality in relations of power and knowledge. It also studies how individuals, in the process of history have come to think about themselves as sexual objects. By focusing much on the past, the book presents a history of the present. It focuses back to a period encompassing the centuries immediately before and after the death of Jesus Christ. It analyses the Graeco-Roman and Christian texts.

Foucault begins his analysis by examining the widely accepted conceptions of sexual experience and practice. In fact, Foucault intended to study the repressive hypothesis for understanding the modern history of sexuality and the relations between power and sex.

In the view of Foucault, the repressive hypothesis depicts the history of Western European societies since the seventeenth century. Seventeenth century was a period in which a series of prohibitions were imposed on the individuals and their bodies. The Victorian regime regulated, confined and censored sexuality. The expressions of sexuality are restricted to home and legally contracted procreative people. Malcolm Water says, 'The bourgeoisie, revolution 'liberated' sex from kinship and redefined it as sexuality, that is individual, personal, sexual expression.'[34]

The association of sex with sexuality opened up disciplinary control. Malcolm identifies four strategies in Foucault's analysis of disciplinary control. They are :

* "*The Medicalization of women's bodies* : Foucault describes this as the 'hysterization, linking women's entire organic and psychological being to the womb, thus define them by sex and opening up to expert medical control.

* *The Sexualization of Children* : Experts began to define children's sexuality as normal or unnatural and thus opened up childhood and family life to expert interference.

* *The control of population* : The social functions of procreation in relation to population size and environment effects were recognized, which opens procreative sex to state and expert management.

* *The psychiatric specification of perversion* : Distinctions were made between normal and pathological sex and interfering correctives applied to the latter".[35]

According to Foucault at the closing years of seventeenth century, 'there emerged as a political, economic, and technical incitement to talk about sex. And not so much in the form of a general theory of sexuality as in the form of analysis, stocktaking classification, and specification, of quantitative or causal studies'.[36]

Sex gradually became an object of administration, management, and government.

A concrete form in which sex became an object of administration and inquiry in the seventeenth century was that of 'population'. Population became a possible object of government administration with the revelation that it had its own regulations. This revelation came through the employment of statistical methods and techniques of analysis. The governments that began to be concerned with political, moral and other welfare problems of the populations, simultaneously, stretched their gaze to the analysis of various dimensions of population. These dimensions include birth-rate, legitimate and illegitimate births, age of marriage, frequency of sexual relations, fertility etc., In this process, sex, once confined to privacy of the home to procreation, simultaneously, became a governmental matter between the state and the individual. Sex even became a public issue enmeshed in the web of discourses and analysis. Because of this process, there emerged, in the eighteenth and nineteenth centuries numerous discourses on sexuality. The discourses can be seen in the fields of medicine, pedagogy, criminal justice, psychiatry and social work.

The conclusion that Foucault draws from the above repressive hypothesis is that the last three centuries do not so much reveal a constant and uniform silence over sexuality as the increasing of vast network of discourses on sex. In the consequence, the distinctiveness of modern Western societies is not to be found in the forms of sexual repression but in the fact that sexuality was simultaneously subjected to continuous discourses and exploited as the secret of our being. According to Foucault the plethora of discourse, governed by government aimed at eradicating fruitless pleasures failed. Because in the "nineteenth century there had occurred a dispersion of sexualities, a multiple implantation of "perversions"'.[37]

Barry Smart explains the above issue in lucid terms. He says, 'The privacy, sanctity, and discretion accorded to heterosexual monogamy and associated with the proliferation of discourses on sexuality in the eighteenth and nineteenth centuries has as its corollary an interrogation and incitement to confession of a plethora of sexualities and sensualities which were constituted as unnatural or abnormal counterparts to the regular sexuality of the 'legitimate' couple. In consequence Foucault suggests that power did not prohibit or eliminate nonconjugal, nonmonogamous sexualities, rather they were incited and multiplied'.[38]

Perverse forms of sexualities are conceptualised as the result of the repression over the bodies and pleasures. The extension of power over bodies, modes of conduct, and sex did not produce repression, but a proliferation and encouragement of unorthodox sexualities. With this historical experience, Foucault argues, we have to abandon the repressive hypothesis of increased sexual repression associated with the modern industrial societies.

Lawrence identifies three important themes in "The History of Sexuality". First we see that the relations of power affected even our innermost experience of ourselves and our secrete desires. The character of this effect is not prohibition, rather mobilization and organization of sexual experience. Since seventh century, there has been a screening and control of statements about sex. However, there has been a massive proliferation of discourse concerning sex. The effects of public discourse are to multiply individual sexualities, perversions, to charge parents, educators, doctors and others with a vigilance toward the secret sexual practices of children, students, and patients. This resulted in the saturation of social space, by the nineteenth century.

Foucault traces the second theme in the multitudinous practices of confession by which the individuals have been obliged to render their desires in speech. Because of this practice, the individuals subjected them- selves to interpretation. In fact, the process of individual becoming as a subject to interpretation began in the early Christian monastery, simultaneously spread to law, psychiatry, medicine, pedagogy and family relations. It is through confession that truth and sex are joined, through the obligatory expression of an individual secret. It is this endless process of the individual self as the subjects of desire impedes the extent to which the very practices of self-interpretation and self-revealing have a political history.

In the first volume of "The History of Sexuality" Foucault argues that at one time the Christian confession was the locus or venue of sexuality. In the middle ages the priests of the church were concerned with what the people did. The faithful people were asked in detail about the sexual activities. With the advent of Reformation on the scene, the discourse of sexuality took another turn. After Reformation the priests simply did not confine their questions to the acts of the individuals, they began to ask even about the intentions. Sexuality, upon that time confined to body, after the Reformation it had been stretched to the mind as well.

Finally, it is through certain political history that Foucault explains the history of western sexual experience. In the eighteenth century governments realized that they are not ruling or dealing just with 'subjects' or 'people' but with 'populations'. The 'populations' are understood with certain phenomenon and its peculiar variables, birth, and death rates, life expectancy and fertility. In this way, one can understand the importance of sex in the western culture over the last three hundred years. Ultimately, it is by disciplining the body and regulating the population that the western civilization persists.

Foucault never accepted a fixed position or fixed theory against which all things could be measured. In his study of sexuality Foucault confronted with the long Christian tradition that had been inherited by the nineteenth and twentieth centuries. In his search for the beginnings of this tradition, Foucault went back to the Greeks. In this context, it is worth quoting Patricia O'Brien,'Foucault emphasized that sexuality and its promise of the fulfilment of the self are not liberation but rather oppressions of a Christian tradi- tion. Rome, in volume three, (The History of Sexuality) represented a transition between ancient and Greece and the Christian world. Sex itself, as distinguished from sexuality, became a product of the discourse, not "the thing itself". This analysis is stunning reversal intended to highlight through differences the shift in discourse'.[39]

In " The History of Sexuality" Foucault examines the way in which discourses on sexuality contribute to the constitution of human being as subjects. He tries to understand the complex power / knowledge nexus. He says, 'What is said about sex must not be analysed simply as the surface projection of... power mechanisms. Indeed, it is in discourse that power and knowledge are joined together'.[40]

According to Foucault at the beginning of twentieth century, sex became a matter of science. His example is psychoanalysis or discourse on sexuality. As there were confessions in the Christianity, in the twentieth century, a new scientific confession came on to the scene in the name of psychoanalysis. That is why there is an attack on Freudo-Marxiast position in "The History of Sexuality". In Foucault's view, by positioning a sexual instinct Freud opened up a new realm for the domination of science over sexuality. He calls this a repressive 'hypotheses'.

The opinion of Madan Sarup on the essence of the book "The History of Sexuality", is appealing. He says, "The fundamental thesis of the book is that sexuality is not a natural reality but the product of a system of a discourses and practices which form part of the intensifying surveillance and control of the individual. Foucault suggests that liberation is a form of servitude, since our apparently 'natural' sexuality is in fact a product of power.

In fact, in "The History of Sexuality" Foucault once again returned to the complex issue of the subjectivity by questioning how a human being actively participates in the process of becoming a subject, rather than passively suffering the effects of domination. Foucault has analysed this aspect in the latter writing, "The Discourse on Language". Foucault examines the role played by language in transformation of the individual into a subject.

According to Judith Butler, Foucault's "The History of Sexuality" 'questions whether the history of Western desire can adequately be explained within a dialectical framework which relies on the binary oppositions'.[41]

The binary configuration of power in terms of repression/emancipation reduces the multiplicity of power-relations into univocal alternatives that disguise the variegated texture of power. These constructions, even if they seem emancipatory, ultimately result in the restriction of political imagination. That is why Foucault was very critical about Marxism.

In the view of Foucault, Marx's analysis of the formation of capital is for a large part governed by the framework of Ricardian economics. In fact, Marx could not break away from the epistemological frame established by Ricardo. Foucault says, 'But the alternatives offered by Ricardo's 'pessimism' and Marx's revolutionary promises are probably of little importance. Such a system if options represents nothing more than the two possible ways of examining the relations of anthropology and History as they are established by economics through the notions of scarcity and labour.... At the deepest level of Western knowledge, Marxism introduced no real discontinuity; it found it place without difficulty, as a full, quite, comfortable and , goodness knows, satisfying form for a time (its own), within an epistemological arrangement that welcomed it gladly (since it was this arrangement that was in fact making room for it) and that it, in return, had no intention of disturbing and, above all, no power to modify, even one jot, since it rested entirely upon it. Marxism exists in nineteenth century thought like a fish in water : that is, it is unable to breathe anywhere else'.[42]

Foucault radically opposes the Marxist notion of ideology. According to Madan Sarup, there are three reasons for Foucault to reject Marxian notion of ideology[43]. "The first is that it stands in virtual opposition to something else which is supposed to count as truth. Second one is that the Marxian analyses always presuppose a human subject on the lines of the model provided by classical philosophy. Finally, ideology stands in a secondary position relative to something which functions as its base, as its material economic determinant.

Foucault did not say anything about class-consciousness, class ideology, class interest or class struggle. The reason for this is that Foucault did not believe in class. Foucault declared very concretely, 'one should not assume a massive and primal condition of domination, a binary structure with "dominators" on the one side and "dominated" on the other side, but rather a multiform production of relations of domination…'[44]

Foucault was also very critical of those who call "Marxism as science of sciences".[45]

In place of the totalizing discourses, Foucault proposes his genealogy. The genealogy of knowledge consists of two separate bodies of knowledge : First, the dissenting opinions and theories that did not become the established and widely recognized and, second, the local beliefs and understandings. The genealogy is concerned with bringing these two knowledges, and their struggles to pass themselves on to others. Genealogy does not claim to be truer than institutionalised knowledge, but merely to be the missing part of the puzzle. It works by isolating the central components of some current day political mechanism. Foucault says,' Let us give the term 'genealogy' to the union of erudite knowledge and local memories which allows us to establish a historical knowledge of struggles and to make use of this knowledge tactically today. This then will be a provisional definition of the genealogies, which I have attempted to compile with you over the last few years'.[46]

The genealogy explores what was not evident because of the institutionalisation of knowledge by those in power. Archaeology studies the practices of language, whereas genealogy uncovers the creation of objects through institutional practices. The archaeological historian claims to write from a neutral, disinterested perspective, Foucaultian genealogist admits the political and polemical interests motivating the writing of the history.

Foucault wrote essays on literatures and other forms of creativity in his early career. His book, "The Order of Things" includes an essay on Velázquez's *Las Meninas*. Velázquez was Diego Rodríguez de Silva (1599-1660) is Spanish painter. The painting *Las Meninas* is from the series of royal portraits, representing the royal family, court functionaries, and the artist himself.

In 1963 Foucalut wrote a monograph on the French experimental novelist Raymond Russel. In the same year. Foucault was involed in many literary activities that are associated with the magazine *Tel quel. Tel quel* was founded in 1960s by the novelist and critic Phillepe Sollers.It was deveoted much to the publication of *avant-gardist* literature. However, Foucalut was not in search of beauty : he was not an aeshetician. In the works of Roussel, Georges Bataille, Mourice Blanchot and even in the writings of Surrealists Foucalut finds an obscure but articualte engagement with the experience that has been marginalized or neglected. Fiction, for Foucaltu has heteregenous causes and serves multiple purposes. Fiction fills a horrible expressive vacuum.

As a postmodern and poststructuralist philosopher Foucault attempted to show that the basic ideas that people usually take to be permanent truths about human nature and society change in the course of history. His readings challenged the influence of the German political philosopher Karl Marx and the Austrian psychoanalyst Sigmund Freud. Foucault offered new ideas that challenged our assumptions about prisons, the police, care of people with mental illnesses, gay rights, and welfare.

Foucault's thought explored the shifting models of power within a society and the ways in which power relate to the self. He probed the changing rules that govern the kind of claims that could be taken seriously as true or false at different times in history. He also studied how everyday practices permitted people to define their identities and systematize knowledge.

Foucault's last period was inaugurated by the publication of *Discipline and Punish* in 1975. It apparently questions whether imprisonment is a more humane punishment than torture, and it is concerned with the way society orders individuals by training their bodies. In all the books of his last period, Foucault seeks to show that Western society has developed a new kind of power Foucault calls as *bio-power*—that is, a new system of control that traditional concepts of authority are unable to understand and criticize. Rather than being repressive, this new power increases life. Foucault wants people to refuse to go along with the welfare state by developing individual ethics in which one turns one's life into something that others can respect and admire.

Foucault himself resisted any attempt to label him as a structuralist, postmodernist or poststructuralist. However, his work, iconoclastic in spirit and letter, is an indispensable component in the postmodern philosophy. According to Megil, 'His cut across accepted categories generating tension with analyses of more conventional kind, they are not only intriguing but also sharply illuminating'.[47]

Jacques Derrida

The most innovative philosopher of the twentieth century is Jacques Derrida. The name of this French philosopher almost became synonymous with Deconstruction, often described as a 'method' of analysis, a type of critique or an act of reading. Derrida's method as a philosopher and literary critic involves a radical critique of Western metaphysic and a revision of traditional concepts of language. While writing on Derrida Richard Kearney says, 'Few moderns have generated so much international celebration or censure as this French exponent of the 'textual revolution'. He has been both reviled and revered for his anarchic play with eccentric ingenuities of language. Ns sacred concept of traditional thought has been spared a prod from his dissecting scalpel. He danced on the graves of all our hallowed certainties. To some, he no more than a mischief-maker, to others, he is the most revolutionary philosopher of the twentieth century'.[48]

In a series of seminal works like "Of Grammatology" (1967), "Writing and Difference" (1967), "Dissemination" (1972), Margins of Philosophy (1972) Derrida forcefully destabilizes the traditional notions of thinking and attempts to go beyond the conventional division between philosophy and aesthetic discourse. Derrida refuses to be placed within the existing philosophical categories. His influence has extended far beyond philosophy to such dissimilar disciplines as literary criticism, sociology, political theory, psychology, anthropology, theology and many more. The motivating impulse of his work has been to disrupt all univocal classifications and fixed identities.

Derrida's deconstruction took much of its inspiration from the phenomenology of the German philosophers, Edmund Husserl, (1859-1938), and Martin Heidegger (1889- 1976). Derrida himself acknowledged the influence of these two phenomenologists on him in an interview. He said,'My philosophical formation owes much to the thought of Husserl and Heidegger and Hegel. Heidegger is probably the most constant influence, particularly his project of overcoming/ deconstructing Greek metaphysics. Husserl, whom I studied in a more detailed and painstaking fashion, taught me certain methodological prudence and reserve, rigorous techniques of unravelling and formulating questions'.[49]

Deconstruction is best understood as a textual strategy. Derrida's writing refuses to accept a distinction between "literature" and "criticism." Derrida feels that deconstruction is not reducible to a method. Deconstruction is not something critics do to a text, but a way of highlighting things that texts do to themselves and each other. It questions the priority of things, which are set up as original, natural, and/ self-evident. Deconstruction shows how texts subvert, exceed, or even overturn their author's stated purposes or intentions. In the contemporary scene, specifically in the literary scene Deconstructive readings are part of larger interpretive strategies. This theory often destabilizes hierarchical or binary oppositions like male and female, elite and popular culture, straight and gay, etc.,. Though much of Poststructuralist thought inspired by Derrida it is a philosophical development with which Derrida's work is associated.

Derrida is an inheritor of the thought of Nietzsche. His reading of Saussure takes the form deconstruction of metaphysics that seem functioning in Ferdinand de Saussure's "Course in General Linguistics"(1916). This metaphysic can also be seen in operation in the writings of Saussure's structuralist inheritors. Allen Thiher says,'Derrida's basic project demands the attempt to think through metaphysics to a position that cannot be easily defined within the limits of language, since language itself is a product of metaphysic'.[50]

However, Derrida's work is not another theoretical activity. In fact, his essays are closer to a literary form of contestation and questioning. His essays act like disfiguring mirrors that reflect back toward theory of distorted image that reveals what was concealed in his thought. In Derrida's writing, the distinction between philosophy and literature is blurred.

Derrida demonstrates the persistence of *logocentrism* in Western thought and the intractability of its paradoxes. He thinks that *logocentrism* has been an inescapable horizon of Western metaphysic, since any critique relies on logocentric concepts. According to Derrida, Saussure's "Course in General Linguistics" is a repetition or continuation of the Western metaphysics. In Saussure's attitude towards writing in opposition to speech, Derrida finds one more instance of Western metaphysics. The Western metaphysics always denigrated writing as a mere representation of the spoken word. This denigration constitutes, in the view of Derrida, *Logocentrism* or *Phonocentrism*

Derrida first came to the attention when he published two long review articles on books on the history and nature of writing, in the Parisian journal, *Critique*. These pieces formed the basis of Derrida's most important and well-known book, "Of Grammatology"[51] . This book has been considered one of the key texts in the Poststructuralism.

In a way, "Of Grammatology" is the story of how in the west *speech* has been seen as centre and the *writing* its margin or the other. In the view of Derrida, the entire Western tradition of thought from Plato to Rousseau, and the modern structuralist linguist Ferdinand de Saussure and even the anthropologist Levi-Strauss privileged speech over writing. Derrida calls this privileging as '*Logocentrism*'.

Derrida's essay "Structure, Sign and Play in the Discourse of Human Sciences[52] " is an important document in the Postmodern or Poststructuralist philosophy. The essay begins with the word "perhaps[53] ", before that Derrida quotes Montaigne's statement, "We need to interpret interpretations more than to interpret things". The word "perhaps" signifies that in the world of deconstruction everything is ambiguous, one cannot make definitive statements. It is a world of uncertainty. The meaning is contingent and nothing is stable.

According to Derrida, there is a major shift or break in the basic structure of the Western philosophy. This break is a moment where the whole way of philosophy thought about itself shifted. This shift or rupture was that it became possible to think about "the structurality of the structure"[54]. In other words, this is the moment when structuralism pointed out that language was indeed a structure, when it became possible to think about the idea of structure itself, and how every system had a structure. Derrida, here is talking about the moment when philosophers began to see their philosophical systems, not as absolute truth, but as systems, or as structures.

Derrida declares that all structures have some sort of centres. He says, 'Nevertheless, up to the event which I wish to mark out and define, structure-or rather the structurality of structure-although it has always been at work, has always been neutralized or reduced, and this by a process of giving it a centre or of referring it to a point of presence, a fixed origin. The function of this centre was not only to orient, balance, and organize the structure-one cannot in fact conceive of an unorganised structure- but above all to make sure that the organizing principle of the structure would limit what we might call the *play* of the structure'.[55]

Though Derrida was talking about philosophical systems or structures, his idea is applicable to almost every structure. There is something that all elements in the structure refer to, something that keeps its shape or parts together. This something is the centre that holds the whole structure together, and in this way limits the movements of the elements in the structure. Derrida calls this movement "play". In the view of Derrida, the holding together of the other elements is acceptable in the case of a concrete structure like a building, but it is unacceptable in the case of philosophical systems. The lack of "play" is not good to any philosophical system.

Derrida says the centre is the crucial part of any structure. It is the point where one cannot substitute anything. An example for this may be philosophical system or belief system. In the belief system or religion god is the centre of everything. Anything that happens in the world will be referred back to god as the central cause of the event. Nothing in the religion is equal to god and nothing can replace Him, the central cause of all things.

The centre of any structure or system is something that has no equivalent value; nothing can be exchanged for it. It is the ultimate referent for everything in the system. The centre a strange part of a structure. It is strange because it is a part of the structure, at the same time it is not part of it, because it is the governing element. Hence, it is able to escape the structurality of the structure. Derrida says, 'Thus it has always been thought that the centre, which is by definition unique, constituted that very thing within a structure which while governing the structure, escapes the structurality. This is why classical thought concerning structure could say that the centre is paradoxically, *within* the structure and *outside* it'.[56]

As the centre limits the play, it has been considered useful. According to Derrida, all systems want ultimately to be fixed, to be stable and to have play. Before the "rupture" (that happened with the advent of structuralism), what happened in the history of philosophy was a continual substitution of one centered system for the other centered systems. The eantered systems in the western philosophy can be classified. From the early Christian era to the Eighteenth century god has been positioned as the centre and cause of all things. From eighteenth century to the Enlightenment or to the late eighteenth century : In this period god has been removed from the centre and rationality or reason was positioned as centre and the cause of all things.

In fact, it is structuralism that made possible to see philosophical systems as all insisting on a centre, though a different kind of centre. The event or the rupture that Derrida was talking is the moment when it was possible to see for the first time that the centre was a construct. The assumption that the centre, either god or rationality, is the basis or origin for all things in the system makes the centre irreplaceable and gives centre what Derrida calls "central presence" or full presence. This central presence is never defined in relation to other things, by negative value.

Derrida calls the idea of centre, in semiotic term, as "transcendental signified. This is ultimate source of meaning and cannot be represented by any other signifier. The word signified contains another word "sign". For example, the "sign" 'dog' is made up of the sound 'dog'-which is the signifier –and the concept or meaning of 'dog', which is the "signified". The actual animal is called the referent. A "transcendental signified" is a meaning that lies beyond everything else. The best example for the "transcendental signified" is *logos* or the idea of god. The *logos* lies beyond entire universe. But it is this *logos* that limits the free play of the whole structure of universe. However, the god cannot be represented by any signifier, yet god is the thing that all signifiers in a system ultimately refer. It is He who makes the rules, but He is beyond the rules. Though He is beyond the structure of the world, He is its centre.

Derrida says that the thinkers like Nietzsche, Freud and Heidegger tried to talk and think about systems without making a new system with centre. They failed in their attempts, because they positioned their own new systems. Derrida says, 'We have no language-no syntax, no lexicon-which is foreign to this history; we can pronounce not a single destructive proposition which has not already has to slip into the form, the logic, and the implicit postulations of precisely what it seeks to contest'.[57]

Derrida's example is to think about the concept of "sign". As soon as one tries to say that all signs are equal and that there is no "transcendental signified" that holds together any semiotic system and signifying systems have no centres one is implicitly telling that all signs have infinite play. If anybody assumes that sign has some fixed meaning that one is back in the system one is trying to deconstruct.

According to Derrida, during the long history of philosophy some names like Ideal, the World Spirit, Mind, the Divine Will, and Consciousness acted as centres. Western thought is based on the idea of a centre, an Origin, a Truth, an Ideal Form, a Fixed Point, an Essence, a God and a presence have stood for an inner "transcendental signifieds. These inner principles of words express themselves as centres, hence they involve "metaphysics of presence". Derrida's contention is that almost all Western philosophers rely on the assumption of an immediately available area of certainty. For example for hundreds of years, much of Western culture cantered on Christianity and Christ. In the view of Derrida, the problem with the centres is that they attempt to exclude others, in doing so they repress, marginalize others.

Derrida tries to put in question the entire metaphysical assumptions of Western Philosophy. As we have already seen the concept unity, centre and presence have been basic issues in the Western philosophy. Structuralist also treated the term 'structure' as an unproblematic and stable centre of meaning. Derrida advocates that we have to resist the thinkers who tried to impose upon us one pole in the binary oppositions like body/ soul, good/bad, nature/culture, and man/woman. Recently many writers found out numerous binary oppositions. The list is unending : Good/ evil, original/copy, primary/secondary, inside/outside, reality/appearance, essence/accident, soul/body, pure/corrupted, father/son, male/ female,speech/writing,centre/margin,normal/deviant,natural/ unnatural,white/black,self/other,truth/faction,Philosophy/myth,sciences/ humanities,master/slave, base/superstructure. These binaries are in operation in the Western thinking since Plato. Derrida's analysis undermines the binary opposition in the Western thought, allows the free flow of signifiers, and breaks the structured thinking. Derrida deconstructs the binary oppositions of the Western philosophy. Binary means "composed of two, or twofold."[58]

As we have already seen, the concept of binary oppositions is central to structuralism. For deconstructionists and postmodernists the concept binary opposition represents nostalgia for 'self'-presence' or 'self-centring'. In fact, deconstruction undermines such analogical oppositions and reveal how a text undermines the imposition of binary structure on it through *aporia* and indeterminacy.

For example Western thinking privileges 'speech' at the expense of 'writing'. It believes that 'speech' offers true 'presence' while 'writing' is impure and supplementary. Derrida calls this privileging of speech "Phonocentrism', which is a particular example of what he calls *logocentrism*.

Logocentrism and Phonocentrism

'*Logocentrism* is coined by Derrida. It comes from the Greek word *logos*, which means word, truth, reason and law. The Greeks thought of *logos* as a cosmic principle hidden deep within human beings, within speech and within the natural universe. "*Logocentric* means literally 'cantered on the word'"'[59]. But in Derrida, *logocentrism* implies all forms of human thought that is based on a desire for truth. Derrida proves how *logocentrism* has been the characteristic of the western thought since Plato. In the view of Derrida *Phonocentrism* is sub category of *logocentrism*. *Phonocentrism* means centred on the sound/speech. *Phonocentrism* indicates the primacy of speech over writing. *Phonocentrism* has also been another characteristic of Western thought since Plato. The *logocentrics* believe that truth is voice, the word, a central idea or an origin.

Logocentrism is the supposition that words can unproblematically communicate meanings present in the individual's mind such that the listener, or reader, receives them in the same way as the speaker/hearer intended. Words and meanings are therefore considered to have an internal stability. This is a standard assumption of discourse in Western culture, but one that has come under attack from Derrida.

In his "Of Grammatology" Derrida looks particularly at the opposition speech/writing, saying that speech always is seen as more important than writing. In all most, all the linguistic theories speech has been positioned as the primary form of language, and writing is just the transcription of speech.

According to Derrida speech gets privileged because it is associated with presence-for there to be spoken language, somebody has to be there to speaking. The idea is that the spoken word guarantees the existence of somebody doing the speaking; hence, it reinforces all those great humanist ideas that there is self, which the origin of what is being said is. Derrida calls this idea of self that has to be there to speak as a part of the metaphysics of 'presence'. The idea of 'presence' is central to all systems of Western philosophy, from Plato to Saussure. Presence is part of a binary opposition, presence/absence, in which speech is always privileged over writing. Derrida calls this privileging of speech over writing as *logocentrism*.

Writing on Derrida's concept of '*logocentrism*', Christopher Johnson says, 'Probably Derrida's most sustained and systematic critique of *logocentrism* is to be found in "Of Grammatology", published 1967. In this now seminal work, Derrida demonstrates how, throughout the history of the Western thought, writing in the common sense of the word has been consistently involved in a series of oppositions assigning to it only secondary status in man's spiritual, intellectual and practical experience...In "Of Grammatology", Derrida's critique of this reduction or repression of writing takes the form of a critical engagement with a series of examples or 'symptoms' of the logocentric paradigm, from Plato and Rousseau through to Saussure and Levi-Strauss'.[60]

According to Derrida, one of the most effective ways in which the logocentric bias of Western metaphysic operates is in the conventional priority of speech over writing. Derrida equates *logocentrism* with Phonocentrism. This can be seen in the Western thought. In "Plato's

Pharmacy[61]" Derrida begins his dissemination of Western metaphysic. In fact, it is Derrida's unique reading of the *Phaedrus*. *Phaedrus* is one of the dialogues of Socrates, which were written by Plato.

As Socrates and Plato are seminal and the fathers of meaning in the Western thought, Derrida disseminates them in his book. He takes a lot of pain in this dissemination. According to Christopher Norris,' A good place to start with 'Plato's Pharmacy', the reading of Plato's dialogue the *Phaedrus,* which occupies Derrida for some hundred pages of closely argued textual and analytic commentary. It is an obvious jumping-off point for several connected reasons. First, because Derrida is here engaged with something like a mythic inaugural moment in the 'logocentric' epoch whose effects (as he argues) reach down from Plato to the present day'.[62]

In Plato Derrida discovers a certain ideal scene of instruction, one that concerns the priority of speech over writing and the philosophical, political and even moral dangers of thinking to invert that priority. In the view of Norris this essay of Derrida is the most challenging to traditional philosophy. According to Derrida, Plato believed that truth being expressed in a "silent dialogue of the soul with the self", that is, an immediate presence of the speaker to himself. He thought that truth is still pure of self-immediacy. Because it has not yet be corrupted or contaminated by the alienation or confusion. In such a silent speech meaning is still identical with it self. There is no difference between what it is and what it says. As it could keep other at a distance, the self here can claim to the uncorrupted sovereignty of a single truth.

In analysing, the *Phaedru* Derrida's method can be understood as twofold : first, he gives a reading of the Phaedrus as Plato would have us read it and then he analyses Plato's views on *writing,* especially as Plato and Socrates use it in the binary opposition, speaking/writing. Plato prioritised speech, as it is existential witness to the immediate experience, condemned, and treated writing with great suspicion. He accuses writing of a certain parricide. For Plato,' written signs are like illegitimate offspring who have divested themselves of the authors who originally fathered them'.[63]

Plato often calls writing a *Pharmakan.* The word *Pharmakan* got several meanings like, *allurement, magician, poisoner and wizard.* Derrida identifies some more meanings to the word like *charm, philter, drug, and remedy.*

For Derrida the term *Pharmakan* is ambiguous, as it gives the meaning of both *cure* and *poison.* Writing for Plato is also an evil disease. It is corrupted as it is removed from the authoritative presence that is from the original intension of the speaker. Writing displaces the meaning outside of its author, in this way it is depriving of its paternal tutelage and exposing it to error. In short, for Plato,' writing is *both* the disease which alienates speech as immediate self-presence and the cure which permits it to achieve a durability beyond to temporal /spatial confines of its original expression'.[64]

Derrida deconstructs Plato's metaphysics by demonstrating that Platonic metaphysic requires writing to preserve speech, and to re-present its original presence in its very absence. According to Derrida, Plato's treatment of writing sets a pattern for similar encounters down through the history of Western thought. Derrida traces this tradition in much more intense manner in the works of Kant, Rousseau, Hegel, Husserl and other thinkers. As Rousseau had much to say about writing, Rousseau figures so central in the texts of Derrida. Writing for Rousseau was a dangerous supplement. It always threatens to poison the springs of authentic human understanding. Writing belongs to a stage of cultural development, which emerged by spoiling natural state of human communication in face-to-face contact. Writing invades the happy sphere of one-to-one familiar address, and separates individuals and imposes an alien order on them. According to Derrida, Rousseau is repeating the same logocentric logic of Plato. Derrida says, 'Self-presence, transparent proximity in the face-to-face of countenances and the immediate range of the voice, this determination of social authenticity is therefore classic : Rousseauistic but already the inheritor of Platonism…'[65]

Derrida argues that writing, which Rousseau thought as an instrument *par excellence* of social control, was always there in Rousseau's reflection on society and language. As it is there with Plato and Saussure, it is there in Rousseau also. In the view of Derrida, 'Rousseau condemns writing as destruction of presence and as disease of speech. He rehabilitates it to the extent that it promises the reappropriation of that of which speech allowed itself to be disposed. But by what, if not already a writing older than speech and already installed in that place?'[66]

Drrida quotes some important paragraphs from the "Confessions" of Rousseau, which bring out his dependence on writing. In these paragraphs, Rousseau seeks to guarantee the reality of his experience. Norris explains, 'Writing is the act of belated self vindication by which Rousseau will at last show up in a favourable light, freed from the irksome constraints of everyday behaviour'.[67]

Derrida deconstructs the Platonic hierarchy of speech over writing. Richard says, 'Derrida also battles against the 'homocentric' bias that privileges speech over writing in the Western philosophical tradition. Beginning as far back as Plato, writing has been viewed as a poor substitute for the spoken word because the speaker is no longer present to 'correct' misunderstandings. However, Derrida challenges this trust in phonocentricity, pointing out what that '*différance*' exists even when we speak to ourselves with the ideal of self-presence as soliloquy. Thus in speech there is '*archi-writing*'.i.e an essential difference between distinct (and absent) acoustic signifiers allowing for possible meaning. By contrast, a text exhibits an autonomy that openly admits it requires neither the presence of a speaking subject nor the referential presence of the 'matter' of the text'.[68]

The term 'différance' is coined by Derrida, both signals how language works and is also another term for manoeuvres and movements of deconstruction. Derrida uses it to illustrate, following the example of Saussure, how a word always depends for its meaning not on its natural bond with the real, but on which it is different from. It indicates the perpetual movements and the potential slippage of meaning in the language. In a way, the French word 'différance' means 'to differ, 'to delay' and 'to postpone'. "Spoken French makes no phonetic distinction between the endings'-ence' and '-ance'; the word registers as *difference*. This undetected difference shows up only in writing"[69] . When spoken all the différance is lost, the différance can be seen but not heard.

In fact, Derrida coined the word in order to name how signs function differentially in opposition to other signs and that at the same time they depend on deferring and referring to other signs for their meaning. Toril Moi explains Derrida's neologism in lucid terms. She explains: 'The basic significance of the Derridean term '*différance*'... Spelt with an 'a' to distinguish it-in writing, not in speech-from the normal French word difference (différence), it acquires more active sense of ending '-ance' in

French, and can therefore be translated both as 'difference' and 'defferal' in English.

As we have seen, the interplay between presence and absence that produces meaning is posited as one of *deferral* : meaning is never truly present, but is only constructed through the potentially endless process of referring to other, absent signifiers. The 'next' signifiers can in a sense be said to give meaning to the 'previous' one, and so on *ad infinitum.* There can thus be no 'transcendental signified' where the process of deferral somehow would come to an end. Such a transcendental would have to be meaningful in itself, fully present to itself, require no origin and no end other than itself. An obvious example of such a 'transcendental signified' would be the Christian concept of God as Alpha Omega, and the origin of meaning and final end of the world. Similarly, the traditional view of the author as the source and meaning of his or her own text casts the author in the role of transcendental signified".[70] The ultimate aim of Derrida in introducing the concept *différance* is to declare that writing is not a copy speech.

The process of deferring applies to the written and spoken word : defferal/*différance.* Thus, meaning is endlessly differed since each word leads to another word in the system of signification. In Derrida's view, a text, be it philosophical or literary, is an endless sequence of signifiers. These signifiers have no ultimate or determinate meanings.

Quite interestingly Derrida himself explains the reason and intention in introducing the concept 'différance' in an interview given to the French post-structuralist feminist Julia Kristeva. He says, ' The reduction of writing-as the reduction of the exteriority of the signifier-was part and parcel of phonologism and *logocentrism*. We know how Saussure, according to the traditional operation that was also Plato's, Aristotle's, Rousseau's, Hegel's, Husserl's, etc., excludes writing from the field of linguistics-from language and speech-as a phenomenon of exterior representation, both useless and dangerous'.[71]

Derrida further says,' Actually, it could be shown, as I have attempted to do, that there is no purely phonetic writing, and that phonologism is less consequence of the practice of the alphabet in a given culture than a certain ethical or axiological *experience* of this practice...

Of course, it is not a question of resorting to the same concept of writing and of simply inverting the dissymmetry that has now become problematical. It is a question, rather, of producing a new concept of writing. This concept can be called *gram* or *différance*.[72]

In fact, signification is always a function of largely unconscious differential relations among signifiers, speakers, hearers, situations and contexts. These situations unfold in social spaces and historical times. It is not possible to master them completely. The process of signification is a play of differences. In that way no sign can function as sign without referring to other elements, which are not themselves present. In fact, every element is : 'constituted on the basis of the trace within the other elements of chain'.[73]

As every signifier carries with it a trace of the differences it is impossible to achieve the univocal meaning. Beyond any present meaning lies the absent, unspoken and unthought, and uncomprehended network of conditions on which it depends. As a result, our meaning always escapes any unitary conscious grasp we have it. Because language as writing inevitably harbours the possibility of an endless dissemination of sense, an infinite multiplicity of reinterpretations.

Philosophy is a kind of writing, according to Derrida, that has been interpreted on the lines that deny the play of *différance*. Throughout its history, it has tried one method or the other to freeze up this play of *différance*. This freezing up is a kind of repression. However, this repression has its effects in the form of paradoxes, internal contradictions. The task of Derrida's deconstruction is to shed light on these and expose them. The intention behind this exposition is, not to produce a new method or theory; rather it is aimed at undermining the pretensions of theoretical mastery. According to Derrida, 'it inaugurates the destruction, not the demolition but de-sedimentation, the deconstruction, of all the significations that have their sources in that of the logos. Particularly the signification of *truth*'.[74]

In the structuralist thought, specifically in the thought of Saussure, the relation between signifier and signified is a stable one. But for Derrida, the poststructuralist, the meaning is always a state of flux and contention. When one thinks of a 'dog', one is thinking what it is not : a cat, hog, or whatever. When one tries to fix a meaning or tries to impose, something singular one is achieving it by silencing the other or different meanings. It is not possible to have the idea of 'good' without it's opposite 'bad'. Likewise, one cannot have the idea of 'man' or 'maleness' without 'woman' and 'womanliness'. The more emphatically the meaning is articulated or asserted the more significant are the areas of difference that enclose it. Derrida's Deconstruction can be described as a theory of reading which aims to undermine the logic of opposition within texts. According to Derrida, texts are not about what they seem to be, he searches weak points or margins or fractures in the texts where the otherness of the text is concealed. Derrida reads the texts to bring out the concealed thing or meaning out. This kind of fracturing to reveal the otherness of meaning is called *aporia*, which means in Greek 'doubt'.

For Derrida there is always a logic of the 'supplement' inscribed in any pretext toward clear conceptual identity. There is always something, which escapes and subverts the logic of binary opposition and it is these excesses and resistances, which Derrida turns against metaphysical thinking. By immersing himself within the very structure of a texts argument, Derrida attempts an immanent critique, which would expose its contradictions, limitations and presuppositions. It is not that a text can be deconstructed because of weakness or flaw in a thinker's argument, which can then be remedied. It is rather that there is something structural in the very nature of writing that necessitates contradiction and logic that Derrida attempts to articulate.

By seizing on authorial repressions, footnotes, and other seemingly minor details, often confined to the margins of a text, Derrida tries to demonstrate by a reversal of traditional logic how what has been posited as central, or primary, and therefore dependent upon, what has been constructed as secondary, marginal or derivate. What Derrida call *aporias* are those moments where oppositions are held in mutual suspension, neither term of which can be guaranteed structuring qualitative superiority. Hence, Derrida's logic replaces the logic of either/or with a logic of both/and and neither/nor.

Derrida undermines the idea of finding a correct meaning in text in two ways. First, because the language, which makes up a text, is never self-contained, rather it is always spilling over into different meanings : it is liable to *dissemination*. Secondly, the language of criticism or interpretations is itself subject to the conditions of *différance* and the more it attempts to a specific closure, the more other meanings which are excluded demand to be heard. That is why texts do not have just one meaning, rather they have multiple meanings.

The significance of Derrida's writing is that in his work he raised questions which are pertinent to writing and to textuality that tend to be ignored or sublimated in metacommentary on texts. In addition, he has developed a particular alert and influential reading method. But he never treated his method as absolute. In fact, he never agreed to call it a method. In a way, his work epitomizes tremendous self-limitation. In this context the opinion of the American philosopher Richard Rorty (1931-) is very important. He says, ' Derrida has no interest in bringing "his philosophy" into accord with common sense. He is not writing a philosophy. He is not giving an account of anything : he is not offering a comprehensive view of anything. He is not protesting against the *errors* of a philosophical school. He is however, protesting against the notion that the philosophy of language hooks on to the world, is something more than one more quaint little genre, that it is first philosophy. But the protest is not because he has a different candidate for the position of "first philosophy," it is against the notion of "first philosophy'.[75]

Jean Françoise Lyotard

Although a political activist of Marxist persuasion in the 1950s and 1960s, Lyotard became the non-Marxist philosopher of Postmodernity in the 19080s. The early works of Lyotard were strongly influenced by Phenomenology, Marxism and Nietzsche. But in 1980 he carried a resolute postmodern turn in theory. He is celebrated as the postmodern theorist *par excellence*. His book "The Post-modern Condition" introduced the term 'postmodern' to a wider public. Lyotard published a series of books that promote postmodern position in theory, politics and aesthetics. More than anyone else, Lyotard has championed a break with modernity, modern theories and methods. It is Lyotard who has championed, popularised and disseminated postmodern alternatives.

His "The Postmodern Condition" attacked the legitimating myths of modern age, the progressive liberation of humanity through science, and the idea that philosophy can restore to unity, to learning and develop universally valid knowledge for humanity. His theory is identified with the critique of universal knowledge and foundationalism. Lyotard believes that we can no longer talk about a totalising idea of reason for there is no reason only reasons. In an interview given to Willem Van Reijen and

Dick Veerman he said, 'I think that, in effect, a part of the attack against the position developed in "The Postmodern Condition" my critics generally not having read the other works-bears the marks of a summary and totalising idea of reason. I would oppose simply with the following principle (which seems to more rationalist than they think) : there is no reason, only reasons'.[76]

Lyotard in "The Postmodern Condition" reflects on science, the changing nature of knowledge in computerized world, the difference between narrative knowledge and scientific knowledge. He says that in the last four or five decades the leading sciences and the technologies have become increasingly concerned with language. For example, the theories of linguistics, problems of communication, concepts and their languages, cybernetics, problems of translation, information storage data. The nature of knowledge is also changing in this context of general transformation. The status of knowledge alters as societies enter what is known as the postmodern age. Lyotard says, 'Our working hypotheses is that the status of knowledge is altered as societies enter what is known as postindustrial age and cultures enter into what is known as postmodern age'.[77]

Locating the beginning of the postmodern age in 1950s, Lyotard argues that the era is marked by the demise of *grandes histories* or grand histories, or 'an incredulity towards metanarratives'[78] and the emergence of *petites histories* or micro narratives in their place. In fact, there is disillusionment with the ambitious 'total explanations of reality, such as those offered by science, or religion or political projects like communism. In place of these, there is a growing awareness and preference for small-scale and singles-issue preoccupations.

Lyotard makes a number of predictions. He says that the old principle that the acquisition of knowledge is indissociable form the training of minds or individuals is becoming obsolete and knowledge ceases to be an end itself. In fact, it is produced in order to be sold. Computerized knowledge had already become the principle force of production. Knowledge will be the major component in the worldwide competition for power and it is imaginable that nation states will one-day fight for control over information, just as they fought for control over territories in the past.

Lyotard's book is a highly polemical attack on the discourse of modernity. As we have seen earlier, for Lyotard the postmodern condition is marked by a crisis in the status of knowledge in Western societies. This is expressed in the observation of the book as 'incredulity towards metanarratives' and obsolesces of the metanarrative apparatus of legitimation. In other words, knowledge in the postmodern era can no longer be legitimised according to the great narratives that have the Western knowledge to date, like the notion of progress embedded in the Enlightenments, or the notion of social liberation through history embedded in Marxism or the release from unconscious trauma harboured by Freudian theory.

Lyotard considers the above narratives violent and tyrannical as they impose a totalising pattern and universality on actions, events and things. Instead of these totalising patterns, he suggests to utilize local narratives to explain things. In that way knowledge can only be partial, fragmented and incomplete. Lyotard's proposal is regarded as a radically new form of epistemological freedom, which resists the dominance of overarching patterns.

Lyotard is suspicious of all claims of proof or truth. In his view, 'Scientists, technicians, and instruments are purchased not to find truth, but augment power'.[79]

Beneath the conspicuous objectivity, in the truth claims, there lies a buried and dominant discourse of 'real politik'. He calls it 'the exercise of power'.[80] In the view of Lyotard, metanarratives operate through inclusion and exclusion as homogenizing forces and marshal the heterogeneity into ordered realms. In the name of universal principles and general goals, these metanarratives silence and exclude other discourses. Postmodernism signals the collapse of all universalistic metanarratives with the privileged truth to tell. It invites the plurality of voices from the margins, insists cultural diversity, accepts heterogeneity, and rejects homogeneity.

Legitimation of any sort is always an issue of power. The book "The Postmodern Condition" deals with that aspect. Delegitimation of grand narratives is the basic argument of the book. Lyotard thinks, 'We no longer have recourse to grand narratives, we can resort neither to the dialectic of Spirit nor even to the emancipation of humanity as a validation for postmodern scientific discourse. But as we have just seen, the little narrative (petit récit) remains the quintessential form of imaginative invention, most particularly in science".[81]

Lyotard focuses much on science in the book, as it is assigned an important role in the Enlightenment. The thinkers of Enlightenment thought that science would play a central role in gradual emancipation of humankind. Because of this view, science has assumed the status of a metanarratives. Lyotard, on the contrary thought that science has lost its way, and 'its goal is no longer truth, but deformity'.[82] 'Science has become less philosophical and more pragmatic'.[83]

In the view of Lyotard, scientific knowledge does not represent the totality of the knowledge. It always existed in competition and conflict with another kind of language. Lyotard calls this knowledge as narrative knowledge. The pre-eminence of narrative forms, like popular stories, myths, legends, can be seen in traditional societies. Lyotard makes distinction between scientific discourse and non-narrative discourse and discusses the retreat of narrative in the face of those abstract, logical and denotative procedures generally associated with science. He even says that scientific knowledge cannot know and make known that it is true knowledge without resorting to the narrative knowledge, which from the point of view of science no knowledge at all.

In "The Postmodern Condition" Lyotard explains the difference between modern and postmodern aesthetics. The difference is that Postmodernism is characterized by a new concept of sublime, which attempts to put forward the unpresentable. In the appendix to the book "The Postmodern Condition", titled "Answering the Question : what is postmodernism?" Lyotard makes a paradoxical claim - 'A work can become modern only if it is postmodern. Postmodernism is thus understood is not modernism at its end but is the nascent state, and this state is constant'.[84]

In his view, modernism is an aesthetic of the sublime, though nostalgic one. It allows the unpresentable to be put forward only as the missing contents, but the form, because of its recognizable consistency, continues to offer to the reader or viewer matter for solace or pleasure.

To be specific, Lyotard's concept of postmodernism is aesthetic rather than the 'historical'. He considers postmodernism a particular form rather than a particular epoch and reads it as less a period of time than as a set of strategies employed by artists to infuse a sense of the sublime.

His argument for the little narratives is in the interest that the little narratives resist closure and totality and emphasize the specificity and singularity of every event, whether ethical, political or aesthetic. According to him there is no longer an ultimate authority that speaks for all human beings from universal perspective without already invoking some ideological formation, hence he opposes any kind of global categorization.

Tim Woods summarizes the important concepts of Lyotard's postmodernism in the following way :

1. "It is primarily' incredulity towards metanarratives and an anti-foundationalism.
2. Although it presents to unpresentable, it does not do so nostalgically, nor does it seek to solace in so doing.
3. It contains pleasure and pain, in a reintroduction of the sublime.
4. It does not seek to give reality but to invent allusions to the conceivable, which cannot be presented.
5. It actively reaches out heterogeneity, pluralism and constant innovation.
6. It is to be thought of not as an historical epoch, but rather as an aesthetic practice.
7. It challenges the legitimation of positive science".[85]

Even though Lyotard rejected grand narratives or central authorities of any kind, he believes that there is a scope to construct value judgments. Lyotard discusses this problem is his book "Just Gaming" (1979), which he wrote in collaboration with J.L.Thebaud. The book argues that it is possible to make value judgments, but based only on specific cases or to make these judgments on a 'case by case' basis. In this kind of situation, one is admitting the absence of any absolute criterion. In this type of condition, Lyotard refers us to paganism. In his view paganism is an ideal of how we ought to operate in a postmodern world

Stuart Sim explains Lyotard's paganism in a concrete way. He says, 'Lyotard terms the state where we make judgments without criterion as paganism. In effect, this describes the postmodern condition, since in that we no longer have any universal theories to fall back on in order to validate our criterion (whether they be theories of truth or politics). We are reduced to making judgments on a case by case basis, which for Lyotard is the only honest way to proceed...Lyotard wishes to introduce this kind of pragmatism into public life in a more general way, since it moves away from an uncritical and slavish reliance on universal theories(grand theories). In his reading of recent history, it has been this uncritical reliance, which has been the source of most of our socio-political problems, in things done in the name of theories such as Marxism, Communism and Socialism. A 'pagan' society would reject such authorities and examine each demand for political action on its own merits, the assumption being that this would result in a more just society than one based on rigid rules and regulations. Judgments without preconceived criteria thus become one of the defining characteristics of a postmodern society'.[86]

What Lyotard, ultimately espousing, here is anti-foundationalism, a rejection of the idea that there are foundations to our system of thought or belief that they lie beyond question.

Lyotard's another important work is "The Differend". A 'differend' in his view, is a dispute that arises when each part is employing a form of language or discourse incommensurable with the other. Each party inhabits what Lyotard calls a 'phrase regime', whose objections are incommensurable with the other and neither of which has any ethical right to make the other conform to its desires. According to Lyotard, the 'phrase' constitutes the basic element of discourse, and it is to consider being open, since it can link to other phrases, thus creating new states of affairs. The term can also be translated as a 'sentence'. 'Phrase regimes' have serious consequences in social and political life.

In political practice, one part to the dispute enforces its view on the other 'resolving' the dispute to its own advantage. One 'phrase regime' exerts domination over the other. In the every day life, the life of an exploited employ can be referred. If an exploited employ who cannot gain redress for her/his exploitation if she/he brings an action against her/his employer. This is because the court that hears her/his plea is set upon the principle that such exploitation is legal. Here the employer's 'phrase regime' is excluding the other from having a proper voice.

The ultimate aim of philosophy or the business of philosophy is to help suppressed 'phrase regimes' find their voices. Lyotard thus brings philosophical politics on the scene. Stuart Sim says,' Philosophical politics, the search for the new, counter-cultural, phrase regimes, can be considered the highest expression of Postmodern philosophy.[87]

Jean Baudrillard

Jean Baudrillard is the most radical among the postmodern philosophers. Baudrillard's conception of postmodernism is founded on three key ideas : simulation, implosion and hyperreality. Like Lyotard, Baudrillard claims that we have entered a new postmodern era of simulations, which is governed, by information and signs and a new cybernetic technology. Baudrillard has moved from being a sociologist of consumer society to being the most notorious and immoderate of the thinkers associated with Postmodernism.

The account Baudrillard develops of contemporary mass culture and the mass media is far-reaching and extravagant in its claims, and has had an important influence across a number of disciplines, especially Cultural Studies, Film, and Literary Criticism.

Although Baudrillard utilises the language of various disciplines in his works, his application of semiotics to the structure of society is widely considered his most significant contribution to social theory. Semiotics distinguishes between the signifier, usually a word or an image, and the thing itself, known as the signified, or referent. According to Baudrillard, the culture of late capitalism is dominated by simulacra, floating signifiers, cut off from their referents that create a hyperreal effect and destroy the possibility of true knowledge.

Baudrillard's writing career began, like that of many French theorists in the 1960s, with a complex argument with Marxism. The shape of Baudrillard's social theory is determined by the route of his detachment with Marxism. In a series of books Baudrillard undertakes to liberate social analysis from the narrow determinism of a Marxism that reduced culture to the secondary effects of economic factors and relations. In "The System of Objects" (1968) and "Consumer Society" (1970),[88] Baudrillard argues that in a society organized on the principle of consumption, rather than production, the economic categories of need, supply, distribution, and profit are inadequate for analysing the nature and function of objects and commodities.

According to Baudrillard the circulation of material goods in late twentieth-century developed economies is comprehensible only as the operation and diversification of linguistic codes. His most important contribution to the theory of consumer society is his insistence that consumption has little to do with the satisfaction of needs, actual or artificial. His argument is that consumer culture creates and maintains a universal code or system of exchangeability between commodities. The desire of the consumer is not for this or that object or element within the code, but rather for inclusion within the system of consumption as a whole. Such inclusion is a powerful means of social control and is a logical and necessary extension of the rationalization of the means of production.

In his "For a Critique of the Political Economy of the Sign" (1972), and "The Mirror of Production" (1973), Baudrillard mounts a devastating critique on the idea of production, which is so central to Marxist sociology. His main focus in these two books is on the Marxist theory of value, and especially on the fundamental division it draws between use values, which are held to be immediate, authentic, and exchange values, which come into being with the institution of the market, and are artificial, distorted, and exploitative. Baudrillard's argument is that all needs of whatever kind are always produced as the effect of the code of consumption. The notion of use value therefore, offers no political promise of redemption from the artificialities and distortions of the market. Because the use value is produced as a derivative or precipitate of the market. In his view, use value has no autonomy; it is only the satellite and alibi of exchange value.

In another work "Symbolic Exchange and Death" (1976) Baudrillard undermines all the values and principles of radical philosophies. In his view there is no possibility of defining authentic human needs and values under market conditions that seem so totally to have abolished the distinction between the authentic and the artificial. He says, "The era of simulation is thus everywhere initiated by the interchangeability of previously contradictory or dialectically opposed terms. Everywhere the same "genesis of simulacra :" the interchangeability of the beautiful and the ugly in fashion; of the right and the left in the politics; of the true and false in every media message; of the useful and useless at the level of objects; and of nature and culture at every level of meaning. All the great humanist criteria of value, all the values of a civilization of moral, aesthetic and practical judgement, vanish in our system of images and signs. Everything becomes undecidable. This is characteristic effect of the domination of the code, which is based everywhere on the principle of neutralization and indifference. This is the generalized brothel of capital : not the brothel of prostitution but the brothel of substitution and interchangeability."[89]

Baudrillard's view in "Symbolic Exchange and Death" (1976) is that the system of symbolic exchange at work in contemporary consumer society is so all-encompassing. The only principle of resistance lies in the destruction or negation of all value or utility whatsoever. The only alternative value is the negation. In a political sense, highly unpromisingly, the only challenge to the dominance of symbolic value is death. Baudrillard moves close to the extreme political positions. He develops the theoretical analysis of the present with which he has come to be most clearly identified, the analysis of the regime of the simulacrum, a shadowy likeness or a deceptive substitute.

The most influential of Baudrillard's works from the 1980s is the essay "The Precession of Simulacra". In it he suggests that the dominance of signs, images, and representations in the contemporary world is such that the real has been effectively wiped out, and "truth, reference and objective causes have ceased to exist"[90] He provides a useful synopsis of the historical stages by which this condition has been reached. Initially, the sign is "the reflection of a basic reality. In the second stage, the sign "masks and prevents a basic reality" In a third stage, the sign "masks the absence of a basic reality." In the fourth stage, at which the contemporary world has arrived, and from which it can hope neither to progress nor retreat, the sign "bears no relation of any reality whatever; it is its own pure simulacrum'.[91]

Baudrillard shows the difference between simulation and imitation. Imitation keeps the distinction between the real and the false intact, even as it masks it. In simulacrum the either/or logic of real and false, truth and deceit is threatened. In this context he says, 'When the real is no longer what it used to be, nostalgia assumes its full meaning. There is a proliferation of myth of origins and signs of reality; of second-hand truth, objectivity and authenticity. There is an escalation of the true, of the lived experience; a resurrection of the figurative where the object and substance have disappeared. And there is panic-stricken production of the real and the referential, above and parallel to the panic of material production.

This is how simulation appears in the phase that concerns us : a strategy of the real, neo-real and hyperreal, whose universal double is a strategy of deterrence'.[92]

It is not that everything has become purely fictional, or without real effects, since the point about a simulation is that it is both real and unreal.

Perhaps the most telling part of Baudrillard's analysis of the effect of the waning of the sense of reality in the age of the simulacrum is his account of the "escalation of the true" which takes place as a kind of panic-stricken compensation, "a proliferation of myths of origin and signs of reality, of second-hand truth, objectivity and authenticity".[93]

In the epigraph to the book, "The Transparency of Evil" (1990) Baudrillard declares, 'Since the world is on a delusional course we must adopt a delusional standpoint towards the world". Baudrillard adopts a vital metaphor for what ails today's world. He argues that our 'social corpus has lost its natural immune powers—its salutary contact with radical otherness—and thus has been invaded by an invisible evil, pernicious and systemic : "[94] AIDS, terrorism, crack cocaine, or computer viruses . . . contain within them the whole logic of our system.

His theory not only names the various phenomena, like transsexuality, transeconomics, transaesthetics, but it also simply considers them a kind of chain reaction, that makes all valuation impossible. In his view, the 'orgy of modernism, caused the deracination of social exchange : "When things, signs or actions are freed from their respective ideas, concepts, essences, values, they embark upon an endless process of self-reproduction'.[95]

Baudrillard says that ours is an age of universal contamination, where nondifferentiated spheres overlap in a promiscuous circulation. "The law that is imposed on us is the law of the of confusion of categories. Everything is sexual. Everything is political. Everything is aesthetic. All at once".[96]

Interestingly, Baudrillard also casts his critique in aesthetic terms : he argues that in today's "transaesthetic" world, dominated by simulacra, art has been dissolved with a general aestheticization of everyday life, giving way to a pure circulation of images, a transaesthetics of triviality, of market art, designed to sell. He says, 'Art has likewise failed to realize the utopian aesthetic of modern times, to transcend itself and become an ideal form of life. (In the earlier times, of course, art had no need of self-transcendence, no need to become a totality, for such a totality already existed-in the shape of religion.) Instead of being subsumed in a transcendent ideality, art has been dissolved within the general aestheticisation of everyday life, giving way to a pure circulation of images, a transaesthetics of banality'.[97]

Baudrillard critiques the levelling of depth and perspective, claiming that "the possibility of metaphor is disappearing in every sphere [affecting] all disciplines as they lose their specificity and partake of a process of confusion and contagion. The hyper visibility of the similar leads only to the hollow aesthetic of "the look," in a kind of postmodern pornography where the undifferentiated other is objectified by the universal global gaze, as we check out the other's factitious image in a parody of desire.

In the view of Baudrillard, in the contemporary society even violence is a question of image, for the violence produced by our hypermodernity is terrorism, which depends on the medium of dissemination of its acts to create its effects. In his view terrorism is a simulacrum of violence.

Baudrillard declares even the end of political economy and the predictions of Marx on it. He says, 'Along with Marx, we too dreamt of the end of political economy –of the abolition of classes and the advent of Capital. And then we dreamt of the end of the economy in terms of a disavowal of its basic tenets—a disavowal that threw out the Marxist critique into the bargain : on this view, primacy was accorded neither to the economic nor to the political—the economy was simply ushered out as a mere epiphenomenon, vanquished by its simulacrum of itself, and by a superior logic'.[98]

Gilles Deleuze and Felix Guattari

Gilles Deleuze and Felix Guattari were also the exponents of French poststructuralist philosophical ideas. Although they have individually published many works under their own names, it is their two joint works : "Anti-Oedipus"(1972) and "A Thousand Plateaus: Capitalism and Schizophrenia"(1980) that have achieved much popularity. For their project has been a concentrated attack on what they regard as the repressive mechanisms and discourses of modernity. It is their attack on representation, the subject, a critique of the state and party idolatry of Marxism that has earned them a lot of name.

Deleuze and Guattari regard modernity as an unparalleled historical stage of domination based upon the proliferation of discourses and institutions, which seek to legitimate and normalize existing structures and states of affairs. Their critique of the capitalist era is partly based upon a rebellion against Freudian psychoanalysis, since they regard the Freudian unconscious as a capitalist construction, a result of repression produced by capitalism in the family. The tyrannical state and the Oedipalized individual have been fostered by political and psychiatric institutions, to the detriment of the human as a body of varied and unorganised desires. Like Lyotard, they enthusiastically espouse a micro-politics that seeks to precipitate radical change through liberation of desire. Postmodern existence occurs where individuals are able to surmount repressive modern forms of identity and stasis to become desiring nomads in a constant process of becoming and transformation.

"Anti-Oedipus" formed the first volume of "Capitalism and Schizophrenia", in which they developed their notion of 'schizoanalysis'. This approach articulated a new mode of postmodern self,organized around concepts of plural and multiple identities and decentred or displaced consciousnesses. They start from the basis that desire is itself revolutionary and radically subversive. Hence, society has needed to repress and control desire, to 'territorialize' it within demarcated areas and delimited structures : 'to code desire is the business of the 'socius'.. In this view, the 'socius' or communal structure within which we live is a repressive regime : it organizes social harmony not through *enabling* collective action to result from rational debate, but by preventing individual and collective desires from being allowed their freedom.

"Anti-Oedipus" is a historical analysis of the ways in which desire is channelled and controlled by different social regimes. Deleuze and Guattari understood desire as a dynamic machine, which constantly produces new connections and productions. Perceiving the libido as still fluid and as a flow prior to representation and production, 'schizoanalysis' opposes all those discourses and mechanisms, which block the flow of the unconscious. For example, the family structure is one site where individual desires are 'controlled' or 'dammed up', as certain social structures are produced and reproduced through parental roles, sibling rivalries and the imposition of gendered identities.

Contrary to conventional psychoanalysis, Deleuze and Guattari understand desire to be essential, and contend that it does not signify a lack, a subject in search of a lost object. Bodies are construed as 'desiring-machines' because machines arrange and connect flows. This 'deterritorialised' body is called the 'body-without-organs' – a body without organization, a body that casts off its socially articulated, regularized and subjectified circumstances. In this respect, schizoanalysis has various tasks that can be considered postmodern.

"A Thousand Plateaus" is the second volume on Capitalism and Schizophrenia, and continues this project of 'deterritorialising' the body. This book reinforces Deleuze and Guattari's theory of 'non-totalis-able multiplicity' based upon the concept of the 'rhizome', their new term for 'deterritorialised' movement. They argue that hitherto knowledge has been organized by systematic and hierarchical principles, as the metaphor 'tree of knowledge' indicates. In opposition to these structural metaphors of arborescence and trees, they pose the models of roots and rhizomes. In their concern to uproot these philosophical trees and to remove their foundations, the rhizome becomes a model of non-hierarchical lines that connect with others in random, unregulated relationships. Rhizomes flow in myriad directions constituting a network of multiplicities. Hence, 'rhizomatics' is a form of 'nomadic thought' opposed to the thought, which attempts to discipline and control rhizomatic movement.

Deleuze and Guattari's brand of postmodern thought seeks to liberate differences and intensities from the grip of state machines. The schizo, rhizome and nomad are all modes for Deleuze and Guattari's postmodern theme of breaking with repressive, representational identity and producing a fragmented, liberated, libidinal body. They represent emancipated, non-authoritarian modes of existence, which refuse social regulation.

To sum up : in theorizing the micro-structures of domination, Deleuze and Guattari's ideas institute a postmodern logic of difference, perspectives and fragments. According to Tim Woods, the ideas Deleuze Guattari and focus upon the following issues :

1. The institutional appropriation, taming and neutralizing of desire;
2. Championing the liberation of the body and desire;

3. The pursuit of a 'schizoanalytic' destruction of the ego and superego in favour of a dynamic unconscious;
4. The rejection of the modernist notion of the unified, rational and expressive subject and the substitution of a postmodern subjectivity which is decentred, liberated form fixed identities, and free to become dispersed and multiple.[99]

Notes

1 The Norton Anthology of Theory and Criticism, W.W.Norton & Company, New York, 2001, p. 1415

2 The Continental Philosophy Reader, Routledge, London, 1996, p. 306.

3 An Introductory Guide to Post-Structuralism and Postmodernism, The University ofGeorgia Press, 1993, p. 9.

4 The Continental Philosophy Reader, p. 329.

5 Ferdinord de Saussure (Quote page check , p. 120)

6 Modern Movements in European Philosophy : phenomenology, critical theory, structuralism, Manchester University Press, Manchester, 1994, p. 242

7 *Ibid.*, p245

8 Words in Reflection : Modern Language Theory and Postmodern Fiction, The University of Chicago Press, Chicago, 1984, p. 73

9 . Modern Movements is European philosophy, p. 250

10 Douglas Kellenr. *Media Culture : Cultural Studies, Identity and Politics between Modern and Postmodern*. London : Routledge, 1995, p. 22.

11 Douglas Kellenr. *Ibid.*, p. 23.

12 Mark Philip in The Return of Grand Theory in Human Sciences, (Ed), Quentin Skinner, Cambridge, Cambridge University Press, 1990 Canto Edition, p. 67.

13 Michel Foucault. in *Ethics : Subjectivity and Truth : The Essential works of Michel Foucault*, Vol. 1, (Ed), Paul Rabinow, London, Allen Lane, The Penguin Press, 1997, p. 312-313

14 Michel Foucault. *The Order of Things : An Archeology of the Human Sciences*, New York : Vintage Books, 1994, p. xv

15 Mark Phili, p. The Return of Grand Theory in the Human Sciences, (ed) Quentin Skinner, Cambridge : Cambridge University Edition,1990, p. 70

16 Michel Foucault. *The Order of Things*, p. ix

17 Madan Sarup *An Introductory Guide to Post- Structuralism and Postmodernism.* Athens : The University of Georgia Press, 1993, p. 58

18 Paul Hamilton. *Historicism*, London : Routledge, 1996, p. 135

19 Michel Foucault. *The Order of Things*, p. 312.

20 Michel Foucault. *Ibid.*, p, p. 385-386

21 Michel Foucault. *Ibid.*, p, p. 386-387

22 James D. Faubion in the introduction to *Aesthetics, Method and Epistemology : Essential Works of Foucault*, vol 2, (Ed), James Faubion, London, Penguin, p. xxx

23 Richard Kearney. *Modern Movements in European Philosophy*, Manchester, Manchester University Press, 1994, p. 285.

24 Michel Foucault. *Power/Knowledge : Selected Interviews& Other Writings*, (Ed) Colin Cordon, New York, Pantheon Books, p. 114.

25 Gary Gutting. In the introduction to *The Cambridge Companion to Foucault*, (Ed) Garry Gutting, Cambridge : Cambridge University Press, 1994, p. 7

26 Gary Gutting. *Ibid.*, p. 10

27 Gary Gutting. *Ibid.*, p. 11

28 Patricia O'Brien. "Michel Foucault's History of Culture" in *"The New Cultural History"* (Ed) Lynn Hunt, Berkeley : University of California,1989, p. 34-35.

29 Michel Foucault. Quoted by Patricia O'Brien in *Ibid.*, p. 36

30 Michel Foucault. *Power/ Knowledge*. 142

31 Gutting, Gary, *Michel Foucault's Archaeology of Scientific Reason*, Cambridge : Cambridge University Press, 1989, p. 260

32 Lawrence Barth. in *Key Sociological Thinkers*, (ed) Rob Stones. London : Macmillan 1998, p256.

33 Madan Saru, p. *An Introductory Guide to Post- Structuralism and Postmodernism*, p. 71

34 Malcolm Waters. *Modern Social Theory*, London : Sage, 1994, p. 233.

35 Malcolm Waters. *Ibid.*, p. 233

36 Michel Foucault. Quoted by Barry Smart in *Michel Foucault* London: Tavistock Publishers, 1985, p. 96

37 Michel Foucault. *Ibid.*, p. 97.

38 Michel Foucault. *Ibid.*, p. 97

39 Patricia O'Brien in "Michel Foucault's History of Culture" in "*The New Cultural History*" (Ed) Lynn Hunt. Berkeley : University of California,1989, p. 42

40 Michel Foucault.The History of Sexuality, Vol. : Introduction, London, Penguine, 1981, p. 100-101

41 Judith Butler. *Subjects of Desire : Hegelian Reflections in Twentieth–Century.* New York : Columbia University Press, 1987, p. 217.

42 Michel Foucault. *The Order of Things*, p. 261-262

43 Madan Saru, p. *An Introductory Guide to Post-Structuralism and Postmodernism*, p. 79

44 Michel Foucault. *Power/ Knowledge*, p142

45 Michel Foucault. *Ibid.*, p. 65

46 Michel Foucault. *Ibid.*, 83

47 Allan Megill. Prophets of Extremeity : Nietzsche, Heidegger, Foucault, Derrida, London : University of California Press, 1985, p. 256

48 Richard Kearney, *Modern Movements in European Philosophy*, Manchester, Manchester University Press, 1994, p. 113.

49 Jacques Derrida. Quoted by Richard Kearney in *Ibid.*, p. 114.

50 Allen Thiher, *Words in Reflection : Modern Language Theory and Postmodern Fiction*, Chicago : Chicago University Press, 1984, p. 82.

51 Jacques Derrida. *Of Grammatology.* Delhi : Motilal Banarsidass Publishers, 1994,

52 Jacques, Derrida. in *Writing and Difference*, London, Routledge, 2001

53 Jacques, Derrida. *Ibid.*, p. 351

54 Jacques, Derrida. *Ibid.*, p. 351-352

55 Jacques, Derrida. *Ibid.*. 352

56 Jacques, Derrida. *Ibid.*, 352

57 Jacques, Derrida. *Ibid.*, p. 354

58 J.A.Cuddon. *A Dictionary of Literary Terms and Literary Theory.* London : Blackwell, 1998.

59 J. A. Cuddon. *Ibid.*.

60 Christopher Johnson. *System and Writing in the Philosophy of Jacques Derrida*, Cambridge : Cambridge University Press, 1993, p. 66

61 Jacques Derrida. *Dissemination.* London : Athlone Press, 1981.

62 Christopher Norris. *Derrida* : Fontana Modern Masters, (ed), Frank Kermode. London : Fontana Press, p. 28

63 Richard Kearney. *Modern Movements in European Philosophy,* p. 118

64 Richard Kearney. *Ibid.*, p. 119.

65 Jacques Derrida, *Of Grammatology*, p. 138.

66 Jacques Derrida. *Ibid.*, p. 142.

67 Christopher Norris. *Derrida,* p. 101

68 Richard Kearney Mara Rain Water (Ed), *The Continental Philosophy Reader.* London : Routledge, 1996, p. 439

69 Madan Saru, p. *An Introductory Guide to Post-structuralism and Postmodernism,* p. 44.

70 Toril Moi. *Sexual / Textual Politics.* London : Routledge, 2001, p. 104-105

71 Jacques Derrida. *Positions*. London : Athlone press,1981, p. 24-25

72 Jacques Derrida. *Ibid,* p. 25

73 Jacques Derrida .*Ibid,* p. 26

74 Jacques Derrida. *Of Grammatology*, p. 10

75 Richard Rorty. "Philosophy as a kind of writing : An essay on Derrida" in *New Literary History*, vol.X, No.1. Autumn, 1978, p.142

76 Jean Francoise Lyotard. In the Journal *Theory, Culture &Society*, Vol. 5, Number2-3, June, 1988, London, Sage, p. 278.

77 Jean Francoise Lyotard. *The Postmodern Condition*. Manchester : Manchester University Press, 1984, p. 3.

78 Jean Francoise Lyotard. *Ibid.*, p. xxiv.

79 Jean Francoise Lyotard. *Ibid.*, p. 46.

80 Jean Francoise Lyotard. *Ibid,* p. 64.

81 Jean Francoise Lyotard. *Ibid.*, p. 60.

82 Jean Francoise Lyotard. *Ibid.*, p48.

83 John Storey. *An Introductory Guide to Cultural Theory and Popular Culture.* Athens, The University of Georgia Press.1993, p. 160.

84 John Storey. *Ibid.*, p. 79

85 Tim Woods. *Beginning Postmodernism*, Manchester, Manchester University Press, 1999, p. 23-24.

86 Stuart Sim. (Ed.) *The Routledge Companion to Postmodernism.* London : Routledge, 2001, p. 331

87 Stuart Sim. *Ibid.*, p. 10

88 Jean Baudrillard. *Selected Writings*. (Ed.) Mark Poster, Oxford : Polity Press, 1988.

89 Jean Baudrillard. In *Symbolic Exchange and Death. Ibid.*, p. 128.

90 Jean Baudrillard. *Selected Writings* 1988, p. 168.

91 Jean Baudrillard. *Ibid.*, p. 170.

92 Jean Baudrillard. *Ibid.*, p. 171.

93 Jean Baudrillard. *Ibid.*, p. 171.

94 Jean Baudrillard. *The Transparency of Evil : Essays on Extreme Phenomena.* London : Verso, 1993, p. 67.

95 Jean Baudrillard. *Ibid.*, p. 6

96 Jean Baudrillard. *Ibid.*, p. 9

97 Jean Baudrillard. *Ibid.*, p. 11.

98 Jean Baudrillard. *Ibid.* p, p. 94-95.

99 Tim Woods. Beginning *Postmodernism*. Manchester : Manchester University Press,1999, p. 32.

VI

Postmodern aesthetics and its Manifestation In Various Art Forms

According to Kohler and Hassan the term 'postmodernism' was first used by Federico de Onis in the 1930s to indicate a minor reaction to modernism. The term became popular in the 1960s in New York when it was used by young artists, writers, and critics such as Rauschenberg, Cage, Burroughs, Barthelme, Fielder, Hassan and Sontag. Then it was referred to a moment beyond the exhausted high modernism, which was rejected because of its institutionalization in the museum and academy. However, it has its philosophical roots in Europe.

Various authors and thinkers used the word postmodern in various senses. According to Daniel Bell Postmodernism was perceived as a heightening of the adversorial tendencies of modernism with desire, the instinctual and pleasure unleashed to carry the logic of modernism to its further reaches exacerbating the structural tensions of society and disjunction of the realms. Frederic Jameson in his book "Postmodernism or the Cultural Logic of Late Capitalism" uses the word 'Postmodernism' to refer to cultural logic, or cultural dominant, that leads to the transformation of the cultural sphere in contemporary society.

Jameson shows some reluctance in adopting the view of periodisation which assumes a sudden shift and transformation of all aspects of culture. He follows Ernest Mandel's book "Late Capitalism" (1975) and links the stages of modernism to monopoly capitalism and Postmodernism to post-world war II late capitalism. His demarcation between these two stages and their cultural dominants suggests that he used a form of base-superstructure model of Marxism. This becomes much clear when we know that he is a Marxist. However, Jameson argues that postmodernism is based upon the central role of reproduction in the decentred global network of multinational corporations.

The archaeology of postmodern discourse explores the history of the term in its uneven development with diverse theoretical fields. An English painter John Watking Chapman spoke of 'Postmodern' painting around 1870 to designate painting that was more modern and *avant garde*, in his sense, than French impressionist painting. Another writer by name Rudolf Paunwitz used the word in 1917 to indicate the nihilism and collage of values in the modern Europeal culture. Paunwitz described the development of new postmodern men after the second world war. D.C Somervell in his summation of the first six volumes of British historian Arnold Toynbee's "A Study of History" (1947), used the word 'postmodern' to show the break with the modern age.

Later Toynbee himself took up the word to suggest the post-modern age that began in 1875 and he delineated the fourth stage of Western history. The first three stages according to him are; the Dark Age (675-1075), the Middle Ages (1075-1475) and the Modern (1475- 1875). In Toynbee's view the Western civilization had entered a new transitional phase beginning around 1875. He termed it the 'post-modern age'. The striking features of the age are; dramatic mutation and rupture from the previous modern age, which was characterized by wars, social turmoil and revolution. It was an age of anarchy and total relativism, a time of troubles, marked by the collapse of rationalism and the ethos of the Enlightenment. However, Toynbee did not explain the concrete features of the new postmodern era.

Bernard Rosenberg used the term 'postmodern' to describe a new condition of life and mass society. He believed that certain fundamental changes where taking place in society and culture. He gives a vivid description of the postmodern world with its promising and threatening features. In the same year, that is 1957 another writer by name Peter Drucker published "The Land Marks of Tomorrow : A Report on the New Post-Modern World". In Ducker's view postmodern society was equivalent to postindustrial society. Drucker describes a philosophical shift from the modern Cartesian world view to a new universe of pattern, process and purpose.

A negative notion of postmodern age can be seen in C.Wright Mills' "The Sociological Imagination" (1957) According to Mills the Modern Age is succeeded by a Post- modern period and the basic definitions of society and self are being overtaken by new realities. To conceptualise them as new realities, the standard categories of thought and feeling of the previous era are no longer sufficient. Specifically he believed that Marxism and Liberalism are not convincing as they have taken up the enlightenment belief in the inner connection between reason and freedom.

However, all these theorists that are discused above are very much in the modernist paradigm as they claim certain sweeping sociological generalisations, totalising surveys of history and sociology, and a belief in the power of the sociological imagination to illuminate social reality and to change society.

It is Lyotard who tried to a give a concrete definition of postmodernism. Lyotard in his "The Postmodern Condition", argues that in the last few decades the leading science and technologies have become increasingly concerned with language theories, problems of communication and cybernetics, computers and their languages, problems of translation, information storage and databanks. These technological transformations are having a considerable impact on knowledge. In Lyotard's view knowledge cannot survive unchanged with in the above general transformation. He even predicts that anything in the constituted body of knowledge that is not translatable into quantities of information will be abandoned. Knowledge in the postmodern times ceased to be an end in itself. It is and will be produced in order to be sold.

According to Lyotard all modern systems of knowledge, including science, had been supported by some 'metanarrative' or 'grand discourse' about the main direction of history. A metanarrative is a story of mythic proportions and a story big enough to pull together philosophy and research and politics and art, relate them to one another and give them a unifying sense of direction. Lyotard defines the postmodern era as a time of "incredulity towards metanarratives". He suggests that these metanarratives gave way to *Petis récits* or little narratives. There is no longer a final authority that can speak for all human beings from universal perspective. We can rely only on little narratives. Global and universal categorisations must be rejected.

David Harvey in his book "The Condition of Postmodernity" defined postmodernity as the situation in which the world finds itself after the break of the Enlightenment project which lasted from the later part of the 18th century until well into the 20the century. The Enlightenment project aimed at getting all the world's diverse peoples to see things the same way-the rationalist way. Postmodernism questions this very reason and rationalist way and contests the belief in linear progress absolute truths and national planning of ideal social order.

Lyotard celebrates the plurality and diversity. He is for local differences and from the plurality of ways in which humans choose to live. In his view there is no common measure by which such local differences, which he calls "language games", can be compared. It is not possible to declare that one way of life or thought is superior to another or to call one more progressive and the other reactionary. He feels that such differences are incommensurate. He opposes 'progress' as a yardstick as it has been discredited by the fatal damages of war, ecological destruction and weapons of mass destruction, which are the result of scientific knowledge and technological innovation. Humanity would be better if we stop trusting to force the world and its inhabitants into one mould and stop trusting to make history move in one direction.

According to Norman K. Denzin, 'Postmodernism is defined by the terms; a nostalgic, conservative longing for the past, coupled with an erasure of the boundaries between past and the present, an intense preoccupation with the real and its representations, a pornography of the visual, the commodification of sexuality and desire; a consumer culture which objectifies asset of masculine cultural ideals; intense emotional experiences shaped by anxiety, alienation, resentment, and a detachment from others'.[1]

For Denzin postmodern is four things at the same time. First, it describes the sequence of historical moments from World War II to the present. In this he identifies Vietnam war, the economic recessions of the 1970s and 80s, the rise to power of conservation political regimes in Europe and America; the failure of the Left to mount an attack against these regimes; the collapse of the international labour moment : the emergence of a new conservative politics, to totalitarian regimes in Europe, Asia, Latin America and South Africa. Secondly, the postmodern refers the multinational forms of late capitalism, which have introduced new cultural logics and new forms of communication and representation into the world economic and cultural systems. Thirdly, it describes a movement in the visual arts, architecture, cinema, popular music, and social theory, which goes against the grain of classic realist and modernist formations. Fourthly it refers to a form of theorizing and writing about the social.

The contemporary discovery of the postmodernism first emerged in 1960s. This new sensibility defined itself against abstraction and alienation of modernist art and modern forms of literary criticism. The new sensibility or a 'structure of feeling'[2] celebrated the emergent cultural practices, which were characterized by the breaking down of the distinction between high and low art.

Postmodernism manifested in various forms ranging from Philosophy to literature. According Mike Featherstone : In the first place the broad range of artistic, intellectual and academic fields in which the term postmodernism has been used, is striking. we have music (Cage, Stockhausen, Briers, Holloway, Tredici, Laurie Anderson); art Rauschenberg, Baselitz, March, Schnabel, Kiefer and pop art and Bacon; fiction; Vonnegut's 'Slaughterhouse Five and the novels of Barth, Barthelme, Pynchon, Boroughs, Ballard, Doctrow; film; Body Heat, The Wedding, Blue Velvet , Whetherby; architecture;Jencks, Venturi, Bolin; literary theory and criticism; Sapnos, Hassan Sontag, Fielder; philosophy ;Lyotard, Derrida, Baudrillard, Vattimo, Rorty; anthropology;Clifford, Tyler, Marcus; Sociology;Denzin; Geography ;Soja.

According to Wayne Hudson, "Postmodernity may be characterized as the 'post' of whatever 'modernity' is taken to be... Thus postmodernity may be dubbed : the belatedness of modernity, the last phase of modernity, a radicalization of modernity, a retreat from modernity, the transcendence of modernity, a dialectical crisis of modernity, a critique of modernity – to give only a sample of the available possibilities"[3] . Hudson understands postmodernity in fourteen aspects :

1· Postmodernity as a Myth.

2· Postmodernity as a Periodisation.

3· Postmodernity as a Situation.

4· Postmodernity as an Experience.

5· Postmodernity as an Historical Consciousness.

6· Postmodernity as a Sensibility.

7· Postmodernity as a Climate.

8· Postmodernity as Crisis.

9· Postmodernity as an Episteme.

10· Postmodernity as a Discourse.

11· Postmodernity as a Poetics.

12· Postmodernity as a Retreat.

13· Postmodernity as a Topos.

14· Postmodernity as a Project.

Postmodernity may be characterized as a myth. Postmodernity is not a myth in the sense of a falsehood. It may be a term of periodisation. Those who have taken postmodernity as a periodisation term appear unable to agree on when postmodernity began. Thus 'postmodernity' is alleged to have begun 100 years ago or only 25 years ago; to be just beginning and to be still to come; to be now; to be something recently gone; to be a recurrent structural possibility reappearing in determinate periods.

Postmodernity may be differentiated as a situation or condition. In so far as a particular and possible unique condition is alleged to pertain, reference may be made to : the organisation of knowledge and research, consciousness and sensibility, values, culture, the organization of work and leisure, and patterns of settlement. On this account postmodernity may be glossed in terms of alleged changes in society and economy.

Postmodernity, however, may also be characterized more systematically by reference to reorganisation of knowledges and related changes in social organization and institutional structure. It may also be portrayed as an experience or as a set of modes of experiencing. It may be alleged that a new experience (for instance of historical time) has emerged, or that a set of new modes of experiencing already follow in the wake of new media or new technology. Alternatively, the new modes of experiencing in question may be still to come. Postmodernity may be indicated as a historical consciousness. Here the outstanding insight is that new chronopolitical spaces, new horizons of expectation, may be becoming available to human beings.. Postmodernity may be associated with a problematising of linear history in the name of multi-temporality, polyphony.

As a sensibility or syndrome postmodernity may be signified as a non-totalising sensibility which refuses conventional unifications and homogenisations : it is a sensibility which is accepting of disorder, discrepancies, discontinuities and gaps, which delights in paradoxes and contradictions, and which is ready to represent the unpresentable. A sensibility, which refuses a new equilibrium. As a word that indicates a climate postmodernity refers so many endings. The endings are : the end of humanism and the death of the subject, or, in later versions, the de-centring of 'man' or the subject, the end of representation, the end of neo-realism or mimesis, the end of truth, or the contemporary inability to distinguish between truth and falsehood, appearance and reality.

As a term that speaks about the crisis, postmodernity exposes the crisis of authority in Western European culture : a crisis of values, of legitimation, of finalities. At the most general level this crisis may be detailed in Lyotard's terms as a crisis of the metanarratives (meta-récits) that characterise modernity or even of western culture since the Renaissance. Postmodernity on this account involves the detranscendentalisation and delegitimation of western culture. The possibility of any overarching meta-theory or meta-discourse is rejected, and this rejection is widely taken to be characteristically 'postmodernist'. Nietzschean revivalism, and neo-Wittgensteinian talk of incommensurable 'language games'. .

The postmodern episteme may be classified in terms of : epistemological scepticism, antirationalism, antinomianism, pluralism, immanence, relativity, indeterminacy, discontinuity and disjunction, acceptance of chance, the aleatory, disorder, incommensurability. Postmodernist discourse turns out to mean the theoretical discourse of structuralist and post-structuralist French critical theory, above all, a discourse about the subject, the body, desire, and language. On this account Lacan, Deleuze, Guattri and Lyotard become key figures. But the use of 'discourse' here is improper and it is nowhere established that such a discourse exists.

Postmodernity is also characterized as a retreat : a retreat from the project of Enlightenment or the project of modernity. On this account postmodernity is associated with the rejection of the ideals of the Enlightenment : its universalism, its belief in equality and in progress, and its goal of the realization of reason in history. Postmodernity is said in be a retreat from the project of modernity in the sense of the project of realising reason in history and/or the project of achieving a future rational and humane society. Alternatively, postmodernity is associated with a rejection of Marxism and of the dialectic, teleology, philosophy of history and totality central to it.

A linguistic movement in philosophy also characterizes postmodernism. Wittgenstein came to reject his own earlier positivist theory of language, which provides an important transition in charting the move from modernism to postmodernism. Wittgenstein came to recognise that all languages, from the mathematical to our mother tongues, are internally self-referential. Language is understood as a kind of game theory, in which the rules are arbitrary to each particular user-group. What we can talk about is language games within the boundaries of rational, irrational, and other rational. Human reason is a polyglot, cross-disciplinary and cross-cultural. There is, however, no master language of Truth, as the scientific positivists and religious fundamentalists had hoped.

In eschewing foundational theories and focusing on the function of language, postmodernist tends toward philosophical and ethical pragmatism. The truth of a theory or interpretation is understood not through some direct correspondence to reality but through the practical consequences of its applications. In this sense, postmodernism can be seen as having deep affinities with some religious and scientific philosophies. The reluctance of physicists to draw metaphysical implications from quantum mechanics can be seen as a kind of pragmatism.

Feminist Epistemologies are also inspired a lot by postmodernism. A great wealth of postmodernism literature uses gender as a critical theory for assessing the content and culture of the modern biophysical sciences. Critical feminist case studies expose the hidden prejudice and oppression operating within the sciences. Feminist studies also help to explode the complexity of the nature-nurture interpretation problem as applied to sex-gender. And, of course, there is a similar body of feminist literature within religious studies to which one can turn.

Postmodern Feminists borrow a lot from both Derrida and Lacan. From Derrida they borrow his critique of phallogocentrism – the way in which male speech dominates writing, especially the writing done by woman. Western thought since antiquity has tended to privilege speech over writing for the way in which speech brings the listener into what Derrida calls the 'presence' of the world, whereas writing is more mediated and thus somehow less valid. It is clear that Derrida's critique of the philosophy of presence can be used by feminists who resist the male appropriation of language; they argue that male concepts of reason and reasonable language issue in discourses that exclude woman and women's writing, particularly in the realms of speculative philosophy and science. Derrida's own Poststructuralism is self-consciously feminist in his concept and critique of phallogocentrism, refracting his overall critique of western positivism that, according to him, fundamentally ignores the undecidability of language and thus the political and social ambiguities of all social engineering.

The French Feminists like Irigaray (1985), Cixous (1986) and Kristeva (1980) are thoroughly Derridean in the ways in which they understand the aporetic nature of language and writing. They all agree with Derrida that texts may have levels of often-contradictory meaning, typified by the hierarchy of text over subtext. As feminists, they use literary methods of deconstruction, to bring to light the hidden assumptions and contradictions of male texts that purport to speak for women or about them. Feminist theory has focused on the politics of language, a deconstruction of phallogocentric language has been especially pertinent, showing the ways in which men usurp the dialogue chances of women and thus reinforce their own political and social power.

Lacan also energizes Poststructural feminist cultural studies where theorists have utilized his basic distinctions between the realm of the Imaginary and the realm of the Symbolic to suggest expressive differences between women and men writers. Essentially, Lacan builds on Freud's psychoanalytic theory by adding poststructuralist notations about language. He argues that women have more access than men to the realm of non-linear, evocative discourse (so called round writing). Men inhabit the realm of symbolism and language, including the activities of science and philosophy. Linear notions of logic and discourse govern this realm of expression. Lacan develops a complex account of how men and women move between these phases of development, suggesting new ways of viewing the unconscious (which, he argues, is structured like a language).

Susan Watkings Cixous opines that, Irigaray and Kristeva are suspicious of totalising claims. She says, ' along with writers like Jacques Derrida, they are suspicious of the totalising claims of structuralist linguistics to explain the diversity and plurality of language. Derrida's thinking has been hugely influential in literary studies, and many commentators on Cixous's Irigaray's and Kristeva have argued their indebtedness to his work".[4]

In fact, the term 'postmodernism' once confined to literature and architecture simultaneously spread to all most all the aspects of cultural life and it even suggests a mutation in artistic practice and an epistemic shift in western cultural theory. According to Maltby postmodernism is, 'a conjunction of three fields of thought : postmodernist aesthetics, post-structuralist philosophy and literary theory, and post-Marxist sociologies. Third, the extraordinary ascent of the concept must be seen as an ideological matter. The debate about postmodernism is a battleground of competing political visions'.[5]

Maltby recognizes some ten features of postmodernism. They are : Populist Aesthetics, Programmatic Self-reflexiveness, The Limit-Text, The Decentred Subject and the Primacy of Discourse, Difference Vs. Logocentrism, Critique of Universal Knowledge, Radical Democracy, Politics of Information, and Media Society.

The cultural space of late capitalism is suffused with the representations of commodity aesthetics and mass-media entertainment. These are understood to supply the dominant forms of cognition and imagination. The 'debased' commercial mass culture also became the material for the art. This art goes beyond formal restrictions. In this background the distinction between high art and popular art is blurred.

The distinction between aesthetic practice and theory dissolved into aesthetics itself. Aesthetics incorporated theory into itself, hence, the question of self-reflexiveness became unavoidable in postmodern arts. In postmodern literature art is no longer privileged as a source of truth. Like any other discourse it is one among many. The author has no control over the meaning of the text. The postmodern literary theory eulogizes the text, which dissolves the union of signifier and signified, that is, which frees the signifier from its enthrallment to representation. 'The epistemological juncture of postmodernism is defined by a paradigm shift in which post-humanist philosophies of language have superseded Cartesian/phenomenological philosophies of consciousness. Hence, the subject is "decentered" in relation to meaning he/she is not the source or author of (private) meaning but quite the reverse : the subject or, more precisely, subjectivities are "called up" by discourses which position the subject within the social order and construct his/her perspectives on reality'.[6]

The primacy given to discourse in postmodernity leads them to see the subject as facing the world, history, society and identity in the form of narratives.

As Derrida thinks, in the postmodern world *différance* is the play of signifiers that produces differences on which the meaning depends. Because of this, the meaning in a text, be it a literary text or a cultural artefact or of truth is continuously deferred.

Postmodernism understands reality as chaos and pluralistic. It believes in fragmentation rather than in totalising theories. That is why there is a strong criticism on totalising philosophies. In the felids of politics postmodernism strives for radical democracy in place of 'essentialist paradigms' like Marxism. Postmodernism respects the autonomy of diverse political struggles and appeals "democratically" not only to subjects as workers but to a plurality of non-classist subject- positions.

Computerization and a decisive shift toward the commodity production of information have engendered an "information economy" where ownership of, and access to, data banks become a critical political issue. Herbert Schiller says that, 'the definition and presentation of everyday reality, nationally and internationally, have been the prerogatives of a score of media conglomerates. The concentrated control of information by Western monopolies has created enormous difficulties for those seeking economic self-determination and political autonomy. By their information selection and control, the Western media... assist in providing the transnational corporate business system with diverted and disoriented domestic publics.'[7]

In the postmodern mass media society, mass-communication channels have penetrated into domestic space and colonized it. In this context, by borrowing from Jean Baudrillard, Maltby says, 'exposed to the absolute proximity and total instantaneity of communication, the individual becomes "a switching centre for all the networks of influence", a post-alienated consciousness responding "ecstatically" (rather than critically) to media transmissions. This new communicative order marks "the end of the social" whose perspective space— "the sense of conflicts and historical contradictions"—has been replaced by "the space of simulation [which] confuses the real with the model" it is a situation where (media) models of "the real" precede and constitute "the real," whence simulation is under-stood to dedifferentiate (or "implode") basic binary distinctions like "true" and "false" or real and "imaginary"'.[8]

In the view of Mike Featherstone, postmodernism, "has to be understood against the background of a long-term process involving the growth of a consumer culture and expansion in the number of specialists and intermediaries engaged in the production and circulation of symbolic goods. It draws on tendencies in consumer culture which favour the aestheticization of life, the assumption that the aesthetic life is the ethically good life and that there is no human nature or true self, with the goal of life an endless pursuit of new experiences, values and vocabularies".[9]

Postmodernism simultaneously refers to an anti-foundational stance in philosophy and cultural theory. In addition to this, from the sociological point of view postmodernism extends to the consumer culture and the accompanying aestheticisation of life. Hence, in the view of Featherstone, postmodernism as a sociological concern should be identified with life styles of the new middle class.

Deconstruction, as a philosophical and literary concept, is an integral part of postmodernism. In fact, postmodernism has been popularised much by the literary and cultural critics, who drew inspiration from Derrida's deconstructionism. Deconstruction assumes that culture is a text. The boundaries of the literary text are expanded to include all forms of cultural performances and artefacts, from television and film to text books and science. Cultural deconstruction is possible only if we make the assumption that diverse cultural products can be 'read', in much the way that Derrida's read traditional literary texts. Derrida makes it clear that deconstruction applies to all manner of human expressions.

Deconstructors think that every cultural text is undecidable. Hence their critical practice takes this undecidability into account. According to deconstruction meaning is always elusive; in Derrida's terms, it embodies both difference and deferral : the more we attempt to fix the meaning, the more it slips away. The principle of a text's undecidability is the zero point from which deconstruction as a critical practice proceeds.

Cultural deconstruction tries to find the *aporias* in every work or text. *Aporia* means that the works and texts at some level contradict themselves or leave a vacancy of meaning that needs to be filled. The aporetic nature of texts ensures their undecidability- their reduction to single, simple codes of meaning. Language is aporetic. This aporetic nature of language hinders attempts to reduce meaning into transparent codes and neglect the ambiguities.

Deconstructive cultural criticism aims at locating it in the margins of a text. It turns the subtext into text and reads the cultural object at its margins. Derrida's stress on texts' *aporias*, like blind spots, omissions, tensions, and contradictions suggests the methodological principle of deconstructive reading : search for sense in unlikely places, especially in rhetorical gestures that appear marginal to the main enterprise (prose, plot) of the text in questions. In so doing, one can uncover the intended relationship between value and non-value-hierarchy-giving every text a certain direction of meaning, 'Thus, by reading footnotes or endnotes strongly, one can better understand why a writing relegates this material to secondary status by comparison to the primary status of what remains in the body of the text. One might read material placed in parentheses.[10]

Writing on Derrida's deconstruction Ben Agger says, 'Derridean reading... not only restores the value of marginalia like endnotes, parenthetical material and figural gestures but also reverses the priority of main text over marginal text, text over subtext, in a dehierarchaising way. Derrida assumes that meaning is more clearly surfaced by examining these marginalia. For example, in the prefaces and acknowledgment sections in books one can find all sorts of telling first-person declarations about why the book was written, its topic, its progenitors and debts, its relevant speech communities, the lifeworld of its author'.[11]

We live today in a mass media-saturated environment. The mass media are all around us, from morning till night. We wake up to a radio, we read the morning newspaper while eating breakfast, we watch televisions when we come back home in the evening. All this will have tremendous impact on the lives of individuals. The changes in the lives of individuals are profound. In a way, the lines between reality and illusion have become blurred. We live in hyperreality; in a world where images seem more real than reality itself. One of the aspects of postmodernity is the process of mediaisation. There are various aspects of the mediaisation process in postmodernity.

The media culture is increasingly changing from a print culture to electronic culture. Print media, in the first world countries, although by no means becoming obsolete is restricted to certain groups of society. The electronic media are not more real than print media, but they are more reminiscent of reality. Television especially looks like reality; it is one medium whose codes basically every one can understand, even children.

The media are increasingly involved in transnational process. Historically, the media assisted in creating nation states as we have come to know. Through newspapers, people in different parts of a country could feel that they belonged to the same community even though they would never meet. Today the media do not only portray the national culture. Two important changes have occurred. First many countries now import a large proportion of their television output. The import is cheap, and it attracts large audiences. And the second, satellite broadcasting has meant that people can watch other programs than the ones offered by their national broadcasting companies.

The distribution of programs between countries is uneven. Some countries export programs and other countries import. The US is by far the greatest exporter. However, satellite broadcasting has also meant that people living outside their own cultures or countries are also able to keep in contact with their native culture. Through a process a 'reterritorialisation' it is possible for people who have had to leave their home countries to create their specific local version of distant culture.

The media are becoming increasingly commercialised and deregulated profit has always been an important motive that involves in the media and many media business have started solely for that reason. However, there also have been ideological and cultural reasons behind media enterprise. In postmodernity, the commercial angle is stronger than before, the most important issue is that the satellite broadcasting has weekend the public service systems and deregulation is on the agenda in many countries.

Media ownership is increasingly concentrated in a small number of corporations. Those corporations are primarily American, Japanese or increasingly transnational. A key characteristic of these corporations is that they aim for both vertical and horizontal intergeneration. The merge of corporations makes them more larger and dominant. New technology changes the mediaization process, for example, Internet too exemplifies the constant change to which the media environment is subject. The increasing mass media intertextuality, mass media content, and especially television content is becoming self-referential. Things that happen outside the media become less important.

The mass media have drastically changed people's everyday life. A simple indicator of this fact is the amount of time that people spend with mass media everyday. The mass media have taken time away from other social practices. The mass media, no doubt have immediate effect on mass audiences. The media assists in the process of 'identity construction'. The media function as a cultural form. It is through the media that people get impulses about whom they want to be or who they want to become. It should be pointed out that the media output, aesthetic and cultural products are especially important for the process of identity construction. It is when consuming such products that it becomes possible for people to leave their normal lives for a while and cross a threshold for something else. Aesthetic and cultured experience thus affords special possibilities for self-reflection.

The media also assist in the process of sense making. In a world that is being more complex and every event becoming important, the more we have to rely on the media in order to make sense of the world. They set the agenda for what we think about. In this process, both factual and fictional media output are involved.

The media also assist in structuring of everyday life. Every life is based on routines, and the media is used to routinise life. In the process of routinisation of the peoples' lives the media bind together peoples different public and private arenas. Now let us see the manifestation of postmodern spirit in various art forms.

Postmodern Literature

Between 1960 and 1990 the dominant mode of writing was postmodern writing. In the field of literary studies the term postmodernism has received the widest usage. There have been numerous attempts to theorize the consequences and manifestations of postmodernism for literature. Most of these discussions were running into problems of historical or formal definitions. Postmodernist writers stated their creative praxis with a frontal attack on *avant-garde* culture and literature.

'Literally 'avant-garde' means the vanguard, and advance post, a spearhead or the first line of a moving army...The avant-garde gives the distance which separates it form the bulk a temporal dimension : what is being done *at present* by a small advance unit will be repeated *later* by all. The guard is seen 'advanced' on the assumption that 'the rest will follow suit'. it goes without saying that we know for sure on which side is the front and where is the rear, where is 'before' and where 'behind'... The concept of avant-garde conveys the idea of an endlessly orderly space and time, and of an essential condition of the two orders. In a world in which one can speak of the avant-garde, 'forward' and 'backward' have, simultaneously, spatial and temporal dimensions'.[12]

The important change that took place in the 1960s is that the very idea of an *avant-garde* in literature has been considered naïve. The historical experience of the people or writers made them to relinquish the confidence in the sense of direction. They were not certain of the way that would lead them to forward. In this kind of atmosphere 'Literature, turning against itself, aspires to silence, leaving us with uneasy intimations of outrage and apocalypse. If there is an *avant-garde* in our time, it is probably bent on discovery through suicide. Thus, the term anti-literature, like antimatter, comes to symbolize not merely an inversion of forms but will and energy turned inside out".[13]

The aura formerly attached to the *avant-garde* writing has lost in the postmodern times. In fact, the demarcation between high art and popular art has been eroded. Featherstone insists on some of the features of postmodernism in art and literature as 'the effacement of the boundary between art and everyday life; the collapse of the hierarchical distinction between high art and mass/popular culture; a stylistic promiscuity favouring eclecticism and the mixing codes; parody, pastiche, irony, playfulness and the celebration of the surfaces "depthlessness" of culture;

the decline of the originality/genius of the artist producer and assumption that art can only be repetitive".[14]

As Featherstone says, one can find in postmodernist literature self-conscious merger of genres, styles and attitudes. The postmodern literature relishes the blurring or juxtaposition of forms, like fiction and non-fiction; positions like, straight and ironic; modes like, violent and comic, cultural levels like, high and low and ultimately it takes pleasure in the play and ridicules the search for depth as mere nostalgia.

The postmodern fiction is submerged with aesthetic representation of commodities and mass media entertainment. This obsession is too much some times. A German writer declared that, 'here you stood : the peasant read the Bible; the maniacs read *Mein Kampf*. Now people no longer have any opinions; they have refrigerators. In stead of illusions we have televisions, instead of tradition, the Volkswagon. The only way to catch the spirit of the times is to write a handbook on home appliances".[15]

Though the sentence has overtone of grimness, in a way it reflects reality.

According to Cooper the postmodernist fiction writing is a counterrealist writing[16]. In the writings of counterrealist one kind find a general uncertainty about the reality and the hospitableness of the world, a fascination for epistemological dilemma, an yearning for fictional versions of the reality and the simultaneous apprehensions of their dangers. Cooper considers the writers like Thomas Pynchon, Donald Barthelme, William Burroughs, John Hakes, William Gaddis, Ishmael Reid, Susan Sontag, Vladimir Nabakov, and Jorge Louis Borges.

Barry Lewis understands postmodern fiction as a phenomenon that covers numerous authors which includes, Postmodernist fiction as an international phenomenon, with major representatives from all over the world : Gunter Grass and Peter Handke (Germany); Georges Perec and Monique Wittig (France); Umberto Eco and Italo Calvino (Italy); Angela Carter and Salman Rushdie (Britain); Stanislaw Lem (Poland); Milan Kundera (former Czechoslovakia); Mario Vargos Llosa (Peru); Gabriel Garcia Marquez (Colombia); J.M. Coetzee (South Africa); and Peter Carey (Australia).

Though the postmodernist writers were not homogeneous in modes of writing, there are certain identifiable features in their writings. In the view of Ihab Hassan, postmodern literature "Knows silences other than the inhuman imposes. The avant-garde finds ingenious ways to deny language, deny form, deny art. These ways often generate new kinds of art".[17] Hassan identifies some five metaphors of postmodern 'anti-art' :

1· Art cancels itself Beckett's sentence 'How it is' tells that the book is about how it was not.

2· Art deprecates itself and pretends to be observed. The creator repudiates his own creation. This is because he believes that neither art nor reason can clarify existences.

3· Art is a self-reflexive game in which the forms call attention to their miraculous or ludicrous emptiness.

4· Art orders itself loosely and at random, in which form becomes discontinues and decentred. The authors never try to impose their pattern on the material. By inventing participation they increase options of men. In this way the barrier between author and reader melts away.

5· Art rejects interpretation. Fancy pretends to be fact and vice versa. Art confesses its helplessness before the outrages of the day.

In the fiction of Thomas Pynchon, Donald Barthelme, William Burroughs and Jorge Louis Borges we find the portrayal of the human being as a relative fact, insubstantial figure adrift in an alien world. This world is fantastic, grotesque, absurd, mysteriously threatening. Some of these authors are not very concerned with social forces, but their human figures are diminished nonetheless. John Barth, for example, admits that he, 'an't in fiction get very interested" in such things as current world problems, which he calls "the conditions of [life]" but he is very interested in metaphysical constraints. Which he calls "the facts of life'.[18]

Because his absurd cosmos offers no absolute values or ultimate verities. His characters become dwarfed and immobilized not by impersonal powers but, paradoxically, by a superfluity of freedom and choice. 'Jake Horner in "The End of the Road" is so aware of endless alternatives that even if he were a single, coherent self he could not settle on a course of action. The "serpents of knowledge and Imagination," by offering him too much, bind his limbs as they did Laocoon's and literally paralyse him. He is overwhelmed not by external controls but by their complete absence : too many possibilities have the same effect as too few, and he feels "as though there were no Jacob Horner"'.[19]

Donald Barthelme has been considered one of the major friction writers in the postmodern pattern. In the view of Jerome Klinkowitz, 'The key to Barthelme's new aesthetic for fiction is that the work may stand for itself, that it need not yield to complete explication of something else in the world but may exist as an individual object....'.[20]

Sukenick also expresses the same kind of opinion. He calls the new writing of Barthelme as *Bossa Nova*. According to him, 'The Bossa Nova has no plot, no story, no character, no chronological sequence, no verisimilitude, no imitation, no allegory, no symbolism, no subject matter, no "meaning." It resists interpretation. [...] the Bossa Nova is nonrepresentational-it represents itself. [...] Donald Barthelme is a writer who is very bossa nova....'.[21]

Epistemological uncertainty is an important feature in the postmodern fiction. It is also called as epistemological scepticism. Barthelme's fiction is an example for this. Barthelme's story "The Balloon", which is considered as a manifesto of his aesthetic, is a concrete example for the epistemological uncertainty. In the story the balloon inflated by an unidentified narrator in Central Park instigates various thoughts in the minds of numerous people. The balloon eludes interpretation. It assumes a life of its own quite independently of its creator's intensions. This is because, the narrator I disappears in the first paragraph, where he assigns a fixed meaning to balloon and appears only in the last paragraph. The point of the story is that a work of art should be respected as a concrete particular. Any attempt to appropriate it through the process of interpretation is repressive. Because the imposition of fixed meaning robs a work of art of its intrinsic open-endedness.

This story "Balloon" is seen as an expression of aesthetic ideal : the art object which defies meaning. Though this account is correct, but it remains at same time incomplete. 'We may say that the balloon as autonomous art object has aesthetic value by virtue of its capacity to resist cultural integration : it defies definition in the terms of established systems of meaning. Accordingly, the prevailing view of "The Balloon" as a story that illustrates Barthelme's desire for a form of art that eludes meaning *per se* stands in need of two qualifications. The story is typical of Barthelme's stories in general in that it exposes the inability of our established meaning-systems to impose meaning that is other than stultifying or superficial, and it seeks to resist and, ultimately, transcend the habitual modes of perception promoted by those meaning-systems'.[22]

The postmodern fiction is virtually every thing and every one exists in such a radical state of distortion. The characters inhabit a dimension of structureless being in which their behaviour becomes inexorably arbitrary. The expression 'postmodern fiction' has been named differently as 'surfiction', 'post-contemporary fiction' by Jerome Klinkowitz. 'fabulation' by Raymond Federman, 'historiographic metafiction' by Linda Hutcheon.

There is, as we have already seen, a serious attack on neorealism in postmodern fiction. Kurt Vonnegut declares in "Slaughterhouse Five" declares "Everything there was to know about life was in The Brothers Karamazov, by Feodor Dostoevsky. 'But that isn't enough any more".[23] In the view of Vonnegut fiction had arrived at a cul-de-sac in its development in 1970s it self. One way of this dead end of fiction was demonstrated in William Burroughs' novel "The Naked Lunch" (1959), 'The world cannot be expressed, it can perhaps be indicated by mosaics of juxtaposition, like objects abandoned in a hotel room, defined by negatives and absences'.[24] Burroughs' description alludes to the anti-foundationalism of postmodernism.

Linda Hutcheon in her "A Poetics of Postmodernism : History, Theory, Fiction" (1990). Explains that postmodernism is a contradictory enterprise, in which art forms are use and abuse, install and destabilize convention in their critical or ironic re-reading of the art of the past. She argues further that postmodernist writing is best represented by those works of 'historigraphic metafiction', which self-consciously distort history.

The postmodern historical novels involve bogus accounts of famous events. Take Kazuo Ishiguro's "The Remains of the Day" (1989). This novel implies that a butler in a stately home played a small but significant role in the appeasement policy adopted by Britain towards Germany before the Second World War. Anachronism disrupts temporal order by flaunting glaring inconsistencies of detail or setting. In "Flight to Canada" (1976) by Ishmael Reed, Abraham Lincoln uses a telephone, and his assassination is reported on television. Tom Crick, a schoolteacher in Graham Swift's "Waterland" (1983), blurs history and fantasy by combining his account of the French Revolution with personal reminiscences and unsubstantiated anecdotes about his own family history.

According to Tim Wood, in the novels like John Barth's "Sot—Weed Factor" (1960), Robert Coover's "The Public Burning" (1976), Garcia Marquez's "One Hundred Years of Solitude", John Fowles' "The French Lieutenant's Woman" (1969), and E.L. Doctorow's Ragtime (1975) history is demythologised.

Postmodern fiction can also be characterized by its transgression of the cultural boundaries erected between high and popular culture.

Postmodern fiction believes in fragmentation. The postmodernist writer distrusts the wholeness and completion associated with modern stories, and prefers to deal with other ways of structuring narrative. One alternative is the multiple ending, which resists closure by offering numerous possible outcomes for a plot. "The French Lieutenant's Woman" is the classic instance of this. The novel concerns the love of respectable amateur naturalist Charles Smithson (engaged to the daughter of a wealthy tarader) for Sarah Woodruff, an outcast rumoured to have been scandalously involved with a French lieutenant. Although the book is set in Lyme Regis in 1867, and follows several love story conventions, it is far from being a regular historical romance. Fowles disrupts the narrative by parading his familiarity with Marx, Darwin and others. He directly addresses the reader, and even at one stage steps into the story himself as a character. The multiple endings are a part of these tactics.

Paranoia, or the threat of total engulfment by somebody else's system, is keenly felt by many of the dramatic personae of postmodernist fiction. The protagonists of postmodernist fiction often suffers from the 'dread that someone else is pattering his life.

According to Barry Lewis, "Postmodernist writing reflects paranoid anxieties in many ways, including : the distrust of fixity, of being circumscribed to any one particular place or identity, the conviction that society is conspiring against the individual, and the multiplication of self-made plots to counter the scheming of others. These different responses are immanent in three distinct areas of reference associated with the word 'plot'. The first meaning is that of a piece of ground of small or moderate size sequestered for some special purpose, such as a plot for growing vegetables or building a house. A stationary space, in other words, intimidating to the postmodern hero. Randle McMurphy in Ken Kesey's "One Flew Over the Cuckoo's Nest" (1962), Yossarian in

Joseph Heller's Catch-22 (1962) and Billy Pilgrim in Kurt Vonnegut's "Slaughterhouse-Five" (1969) are each confined to their own 'plots' in this sense by the authorities. McMurphy is committed to a mental hospital, Yossarian is conscripted to the air force, and Billy Pilgrim is interned in a German prisoner-of-war camp. A vindictive bureaucracy controls these mavericks by medication, red tape or the force of arms".[25]

Tim Wood categorizes four points in which postmodern fiction can be understood :

1· [26] Historical narrative which usually pits postmodernism as a break with, or a transcendence of, many aspects of modernism;
2. Philosophical argument which describes postmodernism as the cultural practice emerging from an allegiance to the poststructuralist philosophical assault on notions of stable linguistic meaning and the existence of an unmediated objective reality;
3· Pedagogical or ideological impulse which seeks to raise our awareness of the structural armatures of our culture, through a disruption and 'problematisation' or conventional senses of reality and laying bare of the conceptual structures of our world;
4· Series of textual strategies employed by fiction and designed to foreground and highlight the textuality of the work ('metafictional strategies'), to draw attention to the fictional framing devices and the plurality of worlds.

Borrowing form Brian McHale, Tim Wood explains that postmodernist fiction represents a conceptual shift in emphasis from the 'epistemological' dominant of modernism to the 'ontological' dominant of postmodernism. The key characteristics of postmodern fiction may be summarized as follows :

I. An obsession with the viability of systems representation.
II. The decentring of the subject by discursive systems.
III. The introduction of multiple fictive selves.
IV. An open-ended play with the formal devices.
V. An interrogation of the ontological bases of and connections between narrative and subjectivity.
VI. Narrative fragmentation and reflexivity.

VII. An abolition of the cultural divides between high and popular forms of culture.

VIII. An exploration of ways in which narrative mediates and constructs history.

IX. The displacement of real by simulacra.

X. A belief in the linguistic construction of reality.

Magic Realism is another essential feature of Postmodernist fiction. The term, apparently suggested by the Cuban novelist Alejo Carpentier. Later it was introduced into the critical vocabulary by Alistair Reid. Like much postmodernist work, magic neorealist is essentially eclectic. In particular, it mixes realistic narrative with fantastic and fabulous elements, not so much to reconcile them as to play upon their apparent discordance. The challenge to familiar notions of "reality" in extending to a questioning of "truth", and this questioning can in turn deliberately undermine the text and the words, and eventually the authority of the novel itself.

Postmodern Poetry

Postmodern poetry begins with the American poet Charles Olson, a poet and writer who was the rector of Black Mountain College, North Carolina, an innovative and experimental liberal arts college founded in 1933 and at the height of its influence in the early 1950s. It functioned as an interdisciplinary centre for a wide variety of influential figures, including John Cage, Josef Albers, Merce Cunningham, Pierre Boulez and Robert Rauschenberg. Black Mountain poetics was born in this intellectual environment and derived largely from Olson's teachings especially the essay 'Projective Verse'. Olson called for an 'open' poetry, where 'Field Composition' resisted the 'closed form' of main-stream poetry.

Olson's poem the "The Maximus Poems", written between 1950 and 1970, is a long, complex meditation on his metaphysical, cultural, geographical and political environment. In view of Tim Woods this poem, 'is often taken to be the beginning of the postmodern exploration in poetry'.[27]

Though there are certain postmodern elements in the poems of Allen Ginsberg, Gary Snyder, Gregory Corso and Lawrence Ferlinghetti, those elements are seen in them only dilated in form. A group of poets - with fresh willingness to experiment with a potential instability of language, the concern with the poetry as a linguistic resource for knowledge, and investigation to the way language constructed rather than represented human consciousness – produced poetry that can be called postmodernist. This group includes poets like; Kenneth Koch, James Schuyler, John Ashbery and Frank O'Hara.

During 1970s a few poets focused on a group of little magazines like, *L=A=N=G=U=A=G=E, Talks, Tottel's Hills and Poetics Journal,* and handful of presses like Tuumba Books, the Figures began to continue the postmodern elements in their writing of poetry. Poets like Lyn Hejinian, Ron Silliman, Rober Grenier, Clark Coolidge, Bob Perelman, Barrett Watten, Charles Bernstein, Leslie Scalapino, Michael Davidson, Bruce Andrews, Susan Howe and others began to theorize their work in the terminology of the cultural and philosophical ideas. These ideas are from the postmodern theory. Though they refuse to be called postmodernists, in their work it is conspicuous. Most of these poets are influenced by the work of Gertrude Stein, Louis Zukofsky, Russian Constructivists and some aspects of Black Mountain poetry.

Many of the Language poets explored the power structures embedded in language - social reality as well as institutions. Similar kind of trends can be seen in British poets also. The major themes of poetry : the politics of sign, struggle over the means of representation, politic of identity related to class, race, sex and region. Some poets like John Agard, Grace Nichols used language to raise consciousness specifically about racial perspectives. Most poets possess a sense of subjectivity constructed through language. In these practices they are very much influenced by the contemporary debates on cultural and politics.

The postmodern poets denied the centrality of individual artist as the 'genius'. They deconstructed 'poetics of presence' which emphasized the spoken word. The existing conventional ideas of the language are denied. They tried even to strike a balance between poetic practice and theory. There was a tremendous resistance to preconceived forms of dictating the arraignments of language and ideas. Open form has much been used by the postmodernist in the place of orthodox poetic forms. They introduced multiple voices in the poetry than unified voices. An awareness of textual dimensions of the language is conspicuous in the poetry of postmodernist. By denying the dominant linguistic formulations, the postmodernist depended much on linguistic play. They insisted on shared practices of a poetic community in opposition to the modernist ideology of individualism.

Postmodern Painting

Postmodern aesthetics is conspicuous by its emphasis on the figural over discursive. Postmodernism values the impact of art over the meaning of art. For it the sensation of art is much more important than that of interpretation. The literary critic Susan Sontag earlier laid the emphasis on the impact of art 1960s. She thought that modernism in art was in favour of intellect than sensual capability. She believed that interpretation is a "revenge of intellect upon art". Any work of art should not mere be a text, rather it should be a sensory product. This awareness or the focus on the sensory experience over intellectual experience led the way to postmodernism to favour the image over the narrative, figural over the discursive.

The two terms, figurative and discursive are used by Lyotard to distinguish the postmodern art of impact, surface, and sensation and the modernist art of meaning, depth, and interpretation. In the view of Lyotard, the figural is the primary process of the unconscious and the discursive is the secondary process. These two may be compared to Freudian 'id', and 'ego' respectively. Lyotard along with other postmodernists saw all discourses, whether in art, politics or even in science, as language games. These language games codify libidinal desires. The ultimate aim of postmodernists art is decodification and decolonisation of 'libidinal energies' of which language, text, and the intellect codify, censor and suppress.. In the process of achieving this, postmodern art changes from signifiers to signified, because it emphasizes image not narrative. Hence, the postmodern art increases the impact.

The above impact is possible only in the absence of signifiers, which act as mediators. Then art becomes participatory experience an rather than interpretative affair. The audience directly participates in the libidinal energies set free by the artist in the art. The criticism of art in this type of situation is replaced by art supplement. The art supplement is nothing but what the critic or the reviewer creates in his criticism or review. The critic gives just the impact of the art on him. That is why postmodernists are not concerned with what art means, rather they are concerned with what art does. Postmodernists do not equate aesthetics with beauty, rather they suggest an aesthetic of sublime.

One of the aims of postmodernism is the de-differentiation of the boundaries brought in by modernism between meaning and impact, surface and depth, high art and low art and even between art and politics. In this de-differentiation, postmodernism preferences are aesthetics over ethics, image over text. As it considers, the sensation of the present Postmodernism won't believe in the metanarratives of depth and the structural process. Postmodernism believes that sensation of the present will go beyond all socially constructed morals. Postmodern art can be seen as a slight move away from the siding with of abstraction and conceptualisation of modernism. It is also a shift away from domination of *avant-garde* art that has been dominating modern art since its beginning.

Explaining the function of art, according to Lyotard Paul Crowther says, 'First Lyotard holds that the function of painting since quattrocento has been to document the socio-political and religious order of things, by means of the laws of perspective-thus enabling the audience to identify both with the odder represented and with the artist's mastery of it. This tendency continuous even into the nineteenth and twentieth century in the guise of various realist styles'.[28]

In his essay "Postmodernism and Art" Colin Trodd says, 'The criticism of modernism, although taking any forms, cantered on the belief that it was repressive, clinical and self-possessed. Thus, in opposition to the self-cancelling nature of a modernism condemned by its own conceits, postmodernism, through its redeployment of allegory, parody and narrative quotation, could be associated with the revivification of art itself. Including installation art, photography, painting, and sculpture, postmodernism has been examined by such critics as Charles Jencks, Hal Foster, Rosalind Krauss, Douglas Crimp, Craig Owens, Benjamin Buchloh and Achille Bonito Olivia, all of whom were well versed in the writings of Derrida, Foucault and Baudrillard'.[29]

Installation art was the term applied to a set of critical practices, which emerged in the late 1960s, and was concerned with the conditions in which art is displaced. Artists like Marcel Broodthaers, Hans Haacke, Daniel Buren and Michael Asher were associated with the Installation Art. These artists explored the social, spatial and political networks which comprised the art world.

Modern art is monolithic, universal and closed, whereas, postmodern art is diverse, pluralistic and open ended. The dominant model in the modern painting is the progressive exposure of the formal quintessence the medium. Clive Bell, the modernist critic, in 1914 maintained that all great painting registered significant form. His intention, in the declaration was to suggest that the modern works of art possess their own values and criteria. According to Colin Trodd, 'the history of modern painting is the history of self-purification by the eradication of all 'external' influence until we are confronted with absolute form in the pristine and Spartan clarity of post-painterly abstraction'.[30]

Clemanet Greenberg, the American critic is his "Modernist Painting" (1961) spoke about modernist art in philosophical terms. In the view of Greenberg, modernism, in the process of establishing its autonomy of expression, creates the setting for the emergence of a pure art. This pure art will follow its own agenda. To borrow once again from Colin Trodd, 'Greenberg even predicted that the modern painter would devote more and more time to the nature of his medium : to the flatness of his canvas, to the physical reality of picture-plane, to the luminosity or the opacity of his colour, to the shape of his support, to the presence of the frame. Organizing itself as an inward-looking practice, this form of modernism was to develop through the rigorous elimination of all decorative and ornamental elements'.[31]

Scott Lash says, " Roger Fry and Clement Greenberg, for example, played inordinate roles in shaping the sensibility of successive generations of a high modernist audience. For Greenberg who privileged the flatness of the modernist world of art, the masterpiece was 'a universal, transhistorical form'. Greenberg has often been recognized as one who furnished convincing legitimation to the modernist art. In his view, the painting of nineteenth century was under the controlling influence of other arts like literature, the twentieth century was able to find or rediscover what was particular to it. Madan Sarup explains the ideas of Greenberg in clear terms. He says. 'According to Greenberg, the prime characteristic of painting, unlike any of the other arts, is that paint is applied to a flat, two-dimensional surface. Painting is reducible, in the end, to this one characteristic'.[32]

However, modernism has a far more complex history than offered by Greenberg. According to Colin Trodd in the model of Greenberg there is no place even for Dadaism, Surrearialism and Constructivism. These and other art movements tried to connect art and politics to generate visions of social and cultural liberation. But postmodernist artists and critics challenged the established cultural orthodoxy in the field of art, by understanding all the facets of modernism. By employing, various strategies to counter modernist tendencies in painting postmodernists were recognized as iconoclasts.

Though modernism sometimes rejected the idea of single meaning it ultimately believed in the ability of art to put forward profound insights into what humans could mean. As we have seen already, postmodernism considers that meanings are just surfaces, fictions and stories. Postmodernism considers the codes and conventions, which were introduced by modernism in the field of art, restrictive. In the view of postmodernism modernism has often been as an elitist phenomenon and the modernist works are inaccessible to the layman. In contrast to this, postmodernism does not accept any strict rule. In fact, it claims that there is no deep meaning to be known, as the meaning keeps changing all the time. In an interview given to Anders Stephanson, Frederic Jameson says, 'Finally, historicity and historical depth, which used to be called historical consciousness or the sense of the past, are abolished. In short, objects fall into the world and become decoration again : visual depth and systems of interpretation fade away, and something happen to historical time'.[33]

It believes that words, images and signs lead to more and more signs and images, but not to the truth. Meaning, in any art form or text is dependent on the contet in which it is placed. No text or image is unique as it is related to the other text. Postmodern art releases the art, from the rigid and restrictive rules, hence it is art, it is a liberating phenomenon. It emphasizes on multiplicity, difference and rejects the conventional ideals of unity, stability and uniformity. In fact, Postmodernism has radically devalued many long- established and time-honoured western myths and traditions; hence, it marks a crucial shift in the status of art and artists. Postmodernism views reality as a transitory and disorienting space.

Postmodern art encourages multiplication of stylistic norms and techniques. This emphasis on multiplicity is because of its mistrust in modernist aesthetics of omission or exclusion. The observations of Madan Sarup are valid here. He says, 'Some critics have suggested that the postmodern sensibility involves a shift of emphasis from epistemology to ontology. There has been a shift from knowledge to experience, from theory to practice, from mind to body. Some critics wish to describe those contemporary works that tend towards the body and away from the intellect as postmodern'.[34]

Sarup shows the postmodern artistic sensibility in the paintings of Francis Bacon. Francis Bacon was one of the most significant British artists after 1950s. Many of his paintings depict deformed and tormented figures secluded in depressing interiors. A series of his work of art show people screaming in hysteria and some of his other works are inspired by the traditional art. His subjects are linked to newspaper and magazine photographs of contemporary events. Many works are group in sets of three images called 'triptychs'. 'Triptychs' means a painting or carving (especially an altarpiece) on three panels (usually hinged together). This is intended to express multiple aspects of the same experience. Zygmunt Bauman says, 'The most salient feature of contemporary art is its defiance of order'.[35]

Bauman considers the contemporary art as the paradigm of postmodernity. This art has neither synchronic nor diachronic orders. In spite of the fact that artists of diverse styles populate the field of art, Bauman finds certain common suppositions common to the contemporary or postmodern art. The first supposition is pastiche. The artists are consciously or unconsciously invoking and alluding the distant moods, styles and techniques. Borrowing, eclecticism, and plagiarism and other concepts are no more considered derogatory and it was the case in the modern art. Extemporal, extraterritorial resources are used by the artists at random.

The second one is the use of collage. The postmodern artists often use such ordinary items as photographs and ticket stubs to make collages. An artist can create effects not achievable in traditional painting, by arranging the materials in a certain way. A few artists use collage technique to develop colour compositions. It denies the conventional principle of stylistic unity and follows the equivalence of genres and styles. Self-referentiality is another feature of the postmodern art. This feature is quite opposing to the modernist 'reality representation'.

Modern artists struggled to penetrate into the depths of the reality to achieve 'true' or 'correct' representation, and in the process, they depended on science. That is why we can see the influence of optics, theory of relativity and psychoanalysis on impressionists, cubists and surrealists respectively. The postmodern artists reject all the pretensions and negate all conscious intentions in the making of art. In the view of Bauman the postmodern artists, 'aspire to represent nothing but their own practice : the canvas, its flatness, the media and their inherent qualities'.[36]

Bauman understands Marcel Duchamp's rude act of entering a urinal to an art salon as the ultimate triumph of modernism, rather than a gesture against it. Duchamp's 'iconoclastic venture' was aimed at art critics and theorists. It was an attempt to obtain by threat from the hands of those who have achieved that power or authority by the expertise they possessed in aesthetic discourse rather than by practicing art. Unlike Duchamp, the postmodern artist exhibits his conspicuous invulnerability to theorizing.

The postmodern art world devoid of rules and departing cannon may seem chaotic. Bauman believes that one can make sense out of this chaos, as it is an indication of the acceptance of the plurality of human worlds, which modern philosophy refused to acknowledge. In this context, the opinion of Bauman on postmodern art is significant. He says,'More than ever before, the work of art is now blatantly and emphatically construed. It has no authority to invoke in order to legitimise and validate itself, except the decision of its author. It has no ecumenically dominant or ecumenically ambitious code to refer to, in order to reveal its meaning; instead, it has to construct and deploy its own explanatory potential. In the absence of all wider referential frameworks, a postmodern work of art is moreover open to multiplicity of interpretations which are bound to stop short of reaching 'authoritative' status, and thus remain inconclusive'.[37]

Bauman analyses the postmodern art in saying that, 'The multitude of styles and genres is no longer a projection of the time arrow upon the space of cohabitation. Styles do not divide into progressive and retrograde, forward-looking and outdated. New artistic inventions are not meant to chase out and replace extant ones, but to join the others, finding some elbowroom for themselves on the notoriously overcrowded artistic stage. In a setting where synchrony replaces diachrony, co-presence takes the place of the succession and the perpetual present replaces history-competition takes over from the crusades. No more talk of missions, of advocacy, prophesying, of one and only truth bound to strangle all pseudo-truths. All styles, old and new alike, must prove their right to survival applying the same strategy, since they all submit to the same laws that rule all creation, calculated –in George Steiner's memorable phrase-for maximal impact and instant obsolescence'.[38]

Ihab Hassan, the American literary critic had established criteria for distinguishing 'postmodernist' works from their modernist' equivalents. In his view the modernist works of art privilege depth and determinacy, whereas, postmodernist works privilege surface and indeterminacy. According to Peter Wollen, 'Postmodernism was to be defined as 'art about art', not in the modernist sense of the ontological self-examination and research, the testing and probing of the foundations of painting, but in the new sense of citation, translation, 'deconstruction' and neoclassicism'.[39]

Wollen identifies the use of pastiche and parody, anarchic eclecticism, diaristic polyptychs as signs of new postmodern alternative. Speaking on the postmodern art Zygmunt Bauman says, 'The meaning of postmodern art, we may says, is to stimulate the process of meaning-making and guard it against the danger of ever grinding to a halt; to alert to the inherent polyphony of meaning and to the intricacy of all interpretation; to act as a sort of intellectual and emotional antifreeze, which prevents solidification of any half-way finding into an icy canon arresting the flow of possibilities. Instead of reasserting reality as a graveyard of untested possibilities, postmodern art brings into the open the perpetual incompleteness of meanings and thus go a step further, and suggest that the meaning of postmodern art is deconstruction of meaning; more exactly, revealing the secret of meaning, the secret which modern theoretical practices tried hard to hide or belie-that meaning 'exists' solely in the process of interpretation and critique, and dies together with it'.[40]

Postmodern Architecture

Postmodernism in architecture is movement that developed in the late 20th century and that can roughly be said to be characterized by the combination of new forms, materials, and techniques with the subtle and highly conscious use of motifs and conventions from earlier periods. In architecture, it developed largely as a reaction against the starkness and uncompromising modernism of the International Style.

Postmodernism has been a particularly significant phenomenon in architecture, especially during the 1980s, when prominent commissions were given to such leading figures as Robert Venturi, Michael Graves, James Stirling, Terry Farrell, Charles Moore, Hans Hollein, and Arata Isozaki. Their work drew on a variety of styles, including Modernism, classicism, and even vernacular domestic architecture. This eclecticism recognized the essential pluralism of post-industrial society, a particularly important factor in the field of architecture, since most significant buildings are today used by a range of people with very different tastes and cultural preferences.

The desire to appeal to a broad public has led Postmodernist architects to combine scholarly references to earlier architectural styles with more obviously enjoyable decorative features. A particularly fine example of this is James Stirling's and Michael Wilford's Staatsgalerie (1977-1984) in Stuttgart, where brightly coloured fixtures, such as handrails and canopies, adorn a building that also contains allusions to Classical architecture. The element of populism in such buildings can be compared with the narrow appeal of Modernism, whose austere structures were, according to the Postmodernists, enjoyed only by a cultural elite.

Nigel Watson says, 'The starting point for much of the debate about postmodernism is the twentieth century has been architecture. It has even been suggested that the transition from the modern to the era of the post-modern can be specified as 3.32pm on 15 July 1972. This is the time when a prize-winning example of modern housing-Pruitt-Igoe housing development is St.Louis- was blown up because it was considered unsuitable for human habitation even by those on low income. Modern architecture was characterized by the principles of architects such as Le Corbusier who was at his most influential in the 1920s, though his ideas are typified by the high rise flats which came to dominate our cities in the 1960s".[41]

The modernist architects, like the modernists writers, rejected all previous forms and insisted that both traditional and classical forms of architecture should be replaced by building based upon rational and universal principles. In practice it was an emphasis on functional design. Usually these designs were in glass and concrete. The building was decontextualised and universalised. In the opinion of Nigel,'The hearts of cities were flattened to be replaced all over the world by buildings which looked the same. This was metanarratives of modernism'.[42]

Postmodern architects worked in a more emphatically historical style. For example, the J. Paul Getty Museum, built by Langdon and Wills at Malibu, California, U.S.A. was inspired by a Roman villa. At Marne-la-Vallee, near Paris, Ricardo Bofil used prefabricated concrete to produce echoes of Classicism in the columnar architecture of housing developments like Les Espaces d'Abraxas (1978-1983). This interest in historical styles has been accompanied by concern for preserving old buildings and adapting them to new uses. Many government agencies have been created to preserve buildings of architectural value. Such buildings may not be destroyed or altered.

Most of post-modernist architecture are small buildings, such as houses and stores. In 1978, Philip Johnson unveiled the design he created with John Burgee for the first post-modern skyscraper, the American Telephone and Telegraph Company (now AT&T Corp.) headquarters building in New York City. The base of this controversial structure resembles the Pazzi Chapel of the Renaissance. Johnson and Burgee topped the design with a pediment that has a round opening at the peak to allow clouds of steam to escape from the building's heating system.

The Pompidou Centre in Paris was built by Richard Rogers and Renzo Piano. It reflects the modernist belief in exposing a building's structure. All of its structural and service elements, such as beams and lifts, are painted in primary colours and are visible from the outside.

The postmodern architects rejected the industrial, engineering, and functional aspects of the modern movement of its disregard for history. There is a distrust of corporate capitalism among postmodern architects. They pointed out the inhabitability of modernist housing projects and the demolition of cherished civic spaces. Postmodern architects are stimulated by environmentalism.

The Postmodern architects rejected the modernist subordination of form to function and celebrated spectacle. The postmodern architecture in a way reflects a search for fantastic world and it evokes imagination. It puts together a collage of historical styles. Unlike modernist architecture, which sought to rationalize space, postmodern architecture suspends normal categories of time and space, social and rational categories. In a way it is 'irrational'.

Postmodern Music

The impact of postmodernism on music and musicology can be seen only in the 1980s. Derek Scott says, 'Postmodernism began to have an impact upon music and musicology in the 1980s when it came evident that a paradigmatic shift n thought was needed in order to find answers to the theoretical impasses that had been reached in several areas'.[43]

In the view of Derek Scott the idea that mass audience did no more than passively consume the products of cultural industry has lost its credibility. In the contemporary times it is apparent that classical music is as involved in the market place in the jazz music. Conductors and singers are becoming super stars. The evolution of musical style was now contested. The emphasis that was very heavy on the social significance of music now a days is hardly seen. In this contest postmodernism offered a new theoretical perspective.

Postmodernism in the fields of art, literature and music drove out the theory of art for art's sake. It rejected the modernist notions of universalism, internationalism and the art for art's sake. Postmodernism replaced these concepts by emphasizing the local and specific cultures and celebrating the differences. The art for art's sake movement that originated in the nineteenth century, as a movement against industrialization, proved an untranscendable barricade to the production of art that will provide happiness to the millions of populace. However, by 1980s there was a strong feeling to uncover the complicity between art and entertainment. Many middle class families and individuals shifted their attention from high culture to popular culture. In fact, the distinction between the two disappeared or blurred. Since 1960s onwards, there is an excellent similarity in selling techniques used for the classical repertoire and pop music. The dichotomy that has been shown between arts versus entertainment is an ethical one rather aesthetic.

Postmodern Dance

In Dance also postmodernism is a movement that rebelled against the theories and practices of modernism. The term postmodernism has long been associated with dance. In fact, this association can be traced back from from1960s itself. In the beginning, the postmodern dance tried to break away from the Western conceptions of the classical grace and harmony. This breaking away has interesting resonances in the view of Tim Woods. He says, 'This has interesting resonances with the conceptions of the postmodern as a shattering of the harmonies of Euclidean geometry (e.g. postmodern fiction as part of the quantum universe). Dancers and performance artists, like Laurie Anderson, Botho Strauss, Carolee Schneemann, Yvonne Rainer, Lucinda Childs, Meredith Monk, Steve Paxton, Pina Bausch and Trisha Brown, have been instrumental in challenging the strict cannons of physical aesthetics of the ballet floor'.[44]

In the same context, Tim Woods quotes the Michael Kirby's definition of postmodern dance, from the introduction to the special issue of the magazine *Drama Review*, on Postmodern Dance, March 1975 : 'In the theory of post-modern dance, the choreographer does not apply visual standards to the work. The view is an interior one : movement is not pre-selected for its characteristics but results from certain decisions, goals, plans schemes, rules concepts or problems. Whatever actual movement occur during the performance is acceptable as long as limiting and controlling principles are adhered to'.[45]

However, in Dance postmodernism was associated with the work of a group of choreographers, visual artists and musicians who performed at the Judson Memorial Church in New York's Greenwich Village from 1962-1964. The Judson theatre originated out of the work created for a choreography class taught by the musician Robert Duncan at the studio of Merce Cunningham. Cunningham was a dancer and choreographer and the leader of the avant-garde in American dance. Cunningham and John Cage, another American composer, who had an intense influence on avant-garde music and dance, formed a productive association. Cunningham, by rejecting the earlier literary and psychological themes established his own company. He collaborated with other composers and painters like Robert Rauschenberg and Andy Warhol. Rauschenberg, the American painter, played an important role in the transition from Abstract Expressionism to Pop Art.

The Judson Theatre emerged out of the work created for a choreography class taught by musician Robert Duncan in 1960s at the studio of Merce Cunningham. The artist at the Judson theatre revalued or re-examined the nature of dance and contested all the aspects of performance and presentation of choreographic work. They explored new and cooperative methods of working. In fact, the artists were heavily influenced by the philosophical theories of the various schools like existentialism, Zen Buddhism and phenomenology. Immediacy of the moment and presence in the performance and a search for the intrinsic properties of the dance medium were considered essential. They rejected set patterns and codified systems of movement and even specialized body image. They treated dance as its own subject, pure movement and untainted by the personality of its artists.

Yvonne Rainer was one of the key figures among the members of the Judson Dance and authored the most famous manifests of the Theater. 'Aesthetics of denial' was the conspicuous elements in these manifestos.

In fact, Rainer and other members of the group aimed the demystifying and objectifying the dance. They even intended to discard anything that seemed superfluous to them. Other prominent members of the group were Trisha Brown, Lucinda Childs, David Gordon, Deborah Hay and Steve Paxton. However, it is the work of Steve Paxton, which was considered significant after the work of Rainer.

In fact, Steve Paxton was originally a gymnast who turned to dance and was trained to dance with Marce Cunningham and Robert Duncan. Paxton, most of the time preferred to work with small informal groups rather than with formal companies. He devised a form of dance that uses the physical laws of gravity, friction and inertia to explore the relationship between two moving bodies. His style allowed choreographers to explore and develop movement sequences with the dancers. His influence has been spread by the workshops known as "jams".

After the 1960s the new artists resiscovered the traditional techniques of narrative, virtuosity, theatricaltiy and dream,however, they put them together in a diferent way from the earlier times. The radical changes in the audio and visual technology offered new dimensions. The new theories of the thinkers like Roland Barthes, Jacques Derrida, and Jean-Francoise Lyotard influenced the artists. These thinkers who anatomised the language showed them new ways and extended the imaginative capabilities and the possibilities of the artists. The artists concentrated on signs and symbols rather than on the words. This also resulted in an extension of the scope of the imagination of the artists.

Notes

1 Norman K.Denzin. *Images of Postmodern Society; Social Theory and Contemporary Cinema*. London : Sage, 1991, p. VII.

2 Patricia Waugh '*Postmodernism : A Reader.* London : Edward Arnold, 1992, p-3.

3 Wayne Hudson. "Postmodernity and Contemporary Social Thought" in *Politics and Social Theory*.(Ed.) Peter Lassman London : Routledge.1989.

4 Susan Watkins. *Twentieth Century Women Novelists : Feminist Theory into Practice*. New York : Palgrave, 2001. pP. 97-98.

5 Paul Maltby. *Dissident Postmodernists : Barthelme, Coover, Pynchon*. Philadelphia : University of Pennsylvania Press 1991, p. 3-4.

6 Paul Maltby. *Ibid.*,, p. 5.

7 Herbert Schiller. Quoted by *Paul Maltby*. *Ibid.*, p. 7.

8 Paul Maltby *Ibid.*, p. 7.

9 Mike Featherstone. *Consumer Culture and Postmodernism*. London: Sage. 1991 , p. 126.

10 Ben Agger. Cultural Studies as Critical Theory. London : The Falmer Press., 1992, p. 106

11 Ben Agger. *Ibid.*, p. 106.

12 Zygmunt Bauman. *Postmodernity and its Discontents*. New York : New York University Press, 1997, p. 95.

13 Ihab Hassan. *The Postmodern Turn : Essays in Postmodern Theory and Culture*. Ohio : Ohio State University Press, 1987, p. 3.

14 Mike Featherstone. In Pursuit of Postmodern : An Introduction. In M.Featherstone(Ed.), Postmodernism (Special issue). Theory, Culture&Society, 5, 1988, to , p. 203.

15 Quoted by Patricia Waugh. In "Mass Society and Postmodern Fiction" in Postmodernism : A Reader. (Ed.), London : Edward Arnold, 1992, p. 26.

16 Peter L. Cooper. *Thomas Pynchon and the Contemporary World*. 1981, p. 2.

17 Ihab Hassan. *Paracriticisms Seven Speculations of the Times*. Urbana: University of Illinois Press, 1975, p. 21.

18 John Enck. "John Barth" An Interview," *Wisconsin Studies in Contemporary Literature 6,* Winter-Spring 1965, p. 13.

19 Peter L. Cooper. Thomas Pynchon and the Contemporary World , p. 5.

20 Jerome Klinkowitz. Literary Disruptions. Urbana : University of Illinois Press. 1980, p. 80

21 Ronald Sukenick. Quoted by Paul Maltby in *Dissident Post-modernists : Barthelme, Coover, Pynchon.* Philadelphia : University of Pennsylvania Press. 1991, p. 43.

22 Paul Maltby in *Dissident Postmodernists : Barthelme, Coover, Pynchon,* p. 49.

23 Kurt Vonnegut. *Slaughterhouse Five*. London : Vintage 1991, p. 87.

24 William Burroughs'. Quoted by Tim Woods. in Beginning Postmodernism Manchester : Manchester University Press. 1999, p. 55.

25 Barry Lewis. Postmodernism and Literature. in *The Routledge Companion to Postmodernism.* (Ed.) Stuart Sim, London : Routledge, 2001, p. 130.

26 Tim Wood. *Beginning Postmodernism*, p. 58.

27 Tim Woods. *Ibid,* p. 69.

28 Paul Crowther. *Critical Aesthetics and Postmodernism.* Oxford : Clarendon Press, 1993, p. 151.

29 Colin Trodd. Postmodernism and Art. In *Routledge Companion to Postmodernism*, (Ed.) Stuart Sim, London : Routledge, 2001, *Ibid.*, p. 90.

30 Colin Trodd. *Ibid.*, p. 90.

31 Colin Trodd. *Ibid.*, p. 91.

32 Madan Saru, *p. An Introductory Guide to Post-Structuralism and Postmodernism.* Athens : University of Georgia Press. 193, p. 172.

33 Frederic Jameson. In *Universal Abandon? : Politics of Postmodernism*. (Ed.) Andrew Ross. Minneapolis : University of Minnesota Press, 1988, p. 5.

34 Madan Saru, p. *An Introductory Guide to Post-Structuralism and Postmodernism*, p. 172.

35 Zygmunt Bauman. *The Intimations of Postmodernity*. London : Routledge, 1992, p. 27

36 Zygmunt Bauman. *Ibid.*, p. 28.

37 Zygmunt Bauman, *Ibid.*, p, p. 30-31.

38 Zygmunt Bauman. *Postmodernity and its Discontents*. New York : New York university Press, 1997, p. 100.

39 Peter Wollen. *Raiding the Ice Box : Reflections on the Twentieth Century Culture*, London : Verso,1993, p. 183.

40 Zygmunt Bauman. *Postmodernism and its Discontents*, p. 107.

41 Nigel Watson. "Postmodernism and Lifestyles (or : You are What You Buy)In *Routledge Companion to Postmodernism.*(Ed.) : Stuart Sim, London : Routledge. 2001 , p. 61.

42 Nigel Watson. *Ibid.*, p,61.

43 Derek Scoot. "Postmodernism and Music". In The Routledge Companion to Postmodernism, (Ed) by Stuart Sim, p. 134.

44 Tim Woods. Beginning Postmodernism, Manchester : Manchester University Press, 1999, p. 83

45 Tim Woods. *Ibid.*, p. 84

VII

A comparative analysis of modern and postmodern aesthetics

Though there is a possibility in history to show the breaks between one period and another period, it may not be possible to demarcate between one type of aesthetic and another. No culture disappears entirely form the scene and the new emerges. The same applies even to modern and postmodern aesthetics. In spite of the radical brake between modernism and postmodernism, some features and aspects seem to overlap in these two isms.

From the end of nineteenth century to the first half of twentieth century, various 'revolutions' such as the social cultural and sexual, emerged. These movements have their own literary expressions and most of these movements evolved under the banner of modernism. In fact, the revolutions are a part of the modernist project. In the widest meaning of the term 'modern'. This project is basically for the reconstruction of an authentic, higher and essential reality, to be found beyond conventional and arbitrary science system of culture.

The thought of Enlightenment philosophers like Descartes, Kant, Marx, Nietzsche and Freud exposed the illusion of an ideological self-consciousness, and discovered an essential reality in the self propagation of matter and material production, in the life instinct, in the will to power, in the sexual drive and the power of unconscious. These discoveries were all the creation of modernism. On the whole modernism can be defined as revolution, which strove to abolish the arbitrary character of culture and relativity of signs. In the abolition it aimed to affirm the hidden absoluteness of being. This absoluteness can be seen, specifically in the "economics" of Marx, "life" in Nietzsche, "libido" and "unconscious" in Freud, "creative clan" in Bergson, "stream of consciousness" in William James, "being in Heidegger", and the list goes on.

Postmodernism directs its sharpest criticism at modernism for the modernism's adherence to the illusion of "ultimate truth", "absolute language" and "a new style". Postmodernism says all these elements lead to the "essential reality". In fact postmodernism emerged as a new cultural paradigm in the very process of differentiating it self form modernism, as experiment in the self enclosure of sign system, of language folding in upon itself. The absolute notion of reality beyond that of sign system is criticized by postmodernism and considered it as a part of 'meta physics of presence'.

The modernist criticism of the 1920's and 1930's, as represented by the most influential schools, such as Russian Formalism and Anglo-American New Criticism, and later structuralism, attempts to free itself from all historical, social, biographical and psychological moments, integrated into literature, in order to separate the phenomenon of pure literariness. This literariness of literature is analogous to the "elementary particles" of the texture of literature, its ultimate and irreducible essence. This 'purification' is not intended to place literature in an autonomous status; rather it is intended to show how literary or cultural texts can be read without the constraints of various schools, like romanticism, realism, the biographical, psychological and historical criticism, the criticism of naturalism and symbolism and other types of 19th and 20th century criticism. That is the criticism now wanted to free literature from an imposed content and let the literature take its own form. Everything which was valued in literature—the reflection of historical reality, the author's world view, the influence of the intellectual treads of the times, the inferred higher reality of symbolic meanings—all of the now seemed naïve and old-fashioned and extraneous to literature.

Much of the dominant literature of modernist thought can be traced to the work of structural functionalism or totalising theory. A good part of this literature rests on an underlying homeostatic, tension-reduction, or equilibrium model. Freud, for example, rests his views on some conception of tension-reduction as the operative force in social structural development. Perhaps we can trace much of this to Newtonian physics and its influence. The central question is one of order.

Modernist thought is focused on totalising theory, the search for overencompassing theories of society and social development. Some discoverable foundation was said to exist. At the centre, a logos was said to be at play; whether, for example, as in Weber's forces of rationalization, Freud's homeostasis, or as in Hegel's Absolute Spirit. These logics slumbered in anticipation of their correct articulation. These were the transcendental signifiers that were discoverable. Much of the often-mentioned consensus paradigm, too, can be placed within the modernist paradigm. Thus metanarratives are still replete with assumptions of homogeneity, desirability of consensus, order, etc.

Some of the major issues to which the modern literature responded are :

1· A search for secure ontological ground. Ontological ground is that which gives a sense of surety of being itself.

2· Industrialization and consequent displacement of persons from their previous physical and psychic groundings.

3· Capitalism and an oppressive hypocritical moralism.

4· A critical challenge to religious texts and revolutions.

5· The popularization of evolutionary theory.

6· Changes in philosophical thought which suggested that 'reality' was an internal and changeable, not an externally validated, concept, and that what is considered 'real' is based on the desire for power, not on any objective warrant.

7· A sense that the culture has lost its bearings and there is a collapse of values or bankruptcy of values.

8· The society built on power and greed, a shift in paradigms, i.e., models of how the world works from the closed, finite, measurable, cause-and-effect universe of 19th century science to an open, relativistic, changing, strange universe, and a shift from an evolutionary, developmental model to a structural, surface/death model.

9· The basing on the individual judgement and locating meaning in the individual experience.

10· The development of studies and ideas, which have as their focus the nature and functioning of the individual : the discipline of psychology; psychotherapy; movements such as Impressionism and Cubism, which focus on the process of perception.

11· A discovery that the forces governing behaviour, and particularly the most powerful and formative ones, are hidden : this in the realms of psychology, economics, politics—Marx, Freud, Nietzsche, etc. This leads to the search for underlying, hidden structures.

Postmodernist and Poststructuralist responses are radically deviant from the above modernist responses. Neither Postmodernism and Poststructuralism can nor be called as schools, rather they are a group of approaches motivated by some common understanding. In fact these are not sets of theoretical positions, which have at their core a self reflexive discourses. These theories are aware of their tentativeness, the ambiguity and slipperiness.

In contrary to the modernist paradigms, the postmodernists and poststructuralists reject the totalising, essentialist and foundationlist concepts. This rejection is based on the principle that the totalising concept puts all phenomenon under one explanatory concept; for example, the will of God. An essentialist suggests that there is a reality which exists independent of, beneath or beyond, language and ideology, that there is such a thing as 'the feminine', for instance, or 'truth' or 'beauty'. Such a foundationalist concept suggests that signifying systems are stable and unproblematic representations of a world.

Postmodernists challenge the concept of 'man' as developed by Enlightenment philosophy and its cultural manifestation modernism. To be specific, the postmodernist view holds that latest persons are culturally and discursively constructed. The coming term for a person so conceived is a 'subject'.

For the postmodernists, the 'subjects' are created through their cultural meanings and practices and occupy numerous culture based sites, like family occupation, economically and regionally defined, as gendered and of sexually orientated, as members of clubs etc. Every site among these evokes a different configuration of the self, different language usages and different social practices. These subjects are social in their very origin. They take their meaning value and self image from their identity groups in society. Postmodernist understandings of persons are called as anti - humanist, because they are apposed to the humanist idea that persons are isolated and largely material beings, and that humanity is transcendent universal and unchangeable in its essence. One should understand that to be anti-human is not to be anti-humane.

Postmodernism sees reality as being fragmented, diverse and culture specific. That is why they emphasize on specific histories, cultures, and discourses. They pay much attention to the role of language textuality in the construction of reality and identity.

The poststructuralists believe that we live in a linguistic universe, hence, they reject the traditional aesthetic assumptions that language is 'transparent' medium which hands over experience unproblematically. In the linguistic universe reality is only mediated reality. As we live in a world of language, discourse and ideology, naturally our sense of being and meaning is structured by them and none of them transparent.

The postmodernist views that meaning is textual and intertextual. As Derrida says, 'there is nothing outside of text'. Every text, be it literary or cultural acquires its meaning in relation to other texts. This understanding doesn't mean that all reality is textual. It only means that reality is given in the textualised form. Texts are marked by the surplus of meaning. The surplus is identified in the polysemous nature of both language and rhetoric. The meaning of the text is continually differing, overflowing and an influx.

Postmodernists use the term 'discourse' in place of ideology. Discourse is regulated by rules of exclusion, by internal systems of control and delineation, by conditions under which discourses can be employed.

In philosophy 'modernity' begins with Descartes. But in literature and the arts, however, modernism is a 1910-50s phenomenon. In English literature it begins with Joyce, Eliot, Pound, Schoenberg, Corbusier et al. The modern age is brought out by the acceleration in economic activity through "world-system" in the years following 1750 or one could even say the European renaissance. The hallmarks of modern thought are :

Humanism : The human being is the source of meaning and value. Nature is valued only as a useful object to humans. The development of human potential is the highest goal of politics.

Individualism : The individual is both ethically and intellectually prior to society. Humans have rights and the intellectual progress, techno-economic progress is made by the leaps of genius.

Rationalism : There is a natural human faculty of reason, in two guises, theoretical and practical, moving from universal principles to particular applications. Reason and knowledge are antithetical to power, which is centralized and repressive.

Secular moralism: Human reason alone can allow moral actions and moral society, if freed from the superstition and prejudice of religious dogmatism.

Progressive History and Progress : Human history is progressive. Moderns are more humane and moral, because of the public use of reason in governmental rationality, than previous ages.

Postmodernity is specificity of the age that begins after the Second World War. This age starts after capitalism has moved far enough that the conceptual schemes of its early period (1600-1945) are now obsolete and in need of replacement. It redefines and modifies the basic concepts of modernity. In the postmodern age the question of novelty, fashion and tradition are applied to conceptual schemes. In fact, these categories are often used in aesthetics.

Postmodernism radically opposes the modernist logic of "either – or". Postmodernism believes that it is difference that produces identity. Since identities are what we are presented with gender, race class, nation, etc., postmodernism is diagnostic, suspicious, or critical. In its post-structuralist form, postmodernism works back from what seems to an identity to the historical and material conditions of its production and questions the 'rational' and 'logical' identities. Poststructuralists would investigate the ways in which gender, race, class, etc. are produced in material practice. Genders, clothes, hair, race, housing segregation, class, free time, money, inheritances are spaces where identities are formed or constructed.

Realism is one of the driving forces of modernist literature. In opposition to this postmodern writings are counterrealist. Even among the contemporary writers it is possible to show these two extremes. Compared to the writings of counterrealists, the realist writing presents a recognizable, detailed, and plausible social surrounding. A would be writer in Mailer's "The Man Who Studied Yoga" complains that "reality is no longer realistic". The works of the whole range of postmodernist writers echoes this observation. The characters in many of the modernist novels are rounded and individualized characters that are explained or made explicable, through attention to their psychology and motivation. A coherent and consistent narration focuses on their conflicts, introspections, formation of values, personal and social interactions. One has the sense that the characters and their worlds function pretty much by cause and effect, by regular and fixed rules that are familiar or at least knowable in theory. With such characters in such a world, logical explanation is possible.

Generally the modernists show their characters as trying to reach a reasonable mode of being with themselves, with others, and with their civilization. These authors ask us to suspend our disbelief, to concede that the events they describe have happened or could happen to a real person. Writers with an affinity for this kind of realism include Saul Bellow, John Updike, James Baldwin, and Joyce Carol Oates et al. But in postmodernists we recognize their fundamental divergence from the principles and practices of realism.

Postmodern counterrealist characters are dwarfed or shadowed not so much by their social or the cosmic context as by their aesthetic one. The postmodern self-conscious work can metaphysically disturb us. The characters in the postmodern novels are less substantial. These characters are less dimensional than the forces that dominate them. By creating the characters within such position the authors expose the man's position in a public world of technology, institutions and interlocking power structures. According to Cooper, 'Burroughs' played against a backdrop of surrealist filth, makes repeated references to a dynamic universe and often depicts higher forms of life of being broken down into lower forms and those broken again into undifferentiated waste'.[1]

The existentialist literature that emerged in the modernist movement is not a negation of realism, rather its ultimate expansion and a method of rationalistic construction of universal principle of irrationality, designated as 'will' by Schopenhauer, as 'life by Nietzsche, as 'existence' and 'individual' by Kierkegaard. This rationality is much more reasoned and abstract than all the forms of rationality, which divides being into a certain concrete types, into laws and essences. In rationality there is always a dose of concreteness because it is in determinate relation with 'some thing', it is the sense of concrete thing. Again the rationality of this 'some thing' should be explained in the rational point of view. For example, Sartre's novel "Nausea". The novel demonstrates how the unhappy consciousness of Roquentin, not bound by anything and raised to the highest degree of abstractness, suddenly encounters the abstract texture of being of the roots and of the earth, stubborn in its absurdity and inducing nausea. This absurdity which the existentialist consciousness discovers everywhere as the revelation of a 'true' reality, which has not been distorted or generalized, which is given anterior to any act of rationalization, is in fact, "hyperreality". It is a product of rational generalization.

The term 'postmodernism' suggests that the modernist culture has moved into a new phase. The Renaissance which was a movement that was connected with the rise of individualism and the beginnings of the capitalist, bureaucratic industrial order. In the realm of arts and culture modernism is associated with the writings of authors such as James Joyce, Franz Kafka, Marce Proust, Thomas Mann, T.S.Eliot, and Luigi Pirandello. In the visual arts, modernism refers to the work of artists such as Pablo Picasso, Henry Matisse and Jorges Braque and movements such as Futurism, Dadaism, and Surrealism.

In Music, modernism is associated with the work of composers such as Igor Stravansky, Arnold Schoenberg. These creative artists and the modernist movement reflected major changes in the expressive arts. As Featherstone says, 'The basic features of modernism can summarized as : as aesthetic self-consciousness and rflexiveness; a rejection of narratives structure in favour of simultaneity and montage; an exploration of the paradoxical, ambiguous and uncertain open ended nature of reality; and a rejection of the notion of the integrated personality in favour of an emphasis on the destructed, dehumanised subject'.[2]

In the view of Featherstone that some of the features of the modernism in the arts have appropriated by postmodern artists, so it is easy to distinguish the two movements in some cases. He lists some of the features connected with postmodernism in the arts : 'the effacement of the boundary between art and everyday life; the collapse of the hierarchical distinction between high and mass/popular culture; a stylistic promiscuity favouring eclecticism and mixing of codes; parody, pastiche, irony, playfulness and the celebration of the surface "depthlessness" of culture; the decline of the originality/genius of artistic producer and the assumption that art can only be repetitious'.[3]

Todd Gitlin offers a slightly different perspective on postmodernism, 'It self-consciously splices genres, attitudes, styles. It relishes the blurring or juxtaposition of forms (fiction-nonfiction), stances (straight ironic), moods (violent-comic), cultural levels (high-low), ...It pulls the rug out from under itself, displaying an acute self-consciousness about the works constructed nature. It takes pleasure in the play of surfaces, and derides the search for depth as mere nostalgia'.[4]

Modern thought tended toward a totalising 'Truth' centered on apparently discoverable logos. Driven by formal rational methods, one would inevitably end up in a dominant and globalising thought. Lyotard for example, has explained how scientific knowledge has usurped narrative knowledge. Narrative knowledge, on the other hand, is based on myth, legend, tales, stories etc, which provided the means of being in society. Whereas scientific knowledge tends towards closure, narrative knowledge embraces imaginary free play. The search for truth by the modernists was inevitably guided by the ideal of establishing absolute postulates from which all other 'facts' can be explained by linear, deductive logic. Postmodernists on the other hand, view knowledge as always fragmented, partial and contingent. It always has multiple sites of production. Postmodernist celebrate local knowledge. Dominant and global knowledge always subverts voices that otherwise seek expression, either directly or indirectly.

Like modernism, postmodernism subsumes different tendencies. Ihab Hassan in his "Postmodern Turn"[5] shows some schematic differences between modernism and postmodernism in the following division :

Modernism	Postmodernism
Romanticism/Symbolism	Pataphysic/Dadaism
Form(conjunctive, closed)	Antiform(disjunctive, open)
Purpose	Play
Design	Chance
Hierarchy	Anarchy
Mastery/Logos	Exhaustion /Silence
Art Object/Finished Work	Process/Performance/Happening
Distance	Participation
Creation/Tantalization	Decreation/ Deconstruction
Synthesis	Antithesis
Presence	Absence

Centering	Dispersal
Genre/Boundary	Text/ Intertext
Semantics	Rhetoric
Paradigm	Syntagm
Hypotexis	Parataxis
Metaphor	Metonymy
Selection	Combination
Root/ Depth	Rhizome/ Surface
Interpretation/ reading	Against Interpretation /Misreading
Signified	Signifier
Lisible (Redearly)	Scriptable (Writerly)
Narrative/*Grande Histoire*	Antinarrative/*Petite Histoire*
Master Code	Idiolect
Symptom	Desire
Type	Mutant
Genital / Phallic	Polymorphous/Androgynous
Paranoia	Schizophrenia
Origin / Cause	Difference-Difference/Trace
God the Father	The Holy Ghost
Metaphysics	Irony
Determinacy	Indeterminacy
Transcendence	Immanence

Postmodern architecture is regarded as having brutalized people in its attempt to rationalize, to impose a strict and systematic order on, their ways of living. Unfortunately for the idealist, humans are not entirely rational, ordered or disciplined. Their tastes are variable and mostly non-justifiable, and are prone to fits of folly. For these reasons postmodern architecture, with its taste for crazy pastiche, its wild blending of styles, its disrespect for monastic regularity and tolerance for historical referentiality is deemed more human than the rigoros of modernist purism.

The opinion of Baudrillard on the modernist architecture of America reflects of viciousness of modern architecture, 'No, architecture should not be humanized. Anti-architecture, the true sort (not the kind you find in Arcosanti, Arizona, which gathers together all the 'soft' technologies in the heart of desert), the wild inhuman type that is beyond the measure of man was made here-made itself here-in New York, without considerations of setting, well-being, or ideal ecology. It opted for hard technologies, exaggerated all dimensions, gambled heaven and hell…Eco-architecture, eco-society…this is the gentle hell of the Roman Empire in decline'.[6]

The early-century musical *avant-garde* also exemplified the phenomena of vanguardism, radical interventionism, and a defensive disdain for immediate audiences. Like the other avant-gardes of the early century, it aroused public scandal and moral outrage. An infamous occasion was the first performance of Berg's Altenberg songs in Vienna in 1913, which provoked such a riot that the police were called in, as did the Parisian premiere of Stravinsky's "Rite of Spring" soon after. This extreme public hostility caused defensive attempts by composers to get their music played. Schoenberg and his circle founded the "Society for the Private Performance of Music" in 1918. Performances were by invitation and unpublicized, and critics and the public were barred. They thus created an elite group by which their music was judged, closed against the ravages of commercialism and of the mass public.

These early modernist composers supported themselves mainly by private teaching and occasional conducting jobs. They experienced the usual alternation between marginalisation and ostracism, then sudden public acclaim, typical of an *avant-garde*.

Georgina Born summarizes the antagonism between modern and postmodern music at three levels. First, by their different relation music and culture; Second the absence and presence of supraformalist concern with the social and political dimensions of culture; and Third, by confecting technological discourses and the use of different technologies. He classifies the differences in the following manner:[7]

Modernism/ Serialism, Postserialism	Postmodernism/ Experimental Music
Determinism	Indeterminism, nondeterminism.

Rationalism Mysticism.	Irrationalism,
Science, Universalism	Sociopoliticization.
Cerebral, complex Text-centered	Physical,performative, simple Practice-centered.
Linear, cumulative, teleological	Cyclical, repetitive, static.

Within a unity of difference to Popular music

Nonreference, absolute Reference	difference, transformation nonacknowledgment

Within a unity on technology

Scientistic, theoreticist	Empiricist, artisanal
High-tech, institutional	Low-tech bricolage, entre-preneurial

Institutional base

East Coast universities	West Coast, art colleges, art institutions
Institutionally and state-backed	Self-employed, perfor-mance-backed.

The postmodern dance which started as a movement rejecting musicality , meaning, chareterization, mood and atmosphere, simultaneously had gone through several phases. The analytical phase of 1960s and 70s redifined the movement, and in 1980s there was again a rebirth of content. Often the postmodern dance produced a variety of collective or cooperative ventures among artists, like Linda Childs, Sol Lewitt, and Philip Glass, Trisha Brown and Robert Rauschenberg. By reassessing the representaion and discourse, the postmodern dance opened the theatre to other cultures. In that way it celebrated the plurality, which is the spirit of postmodernism.

The postmodernists in dance moved beyond the limits of Cunningham's choreography, questioning every aspect of the art form. They took dance out of the confines of theatre and into the streets, and introduced differences in the types of bodies, styles of mundane movement, and the shapes of the spaces they used. Choreographers such as Brown created works where the dancers were suspended at 90° angles to the vertical, and walked on walls. They took abstraction to the limits, rejecting every sort of extraneous matter and reduced the form to its minimal component parts. Improvisation became an accepted performance strategy as the emphasis turned from product to process. The dance revolution achieved credibility as a form whose innate immediacy and ephemerality made it attractive in a world of pop art, Neo-Dadaism, action painting, and live art.

Aesthetics as a study of beauty and, in particular, the beautiful in art, in a way originated in the eighteenth century with the appearance of the modern individual or Cartesian individual. The disintegration of feudalism and the emergence of capitalism loosened the absolute laws in the social sphere. The new individual began to institute arts and literature as expressions of class identity. In association with this, the romantic theories of beauty also waged war on classical tradition also. The classical tradition understood beauty in terms of set relations and mathematical properties, the romantics, quite contrary to this tradition emphasised a distinctive relationship with nature. The romantics believed that artistic expression transcends prescriptive criteria. In a way romanticism consolidated the individual autonomy and subjective freedom.

The emergence of the postmodern aesthetics, after Second World War, specifically in the 1960s, is a reaction of the Kantian aesthetics. Kant saw a polarization between subjective experience and objective knowledge and constructed a system of thought in which subjective experience and the condition of belonging to a world were shown to be interrelated. Kantian dichotomy has been negated in the postmodern aesthetics.

With the advent of Nietzsche on the scene, aesthetics has been radically altered. He argued that reality is altogether constructed or made : considered facts as *fact-itious*. He felt that the production of reality takes place with fictional means. Nietzsche, according to Welsch, 'points out that we bring forth reality everywhere with fictional means and by the way of metaphorical activity. The talk of 'meta-phorical' activity is to be understood literally in this sense. We transfer an incipient nerves stimulus into an image, that into a sound, finally the sound into a concept. Through such transfer from one sphere to another emerge the cascades of reality, which in everything goes beyond the elementary physical stimulus is a product of human artistry'.[8]

In a way, with the advent of Nietzsche on the scene the belief of Descartes, that all spheres of reality could be apprehended and structured with one mathematical method, had been shattered. In the view of Descartes natural object and human phenomenon could be comprehended uniformly. The implication of Descartes' argument is that there is one method for all issues. In fact, this form of thought remained throughout modernity. All most all the thinkers of modernity proposed one model of solution for all problems. They may differ in expression but in content they were all the same. Whether Hegel's tantalization of history in the name of spirit, or Marx's liberation of humanity through proletariat, they aimed universality and singularity and plurality was very much alien to them. This singularity has been radically opposed by the postmodern aesthetics.

In the view of postmodernists, different perspective modes always participate in the perception of art. The perception of art is on principle 'polyaesthetic', not 'nonaesthetic'

Notes

1 Peter L. Cooper. *Thomas Pynchon and the Contemporary World*, p. 6.

2 Mike Featherstone. In Pursuit of the Postmodern : An Introduction. In (Ed.) Mike Featherstone Postmodernism (Special Issue), *Theory, Culture& Society,* 5, p. 202.

3 Mike Featherstone. *Ibid.*, p. 203.

4 Todd Gitlin. Quoted by Arthur Asa Berger in *Cultural Criticism : A Primer of Key Concepts.* London : Sage, 1995, p. 52.

5 Ihab Hassan. *The Postmodern Turn : Essays in Postmodern theory and Culture*. Ohio : Ohio State University Press, 1987, p. 91.

6 Jean Baudrillard. Quoted in "Postmodernism and Architecture" by Diane Morgan in *The Routledge Companion to Postmodernism.* (Ed.) Stuart Sim. London : Routledge, 2001, p. 84.

7 Georgina Born. *Rationalizing Culture : IRCAM, Boulez, and the Institutionalization of the Musical Avant-Garde*. Berkely : University of California Press. 1995, p. 63.

8 Wolfgang Welsch. *Undoing Aesthetics*. London : Sage, 1997, p. 41.

Conclusion

The postmodern condition radically altered the life styles of the people and their aesthetic norms. 'A lifestyle is first of all the result of all the choices that a person makes concerning his or her life. This includes not only choice of work and leisure activities, but also choice of whether to live alone or not, and, if adult, whether to have children or not. Lifestyle research during the last decade has to a large extent focused upon extravagant lifestyles and on consumption; on lifestyles of people with large amounts of primarily economic but to a certain extent also cultural capital'.[1]

Lifestyle is always visible. A person's identity, at least at the superficial level, asserted with his/her lifestyle. Lifestyle may be manifested in the looks, for example in the dress and manners. It can be seen in the actions of an individual, like the choice of his/her leisure activities. It can also be seen in the use objects like furniture. It can be observed even in one's choice of friends. In a way, lifestyle may be seen as the material expression of self-identity. However, lifestyle is a choice. There may be certain limitations to this choice. All people make choices in their lives, but not all the people have the same opportunities.

Even in the ancient societies, people had opportunities to choose between alternative ways of living. However, the opportunities were rather limited or were not radically different from each other. In the modernity, the changes were somewhat radical. In the postmodernity, the changes pick up the pace. As most of the young people are not growing up in families the impact of parents on them is all most nil, hence they can frequently change their lifestyles. The tremendous freedom the young people got give them an opportunity to experience things in the ways that were unimaginable in the case of their parents.

The social world that each individual inhabits is called life world. The life-worlds in the traditional societies were integrated and unified. This unified element, to some extent can be seen even in the modern societies. But in the postmodern world the life world-has been fragmented or pluralized. The contemporary individual has to move in various private and public arenas. As a result, an individual's life-world consists of various worlds, and in these various worlds, different aspects of lifestyles will come to the forefront. Simultaneously it leads to lifestyles that are more heterogeneous. The frequent changes that are taking place in an individual's life confirm the fact that in the postmodern society lifestyles can never be static. They have to make choices continuously in the rapidly changing or transforming. The options are also too many.

In fact, in the contemporary world everyday life became a matter of personal choice. In a way, it may be considered a process of individualization. The importance given to age, class, and ethnicity are losing their importance. The choices made by the individual are made only in the interests of individuals.

In the postmodern world, people are forced to take responsibility of their own lives, which was not the case in earlier times. Taking decisions is a continuous process in the rapidly changing environment.

The postmodern styling and design is considered retro. Because it shares a self-consciousness about the past and has an ironic sense of playfulness in it. In every object that is used we find a desire to imitate or recreate the mood of and imaginary past. critic sub-titled one of his article as 'You are What You Buy'.[2]

Almost all the public images will make sense by continuous reference to the past rather than to the future. Some writers even go to the extent of appealing to the lost-values. The contemporary experience is rooted in the processes of consumption but not in the production. The personal and collective identities of the people were rooted in the locality around their work places and the workers used to share the values the industry for which they worked.

In the last four or five decades the situation changed radically in the Western world. There has been a shift in the nature of the very relationships in which the Western people live. The lands once housed the large factories now changed into out-of-town shopping areas. Even the lands by the rivers have been transformed leisure marinas, theme parks and heritage museums. In fact, these heritage museums epitomize a process whereby a part is nostalgically recreated. These creations stand as forms of alternate reality.

The comments of Nigel Watson are worth quoting in this context. Nigel says, "We pay our money and are entertained by consuming second-hand experience which once formed the basis of social life. To a significant extent we have become tourists in our own culture. Sunday no longer means a trip to church or chapel, but rather a visit to the cathedrals of consumerism. Shopping malls have become major sites of leisure activity, the pilgrimage is enough even without the act of buying".[3]

In the contemporary social life, there is no space for earlier occupational culture with people rather choosing new lifestyles. The term lifestyles originated in advertising and designer culture. It stands as a corner stone for the free market revolution. The age of mass communication has been taken over by an endless choice and a variety of consumer goods. Though not all the people are exposed to this process, identities are constructed based on consumer goods. Consumption became a way of self-expression. Descartes dictum 'I think, therefore I am' has been contextualised as 'I consume, therefore I am'. The capacity to spend is a kind of power now a days.

The conspicuous growth of consumer markets can be seen in fashion accessories. The human body is also a focus for identity construction in a serious way. The possibilities for changing the shapes of human bodies through cosmetic surgery have been continuously advertised in newspapers and magazines. The body itself became a consumer commodity. A worldwide market has developed to sell the goods that are related to the beautification of the bodies. The aged bodies are considered source of tension and to come of out this tension various measures came on to the scene. People are made to devote much of their leisure to think about their bodies.

All the above discussion boils down to the point that postmodernism lays stress on style and appearance rather than on content. The use value of the objects has been taken over by the sign value. This applies even to the field of art and literature. The distinction between high art and popular art disappeared due to uncertainty in judging the cultural forms. One writer over the other or one art form over the other can never be declared superior. There are no universal values or standards to judge the merit one over the other.

The universal claims to knowledge or truth are no longer accepted. These include religion, science and political theories. Once again, the opinion of Nigel Watson is valid here. Watson says, "The supremacy of Western thinking has been challenged throughout the twentieth century and especially with the decline of colonial empires. The explicit assumption that their cultures and ideas represented the progress of civilization is one that we no longer accept. It is now much more commonplace to assume that we cannot say that one society or culture is better than another one".[4]

The conspicuous features of the postmodern thinking are fragmentation of experience and compression of time and space. There is concrete change in the very structure of multinational companies. This change is the globalisation of production. Even the financial institutions are able to transmit their data electronically to be processed overnight from one corner of the world to the other.

The flows of capital energy, goods, images and money are on large scale. Timothy W. Luke says, "Flows are unbounded by spatial borders, passing along unboundaries without frontiers in the constant flux of exchange. Plainly, a 'transnational' flow of goods, capital, people and ideas have existed for centuries; it antedates even the rise of modern nation-states. However, this historical flow, at least until the 1950s or 1960s, tended to move more slowly, move less and more narrowly than the rush of the products, ideas, persons and money that develops with jet transportation, electronic telecommunication, massive decolonisation and extensive computerization after 1960. It is these greater intensities, rates, densities, levels and velocities in the post-historical flow, which have transmuted it quantitatively into something qualitatively new, complex and different".[5]

By borrowing from Frederic Jameson, Luke says that in the postmodern culture of flow, culture itself has become a product in its own right. The market has become a substitute for itself. The large structural changes or trends involve new socio-spatial codes. To quote Luke once again 'The world systems of transnational capitalism gains its figurations in the televisual/ computational/cyberspatial conduits of the flow. This distinction can also be extended to interpret the workings of many scientific communities, cultural networks, technological innovations, telecommunication links and media markets as they create hyperreal estate out of telematic territory or cyberspatial flow that are 'actually transnational".[6]

The changes that are taking place in the technological and cultural spheres providing opportunities to experience the world is itself an indication of the compression of time and space. Many thinkers have pointed out that the theme parks and places like Disneyland changed the very concept of entertainment and the space of entertainment. In these spaces, some alternative realities are created and they are considered integral parts of shopping experience.

The proliferation of electronic communications that occupy the world of people creating confusion between sight and sound. The continuous flow of information is not allowing people to pay much attention to it. The experiences of the people in this regard are short-lived ones. This short-lived experience can best be illustrated by the hundreds of television channels to which people are exposed. People who are just glancing at or surfing the channels will not have deep impacts. The same is the case with CD-ROMs. The linear flow is always disrupted by the remote control. Here time and content are separated and narrative structures are broken. In fact, the viewer himself breaks these narrative structures. This is a strange experience, which we could never be anticipated some decades ago.

In the postmodern world the activities of the people as consumers define their identities. The implication is that those who are not able to consume or shop do not have any identity.

In the postmodern world, individuals are taking responsibility themselves for their lives. As the traditional bonds have, loosened individuals are not mechanically following the footsteps of their parents. In the earlier societies, the choices for people were rather limited. But in the postmodern world, they have multiple choices. Lifestyles are heterogeneous in the contemporary world. Their behavioural patterns are different from one arena to another. In most of the cases, one is at liberty to change one's lifestyles and habits. For some, the changing lifestyle is a liberating experience. However, it can also be traumatic experience, as each one does not have the same kind of opportunities.

In the postmodernity life styles are highly elastic and dynamic. The distinctions between work and leisure, high culture and popular culture are erased. A key characteristic of the field of lifestyle in postmodernity is that it contains expressivist lifestyles. Postmodern society is a society of signs and images. In the booming of cultural industry expressivist lifestyles are common. Most of the time new lifestyles are manifested in the middle class.

Pluralisation of the lifestyles is another feature in the postmodernity. In the pluralized atmosphere, the hierarchy of any specific style is questioned. In the modern societies, some lifestyles were considered superior to others, whereas in the postmodern societies this superiority is questioned. People with different levels of capital have different lifestyles. Nobody cares.As they are continuously exposed to media people won't find any aura in the lifestyles of others, hence, the symbolic value of preferring one lifestyle over the other disappears. It doesn't mean that there is no significance for the lifestyles; it means that there is only relative significance.

Even a cursory reading of the phenomenon 'aesthetics', since its emergence, reveals the fact that it has undergone radical transformations. Traditionally, the subject has always occupied the margins of philosophy. This was because that in the early days of its origin it dealt with those aspects of experience which art the least agreeable to categorization, i.e., art, beauty, emotion and the other aspects related to senses. The divisions imposed on reality by modern reason and changes brought about by the industrialization of experience have necessitated a rethinking of the relationship between the individual and reality. As Clive Cazeaux says, 'gone are notions of a distinct self in receipt of a mind-independent world and, in their place, are theses to the effect that consciousness and reality are interconnected at fundamental level. One consequence of this shift is that aesthetic experience is redefined. Far from being a mere adjunct to everyday perception, it is shown to be vital to an understanding of the relationship between mind and world"[7] . This shift can be seen in its concrete manifestation in the postmodern aesthetics or in the difference between modern and postmodern aesthetics.

Modernism is a composite term for new aesthetic movements across the arts that date from the late nineteenth and early twentieth centuries. One defining feature of modernism is its basis in a reaction by artists against the prior aesthetic and philosophical forms of romanticism and classicism. This common feature of modernist art is often referred to as the negative aesthetic or simply negation, since the prime motive is a negation of principles of the previous tradition : in painting, a rejection of realist representation and the primacy of subject matter in favour of abstraction, and an emphasis on formal and perceptual experiment; in music. The destructuring and rejection of the earlier harmonic, melodic, and sonata forms of tonality in favour of the extension of dissonance and ambiguity. In literature modernism is marked by experimentation, particularly manipulation of form, and by the realization that knowledge is not absolute. In painting modernism resulted in a profusion of styles and movements in a restless search for new directions and novel principles and in dance it reflects a rejection of existing traditions and a desire to re-examine the fundamental principles of dance as a medium.

The second characteristic of modernism, is linked to the desire for formal experiment, its concern and fascination with new media, technology, and science. The celebration of technology is conspicuous in the early twentieth century movements such as Soviet constructionism and Italian Futurism, both of which advocated new media and drew analogies between industrial production and cultural practice. Technologies were new aesthetic stimulus in terms of the subject matter of art.

The third feature of modernism is theoreticism. Modernism invests an unprecedented power in exegetical or interpretative texts. Examples are the polemical manifestos and writings that accompany many of the early twentieth-century movements. In the early period of modernism art theory and practice were linked. This had a profound impact on the creative writing. In fact, theoreticism had been central to the legitimation of the modernist art practice.

The Fourth defining element of modernism concerns its politics and political rhetoric, its vanguard and interventionist aims. There had been a close relation between avant-garde and the modernism.

The avant-garde got radical political connotations. The avant-garde artists acted in the name of modernity, by its inspiration. Just like modernity itself, they lived at the front line. They always wanted to transgress the frontiers. As Zygmunt Bauman says, most of them took hints and courage from science and technology : Impressionists from the anti-Newtonian optics, the Cubists from the anti-Cartesian relativity theory, Surrealists from psychoanalysis, the Futurists combustion engines and assembly lines. Bauman says, 'without modernity and all it works, the modernists would be unthinkable. They wanted to serve the modernity; it wan not their fault that they had to impose themselves with their offer upon a reluctant or indifferent society. They laid the guilt at the door of the many who stuck to the cannons already left behind : people without dated tastes (that is in the modernist language tasteless people), unable or unwilling to catch up with the insights of the avant-garde'.[8]

The other important feature of modernism is its deification of reason or rationalism and the division of subjectivism/objectivism and the division of high art and popular art.

Postmodernism ousted notions of universalism, internationalism and replaced them with the concerns for the values of specific cultures and their differences. It rejected the separation between high and low or popular culture. It blurred the boundaries between categories and genres. Grand narratives, in all most all-cultural forms have been denounced and regional and local forms have been celebrated. The autonomy of cultural texts has been rejected and they are placed in the specific cultural context.

The postmodernists have repudiated the belief in a universal aesthetic, that art and literature transcend social and cultural contexts. They are understood in specific contexts only. The transcendental status of any text has been questioned. In postmodernism it has become important to ask who the implied readers or audience for a text are.

Modernism was an attempt to defend one universal culture, and it often forced to attack regionalism as parochialism, nationalism as chauvinism. The postmodern alternative is to accept that we are living in an age of cultural relativism. Postmodernism questions cultural codes in order to critique liberal humanist values and moves away from the logic of consumption.

Postmodernism appeared to reflect a radical break with the dominant culture and aesthetics. It substituted disunity, subjectivity and ambiguity, for the modernist unity, absolutism and certainty. The postmodern cultural shift has left its mark on the fashion world through its rejection of modernist tradition, relaxation of norms and its emphasis on individual diversity.

Postmodern literary and cultural texts reflect hyperrealism. In the realm of real the hyperreal, the real and the imaginary continually implode into each other. Rather than a culture of pristine culture, postmodern culture is a pastiche. It has disturbed many of the old certainties surrounding questions of cultural value.

The propositions of Barthes and Derrida are very much essential to any understanding of contemporary culture. In "The Death of the Author' Barthes outlines his theory that 'the Author is an outmoded concept and that texts can operate on their own without reference to authorial objectives and intentions.

Tuning this argument against Barthes, his analysis of the self must call into question the authority of his own utterance : the death of the author is also surely the death of the critic. Criticism, if it is still legitimate to call the practice that in the apparent absence of value judgements is reduced to an exercise in identifying signs in order to reveal their underlying networks of signification. This is an antiauthoritarian argument in more senses than one, and it ends with a firm commitment to the cause of the reader : 'the birth of the reader must be at the cost of the death of the Author'

The social status of the artist has been considerably downgraded by Barthes, and we are at the opposite end of the spectrum from Plato's notion of the artist as an individual dangerous to a well-ordered society. Plato was centrally concerned with the effects of art in his aesthetics.

Barthes pushes structuralism to its limits. If we start with self-regulating grammars and deep structures, it is quite logical to end up with the 'death of the Author'. From this point of view texts are taken on a life of their seemingly independent of human agency. As an aesthetic theory structuralism is vulnerable at several points. Structure remains a questionable concept resting on dubious assumptions.

What has tended to happen in practice of structuralist criticism is that an author's oeuvre is examined in terms of an assumed ideal structure and then each individual work is compared to this ideal structure. As Derrida pointed out, binaries are in operation. There is often a studied avoidance of psychological and social evaluation in structuralism.

The aesthetics of structuralism does not provide the means to evaluate artefacts in a social and psychological sense, ultimately can in fact a disguised theory of value at work in structuralism, and that analytical processes in which the human dimension is suppressed to serve some particular class interest.

Derrida's work is part of a broad intellectual movement, ranging over several disciplines, called post-structuralism, which has reacted against institutional structures and received authority in general. The initial thrust of Derrida's attack had received authority in general. The initial thrust of Derrida's attack is against philosophical structures. His researches repeatedly lead him into the field of aesthetics and criticism, and he has, in fact, spawned a highly influential school of criticism.

Deconstructionist aesthetics involves a very different assumption from those of structuralism. Derrida wishes to replace the search for a for a pre-existent essence or interior design with what he calls "the joyous affirmation of the play of the world and of the innocence of becoming."

The philosophy of Derrida can be classified into the following points:

1. Logocentrism in its developed philosophical sense is inextricably linked to the Greek and European tradition. Though *logocentrism* can be seen in the other cultures, it is not developed systematically.
2. The dominance of the principle of reason, which marks the modern West, is rooted in that original metaphysical response. Derrida says, "Not only does that principle constitutes the verbal formulation of a requirement present since the dawn of Western science and philosophy, it provides the impetus for a new era of purportedly 'modern' reason, metaphysics and technoscience'.[9]
3. The form this takes is an interpretation of the essence of being as objects placed before a subject.
4. 'Philosophy as *logocentrism* is present in every scientific discipline,'[10] progress in the natural and social cannot deliver humanity from the metaphysics.
5. In binary oppositions, every opposition must introduce a 'supplement' to produce a sense of the very thing that the supplement differs. This practice rests on a *différance* and will undo the closure of the *logocentric* oppositions of texts.
6. Deconstruction contrives to dismantle our preconceived notions of identity and expose us to challenge of hitherto suppressed *otherness* or the other side of experience, which has been ignored.

7. There has been nothing that has not been thought that cannot be rethought. There has been no self-evident system of natural signs that cannot rethought or resituated.

Derrida's aesthetic theory derives from his critique of metaphysics, specifically, from his critique of metaphysic of presence. Derrida believes that if metaphysics of presence collapses then arbitrary signs become a real possibility. His argument involves an assault on the 'transcendental signified, that is, a concept which is held to be totally independent of other concepts. Without such a transcendental signified there could be no final meaning to any sign. Logocentrism, in the view of Derrida, assumes an existence of such a transcendental signifieds. God, Platonic forms, Cartesian mind would all stand as examples of the transcendental signified. Derrida rejects this idea of transcendental signified.

Derrida radically negates the concept of binary oppositions. That is why deconstructionist aesthetics is a move away from value judgement. Since meaning is endlessly being produced and just endlessly being erased, there is no scope for fixed points of reference for critics to orient themselves by. In this type of situation there is no possibility for value judgements. The value of reading, be it the reading a text and analysing of a cultural text, in the above context, is seen to be in the active interpretation of the reader. In this type situation, Sim says, Value has shifted from the system to the reader, although this carries the implication that each reader will become increasingly isolated from other readers. If structuralism systematically excludes the human dimension from aesthetic theory-a case of death of the individual subject as well as the death of the author –then deconstruction in some sense reintroduces is, but at the price of individual isolation : 'active interpretation' by their nature remain very private things'.[11] In a way the postmodern aesthetic is anti-aesthetic.

Karl Marx in his 'The German Ideology' compared ideology to a *camera abscura, that* dark rook in which in a pinhole in one wall projects an inverted image from external scene onto its opposite. Marx says, 'If in all ideology men and their circumstances appear upside-down as in camera abscura, this phenomenon arises just as much from their historical life-process as the inversion of objects on the retina does from their physical life-process'.[12]

In view of Martin Jay Marx's reflection of visual metaphor to distinguish upright from distorted knowledge is by no means surprising or unusual, for Western thought has long privileged sight as the sense of most capable of uprising us of truth of external reality. Martin Jay in his essay "Ideology and Ocularcentrism : Is There Anything Behind the Mirror?" [13] Jay identifies a number ocular centric metaphors since the time of Plato : Platonic 'mind eye', Cartesian "Clear and distinct", Baconian 'faith of the eye', Carlyle's 'spiritual optics', Augustine's 'ocular desire'. In all these metaphors 'vision' has served both as the model for the truth and source of the falsehood. Marx's choice of a visual metaphor was a rhetorically powerful ploy at a time Ocularcentrism still reigned supreme. In the view of Jay, the premises of that assumption came under attack. In fact, in the second half of the twentieth century there is a dismantling of the traditional hierarchy of the senses, which placed vision at the summit.

The above assumption has been decried in many quarters. "With its departure has gone the assumption that the alternative to a distorted, ideological sight , inverted and reversed, obscure and opaque, is clear and distinctive vision of the truth as it actually is. In fact, if anything, confidence in the truth telling capacity of vision in any of it various guises has become itself or wisely reproached mark of ideological mystification". [14]

For Merleau-Ponty to Foucault there has been a serious criticism on the above assumption. Jay explains this mistaken concept of ideology or 'God's eye view'.

Jay shows the distrust of the visual or in his own worlds "the metaphysics of reflection" in the Marxian tradition itself. For example Althusser. In the view Althusser ideology is 'representation of the imaginary relationships of individuals to their real conditions of existence. These imaginary relationships are not equivalent to false consciousness. Because they are permanent and inimitable elements of all social systems. His critiques of specularity is a very powerful critique on 'mirror and metaphysics of reflection. (In the view of Derrida 'metaphysics of presence).

Feminists like Luce Irigaray also rejected 'the flat reflecting mirror of western metaphysic which is nothing but the phallocentric privileging of male sexuality. In her view the classical psychoanalytical account of castration anxiety with all sexist implications is also indebted to the privileging of visibility over the sensible. For feminists like Cixous, Irigaray and Kristeva it is ideological to assume sight nobler than senses like touch and smell. The motivating factor behind this kind of awareness came from the postmodern aesthetic phenomena.

Notes

1 *The Politics of Postmodernity*, p. 73.

2 Nigel Watson. "You are What You Buy" *Routledge Companion to Postmodernism.* (Ed) Stuart Sim, London : Routledge, 2001.

3 Nigel Watson. *Ibid.*, p. 55.

4 Nigel Watson. *Ibid.*, p. 58

5 Timothy W. Luke. "New World Order or Neo-world Orders : Power Politics and Ideology in Informationalizing Glocalities" in *Global Modernities,* (Ed.) : Mike Featherstone, Scott Lash and Ronald Robertson, London : Sage, 1995, p, p. 99-100.

6 Timothy W. Luke. *Ibid.*, p. 101.

7 Clive Cazeau . *The Continental Aesthetics Reader*, p. xiii.

8 Zygmunt Bauman. *Ibid.*, p. 97.

9 Jacques Derrida quoted by Thomas Maccarthy in "The Politics of the Ineffable : Derrida's Deconstruction", in *Hermeneutics and Critical Theory in the Ethics and Politics*, (Ed.) Michel Kelly. London, MIT Press, p. 151.

10 Jacques Derrida. in "Deconstruction and the Other" an interview with Derrida, in Richard Kearney , in *Dialogues with Contemporary continental Thinkers,* Manchester : Manchester University Press, 1984, p. 114.

11 Stuart Sim. "Structuralism and Post-Structuralism" in *Philosophical Aesthetics An Introduction.* (Ed.) Oswald Hanfling, Oxford : Blackwell, 1992, p. 431

12 Marx and Engels. The German Ideology. International London : Publishers, 1970, p. 47.

13 Martin Jay. Indidn Jouranal of American Studies, Vol. 18, No.1, Special Issue on Survey ' of Theory, Winter 1988, p. 4

14 Martin Jay. *Ibid.*, p. 4

Bibliography

Alexander, Jeffrey C and Siedman Steven (Eds.) *Culture and Society : Contemporary Debates*. New York : Cambridge university Press, 1996.

Allen, Barry. *Truth in Philosophy*. London : Harvard University Press, 1993.

Allen, Graham. *Intertexualtiy* . London : Routledge, 2000.

Anderson, Water Truett. *The Fontana Postmodern Reader*. London : Fontana Press, 1995.

Aronowitz, Stanley. *Science as Power : Discourse and Ideology in Modern Society*. Minneapolis : University of Minnesota, 1988.

Attridge, Derek. (Ed.) *Jacques Derrida : Acts of Literature*. London : Routledge, 1992.

Barry, Peter. *Beginning Theory : An Introduction to Literary and Cultural Theory*. New York : Manchester University Press. 1995.

Baruch, Eline Hoffman. *Women, Love and Power : Literary and Psychoanalytic Perspectives*. New York : New York University Press, 1991.

Bauman, Zymunt. *Modernity and Ambivalence*. New York : Cornell University press, 1991.

Bauman, Zygmunt. *Postmodernity and its Discontents*. New York : New York University Press,1997.

Baumlin, James S. and Baumlin, Tita French (Eds). *Ethos : New Essays in Rhetorical and Critical Theory*. Dallas : Southern Methodist University Press, 1994.

Beilharz, Peter. *Zygmunt Bauman Dialectic of Modernity*. London : Sage Publications, 2000.

Benjamin, Andrew (Ed.) *The Problems of Modernity*. London : Routledge, 1989.

Bennington,Geoffery. *Interrupting Derrida*. London : Routledge, 2000.

Berman, Marshal. *All That is Solid Melts into Air : The Experience of Modernity*, New York : Penguin, 1988.

Bertens, Hans. *The Idea of the Posmodern : A History*. London : Routledge,1995.

Bertens, Hans. *The Idea of the Postmodern : A History*. London : Routedge,1995.

Birringer, Johanes. *Theater, Theory, Postmodernism*. Bloomington : Indiana University Press. 1993.

Blanning, T.C.W. *Short Oxford History of Europe : The Nineteenth Century*. Oxford : OUP, 2000.

Bloom, Harold. *The Anxiety of Infuence : The Thoery of Poetry*. New York : Oxford, 1997.

Booker, M Keith. *Techniques of Subversion In Modern Literature*. Ganesville : University of Florida, 1991.

Bottomore, Tom. *The Frankfurt School*. London : Tavistock Publications, 1984.

Brenkman, John. "Extreme Criticism" in *Critical Inquiry*, Vol.26, Issue No.1, Autumn, 1997.

Brinton, Crane. *The Shaping of Modern Mind*. New York : A Mentor Books, 1959.

Browne, Ray B. and Browne Pat. *Digging into Popular Culture : Theories and Methodologies in Archeology, Anthropology and Cultural Fields*. Ohio : Bowling Green State University Popular press 1991.

Bullock, Alan and Stallybrass Oliver. *The Fontana Dictionary of Modern Thought* London : Fontana Press, 1990.

Butler, Judith, *Subjects of Desire : Hegelian Reflections in Twentieth – Century*. New York, Columbia University Press, 1987.

Bwehler, Ernst. *Irony and the Discourse of Modernity*. Seattle : University of Washington Press, 1990.

Carrol David, *Paraesthetics, Foucault, Lyotard, Derrida*. New York : Routledge, 1987.

Cavallard, Dani. *Art for Beginners*. Hyderabad : Orient Longman, 2000

Chevalier, Tracy (Ed.) *Encyclopedia of the Essay*. London : Fitzory Dearborn Publishers, 1997.

Claire Colebrook. Gilles Deleuze. London : Routledge, 2002.

Colebrook, Claire. *New Literary Histories*. Manchester : Manchester University Press, 1997.

Crowther, Paul. *Critical Aesthetics and Postmodernism*. Oxford : Clarendon Press, 1993.

Culler, Jonatahn. *Literary Theory : A Very Short Introduction.* Ney York : Oxford, 1977.

Davies, Carole Byce. *Black Women Writing and Identity : Migrations of the Subject*. London : Routledge,1994.

Davies, Ioan. *Cultural Studies and Beyond : Fragments of Empire*. London : Routledge, 1995.

Delanty, Gerard. *Modernity and Postmodernity*. London : Sage, 2000.

Denzin, Norman K. *Images of Postmodern Society : Social Theory and Contemporary Cinema*. London : Sage, 1991.

Derrida, Jacques, *Dissemination*, London, Athlone Press, 1981.

Donoghue, Denis. *Ferocious Alphabets*. Boston : Little Brown Company,1981.

During, Simon. *Foucault and Literature : Towards a Genecology of Writing*. London : Routledge, 1992.

Eagleton, Terry. *The Literary Theory*. Oxford : Blackwell, 1997.

Eliot, Simon and Owens W.R. (Eds.) *A Handbook to Literary Research*. London : Routledge, 1998.

Engstrom, Timothy H. "The Postmodern Sublime? : Philosophical Rehabilitations and Fragmatic Evasions". In *Boundary-2,* Vol. 20, Issue 2. Summer, 1993.

Esterlin, Nancy and Riebling Barbara.(Eds.).,*After-Poststructuralism : Interdisciplinary and Literary Theory*. Illinois : Northwestern University Press, 1993.

Farries, Wendy V. *Labyrinths of Language : Symbolic Landscape and Narrative Design in Modern Fiction*. London : Johns Hopkins University Press, 1988.

Farris, Wendy B. *Labyrinths of Language : Symbolic Landscape and Narrative Design in Modern Fiction. London* : Johans Hopkeis University Press 1988.

Featherstone, Mike (Ed.) *Global Culture : Nationalism, globalization and Modernity*. London : Sage, 1995.

Featherstone, Mike. Lash, Scott. Roberson, Roland (Eds.). *Global Modernities*. London : Sage, 1995.

Featherstone, Mike. (Ed.) *Global Culture*. London : Sage Publications 1995.

Featherstone,Mike. In Pursuit of Postmodern : An Introduction. In M.Featherstone (Ed.), Postmodernism (Special issue). *Theory, Culture&Society*, 5, 1988.

Foster, Hall. Recordings : Art, Spectacle, Cultural Politics. Washington : Bay Press, 1985.

Foster, Hall. *Reçodings : Art, Spectacle, Cultural Politics*. Washington : Bay Press, 1985.

Foster, Mark. (Ed) *Jean Baudrillard : Selected Writings*. Oxford : Stanford University Press, 1992.

Foucalut, Michel. *The Order of Things : An Archeology of Human Science*. New York : Vintage Books, 1994.

Foucault, Michel, *The Order of Things : An Archeology of the Human Sciences*, New York, Vintage Books, 1994

Freidrich, Carl J. *The Philosophy of Kant*. New York : Modern Library, 1949.

Gardiner, Michael. *The Dialogues of Critique : M.M. Bakhtin and the Theory of Ideology*. London : Routledge, 1992.

Giles, Steve. (Ed.).*Theorizing Modernism*. London : Routledge, 1993.

Gilles Deleuze and Felix Guattari. What is Philosophy? London : Verso, 1996 .

Gische, Rodolphe. *Inventions of Difference : On Jacques Derrida.* London : Harvard University Press, 1994.

Gordon Colin (Ed.) *Michel Foucault : Power/Knowledge : Selected Interviews and other Writings-1972-1977*. New York : Pantheon Books, 1980.

Gordon. W. Terrinee. *Saussure for Beginners*. Hyderabad : Orient Longman, 1997.

Graham, Gordon. *Philosophy of the Arts : An Introduction to Aesthetics*. London : Routledge,1997.

Blamirs Harry, *Twentieth Century English Literature*. Hampshire : Macmillan, 1986.

Grams, Eric. "Aesthetics and Cultural Criticism". in *Boundary 2*, Vol. 25, Issue No.1, Spring 1998.

Gutting, Garry (Ed.) *The Cambridge Companion to Foucault*. Cambridge : Cambridge University Press, 1994.

Gutting, Gary, *Michel Foucault's Archaeology of Scientific Reason*, Cambridge, Cambridge University Press, 1989.

Harland, Richard. *Superstructualism : The Philosophy of Structuralism and Poststructuralism*. London : Matheun,1987.

Hartman, Geofferey H. *Saving The Text : Literature/Derrida/ philosophy*. London : John Hopkins University Press, 1981.

Harturan, Geoffrey H. Saving the Text : Literature/Derrida/Philosophy. London : The Johns Hopkins University Press 1981.

Hassan, Ihab. *The Postmodern Turn : Essays in Postmodern Theory and Culture*. Ohio : Ohio State University Press.1987.

Hayward, Susan. *Key Concepts in Cinema Studies*. London : Routlege, 1996.

Heath, James M. Pyne, Michel, (Eds.) *Text, Interpretation, Theory*. Lewisburg : Bucknell Universly Press, 1985.

Hogman, Patrik Colm. *The Politics of Interpretation*. New York : OUP, 1990.

Hopkins, David. *After Modern Art-1945 to2000*. Oxford : OUP,2000.

Howarph, David. *Discourse*. New Delhi : Viva Books, 2002.

Humt, Lynn (Ed.). *The New Cultural History*. Berkeley : University of California Press, 1989.

Hunt, Lynn (Ed.). *The New Cultural History*. Berkeley : University of California Press, 1989.

Hutacheon Linda. *The Political of Postmodernism*, London : Routledge, 2002.

Hutcheon, Linda. *A Poetics of Postmodernsim : History, Theory, Fiction*. London : Routledge, 1992.

Hutcheon, Linda. *The Politics of Postmodernism*. London : Routledge, 1999.

Ihab Hassan. Paracriticisms Seven Speculations of the Times. Urbana : University of Illinois Press, 1975.

Inglehart, Ronald. *Modernization and Postmodernization : Culture, Economic, and Political change in 43 societies*. Princeton : Princeton University Press, 1996.

Jameson, Frederic. "Postmodernism : or the Cultural Logic of Late Capitalism". *New Left Review, 146.*

Jameson, Frederic. *Postmodernism; or the Cultural Logic of Late Capitalism*. London : Verso, 1996.

Jean Baudrillard. *The Transparency of Evil : Essays on Extreme Phenomena*. London : Verso, 1993.

Jencovich, Mark. *The Cultural Politics of the New Criticism*. Cambridge : Cambridge University Press,1993.

Jerome Klinkowitz. Literary Disruptions.

Urbana : University of Illinois Press. 1980.

John Enck. "Jchn Barth" An Interview," *Wisconsin Studies in Contemporary Literature 6,* Winter-Spring 1965.

Johnson, Christopher, *System and Writing in the Philosophy of Jacques Derrida*, Cambridge, Cambridge University Press, 1993.

Jordan, Glenn and Weedon, Chris. *Cultural Politics*. Oxford : Blackwell, 1995.

Karatani, Kojin. Uses of Aesthetics : "After Orientalism". in *Boundary 2*, Vol.25, Issue No2, 1998.

Kearney, Richard. *Modern Movements in European Philosophy*, New York : Manchester University Press,1994.

Kellner, Douglas. *Media Culture : Cultural Studies, Identiy and Politics Between the Modern and the Postmodern*. London : Routledge

Kringer, Murray (Ed.) *The Aims of Representaion : subject, Text, history*. New York : Columbia University Press,1987.

Kuper, Adam and Kuper, Jassscia.(Ed). *The Social Science Encyclopedia*, London : Routledge,1996.

Kurt Vonnegut. Slaughterhouse Five. London : Vintage 1991.

Levenson, Michel H. *A Genealogy of Modernism*. Cambridge : Cambridge University Press, 1992.

London : George Allen and Unwin, 1983.

Lukacs, George. *Essays on Thomas Mann*. London : Merlin Press, 1979.

Lyon, David. *Postmodernity*. New Delhi : Viva Books, 2002.

Lyotard, Jean Francoise. *The Postmodern Condition*. Manchester : Manchester University Press, 1984.

Macolm, Walters. *Modern Sociological Theory*. London : Sage, 1994.

Malcolm Bradbury and James McFarlane (Ed.) *Modernism : A Guide to European Literature, 1890-1930*. London : Penguin, 1991

Malcolm, Walters. Modern Sociological Theory. London : Sage Prelications, 1994.

Martin McQuillan. Paul de Man : London : Routledge 2001

Megill, Allan, *Prophets of Extremity : Nietzsche, Heidegger, Foucault, Derrida* London, University of California Press, 1985.

Miller, J. Hills. *Illustration*. Cambridge : Harvard University Press, 1992.

Mistra, Rajanish Kumar. Buddhist Theory of Meaning. in *Journal Languages Forum*, Vol, 26, Issue, 182, January-December, 2000.

Moi, Toril. *Sexual / Textual Politics*, London, Routledge, 2001.

Nicholson, Linda (Ed.) *Social Postmodernism : Beyond Identity Politics*. Cambridge : Cambridge University Press, 1995.

Norris, Christopher, *Derrida* : Fontana Modern Masters, (ed), Frank Kermode, London, Fontana Press.

Norris, Christopher. *Derrida*. Glasgow : Fontana, 1989.

Ohara, Daniel T. "The Aesthetics of the Real in Paul de Man". in *Boundary-2*, Vol-26, Issue-2,Summer, 1999.

Osborne, Ricahrd and Loon Born Van. *Sociology for Beginners*. Cambridge : Icon Books, 1996.

Paul de Man. *Allegories of Reading : Figural Langue in Rousseau, Nietzsche, Rilke, and Proust*. New Haven and London : Yale University Press, 1983..

Paul de Man. *Aesthetic Ideology*, (Ed.) Minneapolis : University of Minnesota Press, 1996.

Paul de, Man. *Blindness and Insight : Essays in the Rhetoric of Contemporary Criticism*. Minneapolis : University of Minnesota Press, 1979.

Perlloft, Marjhoire. (Ed.*) Postmodern Genres*. London :University of Oklahoma Press, 1988.

Peter L. Cooper. *Thomas Pynchon and the Contemporary World*

Petrey, Sandy. *Speech Acts and Literary Theory*. London : Routledge, 1990.

Pieterse, John Niderveen. (Ed.) *Emanciapations, Modern and Postmodern*. London : Sage, 1992.

Powell, Jim. *Postmodernism*. Chennai : Orient Longman Ltd., 1998.

Powell, Jim. *Postmodernism.* Chennai : Orient Longman, 1998.

Rasamussen, David M. *Hand book of Critical Theory*. Oxford : Blackwell, 1996.

Rasmussen, David M. *Reading Habermas*. Oxford : Basil Blackwell, 1990.

Ronald Sukenick. Quoted by Paul Maltby in *Dissident Postmodernists : Barthelme, Coover, Pynchon.* Philadelphia : University of Pennsylvania Press. 1991.

Rorty, Richard. "Philosophy as a kind of writing : An essay on Derrida" in *New Literary History*. vol. X, No. 1. Autumn, 1978, P. 142

Rosenau, Pauline Marie. *Post-Modernism and the Social Sciences : Insights, Inroads, and Intrusions*, Princeton : Princeton University Press, 1992.

Roseneau, Pauline Marie. *Postmodernism and the Social Sciences.* New Jersey : Princeton University Press, 1992.

Ross, Andrew (Ed.). *Universal Abandon? : The Politics of Postmodernism.* Minnepolis : University of Minnesota, 1988.

Ross, Dorothy (Ed.) *Modernist Impulses in the Human Sciences- 1872-1930.* Baltimore : The John Hopkins University Press. 1994.

Ryan, Michel. *Literay Theory : A Practical Introduction.* London : Blackwell, 1999.

Rylance, Rick. Debating Texts *: Readings in Twentieth Century Literary Theory and Method.* Toronto : University of Toronto Press,1997.

Sayers, Sean and Osborne Peter (Eds.). *Socialism, Feminism and Philosophy.* London : Routledge, 1990

Schleifer, Ronald and Davis, Robert Con. *Contemporary Literary Criticism.* New York : Longman.1984.

Scruton, Roger. *Modern Philosophy.* London : Sinclair Stevenson,1994.

Sethuran V.S. (Ed.) *Contemporary Criticism : An Anthology.* Madras : Macmillan,1989.

Shohat, Ella and Stam, Robert. *Unthinking Eurocenterism : Multiculture and the Media.* London : Routledge, 19994.

Sim, Stuart. (Ed.) *The Routledge Companion to Postmodernism.* London : Routledge, 20001.

Stam, Rober. Burgyone, Robert and Lewis, Sandy Flitterman. *New Vocabularies in Film Semiotic : Struc-turalism, Poststructuralism and Beyond.*London : Routledge, 1992.

Stolitzfus, Ben. *Lacan and Literature.* New York : State University Press, 1996.

Stones, Rob, (Ed), *Key Sociological Thinkers*, London, Macmillan 1998.

Storey, John. *An Introductory Guide to Cultural Theory and Popular Culture.* Athens : The Univerlsity of Georgia Press, 1993.

The University of Georgia Press, 1993.

Thody, Philip and Course, Ann. *The Barthes for Beginners.* Cambridge, Icon Books, 1997.

Tim Woods. in Beginning Postmodernism. Manchester : Manchester University Press. 1999.

Wallace, Elizabeth Kowaleski. *Encyclopedia of Feminist Literary Theory*. New York : Garaland Publishing House, 1997.

Waters, Lindsay. "On Paul de Man's Effort to Re-anchor a True Aesthetics in Our Feeeling" in Boundary-2, Vol-26, Issue-2, Summer, 1999.

Waters, Malcolm, *Modern Social Theory*, London, Sage, 1994.

Waugh, Patricia. (Ed.), *Postmodernism : A Reader.* London : Edward Arnold, 1992.

Waxman, Barbara Frey (Ed.). *Multicultural Literatures through Feminist/Poststructuralist Lenses*. Knoxville : The University of Tennessee Press, 1993.

Webster, Roger. *Studying Literary Theory : An Introduction*. London : Adward Arnold, 1990.

Wellmer, Albrecht. *The Persistence of Modernity*. Cambridge, Massachusetts : MIT Press, 1991.

Wheeler, Kathleen. *Romanticism. Pragmatism and Decon*struction. Oxford : Blackwell, 1993.

Wihl, Garry. *The Contingency of Theory : Pragmatism, Erpressivism and Deconstruction*. London : University Press, New Haven, 1994.

Wolf, Janet. Aesthetics and the sociology of Art.

Wolfreys, Julian (Ed.). *Literary : A Reader and Guide*. Edinburgh : Edinburgh University, 1999.

Wollen Peter. *Raiding the Icebox : Reflections on Twentieth Century Culture*. London : Verso, 1993.

Wuthnov, Robert et al. *Cultural Analysis : The Works of Peter L Berger, Mary Douglas, Michel Foucault and Jurgen Habermas*. Boston : Routledge& Kegan Paul, 1984.

Index

A

B

H

I

J

K

Q

R

T